INTO THE TEETH
OF THE TIGER

SMITHSONIAN HISTORY OF AVIATION SERIES

Von Hardesty, Series Editor

On December 17, 1903, human flight became a reality when Orville Wright piloted the *Wright Flyer* across a 120-foot course above the sands at Kitty Hawk, North Carolina. That awe-inspiring 12 seconds of powered flight inaugurated a new technology and a new era. The airplane quickly evolved as a means of transportation and a weapon of war. Flying faster, farther, and higher, airplanes soon encircled the globe, dramatically altering human perceptions of time and space. The dream of flight appeared to be without bounds. Having conquered the skies, the heirs to the Wrights eventually orbited Earth and landed on the moon.

Aerospace history is punctuated with many triumphs, acts of heroism, and technological achievements. But that same history also showcases technological failures and the devastating impact of aviation technology in modern warfare. As adapted to modern life, the airplane—as with many other important technological breakthroughs—mirrors the darker impulses as well as the genius of its creators. For millions, however, commercial aviation provides safe, reliable, and inexpensive travel for business and leisure.

This book series chronicles the development of aerospace technology in all its manifestations and subtlety. International in scope, this scholarly series includes original monographs, biographies, reprints of out-of-print classics, translations, and reference materials. Both civil and military themes are included, along with systematic studies of the cultural impact of the airplane. Together, these diverse titles contribute to our overall understanding of aeronautical technology and its evolution.

INTO THE TEETH
OF THE TIGER

DONALD S. LOPEZ

Smithsonian Books
Washington

FOREWORD

Flying a shark-mouthed P-40 in the skies over China in 1943–1944, Donald S. Lopez participated in one of the most remarkable air campaigns of World War II. *Into the Teeth of the Tiger*, now revised, gives a vivid account of America's air war against the Japanese in China. Lopez served with the 23rd Fighter Group of the Fourteenth Air Force, the worthy successors of the legendary Flying Tigers.

Lopez's squadron flew countless sorties over the rugged mountainous terrain of China, strafing enemy supply lines and attacking troop concentrations. These bold air operations—perhaps the most distant projection of American air power in Asia at the time—did not go unchallenged: the Japanese launched numerous air raids and a major ground offensive to destroy the American air contingent. Even as the Japanese advanced, American pilots scored many notable victories, a paradox of victory in retreat, which Lopez chronicles in dramatic detail.

Fighter pilots lived a precarious existence in such a remote sector of the war. Intense air action over enemy territory alternated with long interludes of boredom and inactivity. Life was austere, with poor food, bouts of dysentery, rat-infested barracks, and irregular mail deliveries. Heavily laden C-47s and C-46s kept the Fourteenth Air Force going by flying supplies over the Hump (the Himalayas) from India. It took six gallons of fuel to deliver one precious gallon to the beleaguered American air units.

Paul Fussell, author of *Wartime*, has described Lopez's account of the air war in China as "unflappable, humorous, cool." Such adjectives capture the essence of this extraordinary memoir. Lopez blends a pilot's-eye view of the air war with a keen memory of time and place. The narrative captures the characters in Lopez's squadron vividly, conveying both the heroic and tragic nature of the conflict. *Into the Teeth of the Tiger* mirrors as well China at war—the brutality of the Japanese occupation, the nature of partisan warfare, and the unresolved conflict between Chiang Kai-Shek's Nationalists and the Chinese Communist movement.

At the heart of this story is the persona of a talented fighter pilot. This highly demanding profession shaped Don Lopez as a youth and profoundly influenced his perspective as a writer. Lopez possessed the drive to become a military pilot. His aptitude for flying first became evident in his stateside flight training. Later in the skies over China he combined personal courage with his demonstrated flying skills to become an ace, one of the few to earn that distinction in the China theater. His subsequent career included six years as a test pilot, a brief stint in the Korean war to test the F-86 Sabre, and an M.S. degree in aeronautics from the California Institute of Technology. Outside the military, Don Lopez has continued to contribute to the history of flight, working at the Smithsonian Institution's National Air and Space Museum as assistant director for aeronautics and then deputy director. When this world-famous museum opened in 1976, on the occasion of America's Bicentennial, the huge success of the aviation exhibits reflected in large measure the creative work of Don Lopez. *Into the Teeth of the Tiger* is not only an entertaining and insightful memoir but also the introduction to an important contributor to the history of aviation.

Von Hardesty
Editor
Smithsonian History of Aviation Series

ACKNOWLEDGMENTS

I owe a debt of gratitude to Ian Ballantine for suggesting the book and for sharing some of the wisdom acquired during his legendary career; to his lovely wife, Betty, for her skillful editing; and to Dr. Von Hardesty, curator of aeronautics at the National Air and Space Museum, for his careful reading of, and helpful comments on, each chapter. My thanks also go to Lorraine Atherton for her fine copy editing of this revised edition.

My greatest debt, however, is owed to my wife, Glindel; not only for her constant encouragement and support but also for her diligent reading and rereading of the successive versions of the manuscript and her invaluable suggestions for improvement.

1

THE **TEETH**
OF THE **TIGER**

I struggled awake to the clamor of a loud gong being beaten slowly, with a feeling of unfamiliarity with my surroundings. As I awoke more fully I realized that I was in the 75th Fighter Squadron hostel in Hengyang, China, a forward air base on the Siang River, and that it was the morning of December 12, 1943. The clanging was the jing bao (Chinese for "air raid") gong indicating a one-ball alert. One ball was hoisted to the top of a pole when enemy aircraft were reported aloft by the warning net of Chinese observers, who reported by phone. Two balls indicated they were headed in the direction of your base, and three meant that fighters should scramble to intercept the enemy. In addition to the balls, a gong was sounded slowly for one ball, faster for two, and incessantly for three.

My roommate Dick Jones and I were on the flight schedule that day, so we dressed hurriedly in khakis that were still damp from the day before, put on our flying suits, and ran downstairs to the assembly area. Major Richardson, the commanding officer, said that we would have time to eat breakfast, so we joined several other pilots in the mess hall. The Chinese mess boys, sensing the urgency, quickly served our usual breakfast eggs. We gulped them down and hurried out to join the others. It was still dark and quite misty as we piled into the jeeps and weapons carrier to drive to the flight line. Near the flight line we could hear the P-40s being taxied by the crew chiefs from the night dispersal areas into line next to the alert shack.

The aircraft were lined up by flights, after the engines had been run up and checked. At that time the squadron's radio call sign was White, and the flight's call signs were Able, Baker, Charlie, and so on. I was flying as number two, the flight leader's wingman, in the third, or Charlie, flight, led by Lt. Jim Anning, whose airplane was distinguished by a large pair of dice painted on the rudder. This was the last flight, as only twelve aircraft were in flyable condition because of damage inflicted during a Japanese bombing raid two days earlier. Major Richardson was leading White Able flight and the squadron.

At the flight line we rushed to the personal equipment area of the alert shack, got our helmets, oxygen masks, and parachutes, and took them out to our assigned planes. The parachutes were placed in the seats; the helmets and oxygen masks were connected and hung on the stick or the gunsight. Each pilot climbed into the cockpit, adjusted the seat and rudder pedals to his liking, and returned to the alert shack knowing that he could scramble in the minimum time.

It always gave me a thrill to see the now legendary Curtiss P-40 Warhawks lined up ready for action, with their white propeller spinners gleaming and their fierce tiger shark teeth bared, and that was particularly true today as I anticipated my first taste of aerial combat. Now all those long hours of practice dogfights and rat races would pay off. The long courtship would be over, and my desire to be a fighter pilot would be consummated.

My hopes were suddenly dashed as the warning net reported that the enemy had circled back and the one ball was lowered, signaling the all-clear. We all sat around in the shack shooting the breeze and waiting to see if the heavy mist would lift enough so that we could take off on our scheduled strafing mission later that morning. We usually played volleyball to pass the time, but this morning the court was too wet.

About an hour later, just as the mist was dissipating, the one ball went up again and the operations officer, Capt. Bill Grosvenor, told us that the warning net had reported heavy engine noise north of Changsha heading for our base at Hengyang. This time it was for real. About half an hour later the second ball went up; bombers and fighters had been sighted by the net approaching Changsha, which was about forty minutes north of Hengyang. We rushed to our airplanes, climbed into the cockpits, hooked up all our various straps and wires, put on our helmets, and turned on the radios, awaiting the scramble order from the CO. Fuel was so precious in China that we never started our engines or scrambled until the last minute that would allow us to reach the enemy planes even if they turned back, as they often did. I was fairly sure they would continue their attack this time, as we had been bombed heavily just two days before, on December 10. Although I was a veteran of eight combat missions, they were all strafing and bombing missions, and I had yet to see a Japanese plane on the ground, let alone in the air. I was eager to try my hand at air combat since I had been preparing for it, one way or the other, for most of my life. Two of our pilots had been shot down and killed on the tenth, and one of my roommates had been badly wounded, but I had no doubts about surviving the forthcoming battle.

Suddenly the radio came to life and the voice of Major Richardson crackled in my earphones. "White squadron, scramble! Able and Baker flights stay low to intercept the bombers. Charlie flight climb to intercept the fighters." On receiving a nod from Jim Anning, I immediately put my starter switch in the energize position, gave the engine a few shots of prime, turned on the ignition, and engaged the starter. The engine caught right away, and I put the mixture control into auto-rich and adjusted the throttle. To me there is still no more exciting sound than the whine of an inertia starter, followed by the hesitant then deafening roar of a powerful in-line engine.

Since our flight would take off last, we ran up our engines and checked our magnetos while still parked on the flight line. The first element of Able flight lined up on the narrow, crushed-rock runway and started the takeoff roll. The runway was so narrow that we took off in two plane elements with the wing tips overlapping slightly. The wet weather allowed us to take off at close intervals since we did not have to contend with the billowing dust clouds raised on takeoff during dry periods. Also, the haze-reduced visibility made it necessary to follow the preceding element closely to maintain visual contact.

Anning swung into position on the runway, and I lined up on his right wing, slightly to the rear. I signaled that I was ready, and he gave me the head-nod takeoff signal. We opened our throttles, rolled down the runway, and lifted off together. I immediately started the landing gear up and adjusted the cowl flaps for climb. We started a gentle turn to the left to allow the second element to catch up by cutting across the turn. As soon as we reached about 200 feet I switched the fuel selector to belly tank to use as much fuel as possible before having to jettison it if we engaged the enemy. As we climbed I slid out to about 50 feet from the leader so that I could search for enemy planes. In tight formation I would have had to keep my eyes fixed on the leader.

We had reached about 15,000 feet in our climb when I heard Major Richardson call that he had spotted the bombers at low altitude and was going for the attack. I kept searching the sky for Zeros but saw nothing, although the visibility was better at that altitude. Suddenly Anning yelled, "Zeros," jettisoned his tank, and rolled over into a dive. I yanked the tank jettison cable, miraculously remembering to switch to the main tank, turned on my gun switch, and followed him down.

The sight that sprang into my windshield as I started down is etched in my memory. About 2,000 feet below us were about forty Nakajima Ki-43 Oscars (we called all Japanese fighters Zeros, although we identified them correctly for the intelligence officer). The sky seemed filled with them. They were not in formation but in what we called a "squirrel cage," with airplanes climbing, diving, and turning, seemingly without rhyme or reason but evidently well planned, as we never saw them collide. The Oscars looked as though they had been specially waxed for the occasion; they were so beautiful in their light and dark green camouflage, with light blue bellies and enormous bright red balls on the wings and fuselage, that I nearly forgot to fire at them as we dived through. I did manage to fire a short burst, but I was not positioned well and consequently just hit some air. I later learned, after landing, that an Oscar had gotten on my tail and fired at me but had in turn been fired at by our number three and driven off. While he was doing this, the last man in our flight, Lieutenant Beaty, was pounced on by several Oscars, shot down, and killed.

I didn't know Lt. John Beaty well, since he had joined the squadron only a few days before and this was his first combat mission. In 1990, I saw a copy of the following letter he had written to his family on the night before the mission, to be mailed if he was killed.

December 11, 1943

Dear Mom, Dad, Sis and Bud:

Tomorrow morning I go on what I hope will be the first of many missions against the Japs.

I'm a bit excited anticipating a thrill, and content with my lot.

If this first mission, and those to follow, are fortunate for me, you'll never get this. I'm confident it never will be mailed, but should the occasion arise, I want you to have a message from me a little more personal than the adjutant general's—"REGRET TO INFORM YOU."

Naturally, I can't give you the details, nor do I consider them important, but I want to reassure you as to my "feelings" about the matter.

Should you get this, consider me just as alive as when I left the kitchen to milk the cow, or as when I carried the watermelon out to the stone table in the back yard, or as when I left you at the Grand Central that last time.

After all, I have been away for a long time and this will just announce that I have gone to a better tour of duty, which will last a little longer, but which will end with our being together again.

I'd hate to think of your grieving over this prolonged separation, so look on it as I do. I've always yearned for far-off places and so-called adventures, and this is exactly what I want to satisfy that yearning.

There's a war going on and I'm where every man should want to be. What more could I ask? I don't have any particular aim after the war except a vague "I'd like to stay in the army" or "guess I'll go to South America."

The main reason I want to come home is to see you all. So remember when you miss me that, while I'd just as soon live out my normal span and see more of you all, I did to the end what I've tried to do and "fought the good fight."

More than likely they'll send you some of my personal effects—my camera, my diary, my photos of you all and, possibly, my personal pistol, my watch (if they find it) and so I've left enough trinkets behind that each of you should have a souvenir.

Don't weep over these manifestations of my physical existence, if you want me, just sit down in Dad's chair, in front of the fireplace, about midnight, and as the little blue flames dance above the coals, I'LL BE THERE, 'cause that's my favorite place in the world, especially since I hit China and the cold weather.

It really tickles my sporting sense that the handful of us here are holding Tojo and his midget minions at bay. If I go down I hope my buddies get about six for me.

I hope Bud doesn't get into this business. He will make a name for himself in a peaceful world and I'd rather he did not have his sensibilities dulled. But if he does get in I know he'll make us all proud of him.

It would be nice to have a closer view of Sis, as she makes her place in the world. When I last saw her, she was becoming a woman and the sight was good to see.

Mom and Dad, I think the two of you are the best I've ever seen. You have given me the things I don't think I could have found anywhere else. I love and respect you more than anything else in the world and no mere separation of my soul from my body can dim that love.

There are many people I love, and whom I'd like to enjoy life with. It would take a page to name them, but you know who the most important ones are and you'll tell them goodbye for me.

I hope it will be many years before we meet again. Where I am that is but a moment and those years will be sweet for you. I love you all more than I can ever put into words, so until we meet again,

God be with you.

JACK

After passing through the Japanese fighters we went into the haze layer, at about 8,000 feet, and I lost sight of the flight leader and the number three lost sight of me. As I leveled out I found myself alone in the sky with no airplanes in sight. The Oscars must have followed us into the haze. While climbing above the haze layer I kept turning and looking behind to make sure that my rear was clear and not occupied by Oscars. I called my flight leader several times with no response until I realized that my radio must have gone out; there was none of the combat chatter that certainly was taking place.

I had made a number of wide, rather aimless circles, looking for other airplanes of any type, when I saw in the distance in front of me an Oscar chasing a P-40 in a shallow dive. I nosed down, opened the throttle to full power, and headed toward them. Although I was far out of range, I led the Oscar by as much as I could and fired, hoping that the tracers might chase him off the P-40's tail. I was all too successful. He immediately turned directly toward me.

We approached each other head on, he in a slight climb and I in a slight dive. When I got within range I opened fire, and I could see my bullets flashing on the front of his engine. I could also see his guns winking but was not conscious of any hits on my plane. We closed at a tremendous rate, still firing at each other, and at the last split second before we hit nose to nose, he flipped into a vertical right turn. I felt a heavy impact, and my P-40 yawed wildly to the left. I saw that my left wing had struck his left wing as we passed. At first glance I thought that I had lost a big chunk of my wing, but when I got my eyeballs tucked back in I saw that only about three feet was gone, including part of the aileron and the pitot tube; shredded fabric from the aileron was flapping behind. The Oscar's wing had broken off a few feet outside the propeller arc. I glanced back and saw it fluttering in the air and the Oscar tumbling down, out of control, until it disappeared into the haze.

My plane straightened out and seemed to fly normally. I checked the controls; they operated properly. In fact, the good old P-40 flew the same as always as far as I could tell. I gave silent thanks to the designers and builders of this rugged craft. My airspeed indicator read zero, since the pitot tube was gone, but that didn't bother me; I seldom looked at it anyway.

I continued my descent and eventually found two P-40s engaged with one Oscar near the ground. I joined them, and we split up, making successive passes at the Oscar from different directions. He was a good pilot, and he broke sharply at each pass so none of us could get a proper lead on him. Each time he did, however, he would find another P-40 attacking him. I don't think that I ever hit him, but one of the other P-40s finally nailed him, and he burst into flames and crashed into the low hills. That was the first time I'd seen an airplane in flames. It was a spectacular and sobering sight.

The maneuverability of the Oscar was something to behold. We had been told all through our training about the amazing maneuverability of the Japanese fighters, but it had to be seen to be believed. We referred to their turns as flips; when you started a pass and they saw you, they would flip right or left and you would be staring at a pair of streamers in the air where they had been. The Oscar was the most maneuverable of all the Japanese fighters, including the Zero. This was due to its light weight and its maneuver flaps. It weighed only 5,710 pounds, much less than the 6,025-pound Zero and the 9,000-pound P-40.

I lost sight of the other aircraft in the haze, so I climbed until I was above the worst of it. For as far as I could see the sky was empty. I made a few circles but could see no one, so I decided to return to the field at Hengyang. Having made this decision, I realized that I couldn't implement it since I didn't have a clue where I was. I knew I wasn't far from the field, but I had no idea which direction to go, and I couldn't see the river or any familiar landmarks. I throttled back and flew in wide, lazy circles while trying to spot a friendly airplane. After about five minutes, which seemed like several hours, I saw a flight of four P-40s approaching. I couldn't call them as my radio was out, but as they drew closer I could tell from their markings that they were from another squadron based to the south of Hengyang. They had come to support us but had arrived too late. The flight formed up on my right wing in fairly tight formation. I motioned for the flight leader to take the lead but he shook his head and indicated that I should lead. I couldn't understand why, but I found out later that since I was wearing a red scarf they thought I was Captain Grosvenor, our operations officer. Fortunately, in my oxygen mask and helmet, they couldn't tell how frustrated I was about being the only one who knew we were lost. Unless you have very expressive eyebrows, it's almost impossible for someone to read your feelings when you are wearing a helmet and oxygen mask.

I slowed down as much as I dared, hoping he would take the lead, but he stayed right in position. I had made about two more circles when I spotted a lone P-40. I headed toward it and saw, from the dice on its tail, that it was my long-lost flight leader, Jim Anning. I immediately, with my newly acquired flight, joined up on his right wing. I was able to get in closer than usual since part of my left wing was gone. He did a double take that Jimmy Finlayson, of the Laurel and Hardy films, would have envied. He started descending, with me in tight formation, determined never to lose sight of him again, at least until we landed. Soon the field came into view, and our six-plane formation lined up with the runway for the standard low pass to peel off and land.

I should probably have climbed up above the field alone and stalled the airplane to make sure it was safe to land, but neither I nor the flight leader ever gave it a thought. I followed him in, peeled off, and made the standard 360-degree power off pattern, followed by my usual good landing. After I parked and shut down, all the pilots and ground crews crowded around my airplane to inspect the damage. Many thought that I had hit the ground while trying to shoot down the lone Oscar. The whole operation, from takeoff to landing, had seemed like an eternity to me but had lasted only ninety minutes.

On that intercept mission, the squadron had destroyed five bombers and three Oscars—a very successful day, but it lost much of its luster when I learned that my roommate and closest friend, Dick Jones, had shot down two bombers but was missing along with the number four man in my flight. I was worried about Dick, afraid that he had been killed, but after sweating for several hours we got word through the Chinese warning net that he was safe. He rejoined the squadron later that evening just in time for supper. He said that he had shot down one Kawasaki Ki-48 Lily, a twin-engine light bomber, and was attacking a second when its rear gunner hit him in the coolant lines, causing his engine to overheat and forcing him to belly land on a sandbar in the river about twenty miles north of the field. Since the railroad line paralleled the river, the Chinese had taken him to the nearest station where he could catch the next train from Changsha, known to us as the Changshanooga Choo Choo.

In looking back on my first air combat, I don't remember any feeling of fear but rather one of exhilaration, of invincibility and aggressiveness. I could not conceive that I could be shot down or even wounded. I kept a constant lookout to keep from being surprised by an enemy aircraft, but my primary aim was to find something to attack. I never had quite that same feeling on ground attack missions though I never doubted that I would get through them safely. Although we didn't discuss the subject, I'm sure most of the pilots felt the same. We faced ground fire on most strafing missions, but I never had the feeling that I had in air combat of dueling with an opponent.

That evening at the hostel, Maj. Witold Urbanowicz, a Polish officer attached to our squadron, called me Lopez the Destroyer, but I did not intentionally ram the Oscar. I am totally devoid of kamikaze tendencies. I just wanted to keep the advantage that I would have lost had I turned first and allowed him to get on my tail. It never occurred to me that he wouldn't turn, and fortunately, I was correct. As I was to find out in future aerial combat, little real thought and planning takes place in a dogfight. Everything is done by instinct, and as you gain experience your instincts are more fully developed and sharpened, making you much more effective.

2

CHILD OF A GOLDEN AGE

My earliest memory is of an event that sparked both a lifelong passion and my profession. At about three and one half years of age, I was taken by my parents to a major highway in Brooklyn. After sitting on the curb for a long time, in a big crowd, I was caught by a surge of excitement, stood up, and waved at a man in an open car to the accompaniment of loud cheers of "Lindy, Lindy!" Time has erased other details of that incident, but the image of that handsome, heroic figure has stayed with me. Somehow I must have learned that he was a flier. I cannot remember a time since when I was not interested in flight.

I was fortunate in that my growing-up years coincided with the golden age of flight, that period when almost everything that took place in the sky was news. Speed records were set, races were won, oceans were crossed, and the pilots who flew those magical machines were heroes to youths and adults alike.

I was the oldest of three boys, born in a section of Brooklyn known as Canarsie, not far from Jamaica Bay. Canarsie at that time seemed more like a small town than a part of one of the world's largest cities. The groceries and other shops were run by people my family had known for years. My maternal grandfather, Charles Sewell Thall, who died the month before I was born, was a doctor who had practiced in that area for several decades.

Groceries were ordered by phone or by a note carried by me, and delivered to the door. The iceman made his daily deliveries in a horse-drawn wagon, and if we bothered him enough he would give us a small chunk of ice. Fresh produce was also sold from a horse cart. The junkman came periodically with his wagon, backed the horse into the driveway, and collected the bundled newspapers. It was a time when horse and buggy, the horseless carriage, and the new thrill of air travel were all simultaneously present.

Because of the relative proximity of Floyd Bennett Field to my home, I was able to see many of the famous and near-famous aircraft of that era. I saw the gigantic German flying boat the Do.X, Balbo's flight of Savoia Marchetti S.55s, Wiley Post's Vega *Winnie Mae*, Ben Howard's *Mr. Mulligan*, Amelia Earhart's Lockheed Electra, the Thaden-Noyes Beechcraft Staggerwing, and Lee Miles's Granville QED. I also saw Northrop Gammas, Curtiss Helldivers, Vought Corsairs, Pitcairn Autogiros (often towing advertising banners), Wacos of all types, Ford Tri-Motors, Curtiss Condors, and many others—quite a contrast to the Space Shuttle I saw launched in 1984.

Floyd Bennett Field was quite new in my childhood, and as I recall it was a vast expanse of white concrete with red brick hangars and administration building. There were no commercial airlines operating there, so most of the flying consisted of hopping passengers (taking them up for short sightseeing flights), charter and business flights, skywriting, towing advertising banners, and aerial photography, often for the newspapers. The passengers and airplane watchers could walk up and down the ramp in front of the aircraft, separated from the planes only by a chain-link fence. On weekends and holidays airplanes would be lined up on the airfield side of the fence waiting to take up passengers for short flights for $5 per person, I think. The pilots were usually sitting in the planes while an assistant stood by the gate trying to attract passengers. The only pilots whose names I remember (besides Buster Warner, of whom more later) were Roger Q. Williams and Clarence Chamberlin, who in 1927, shortly after Lindbergh's flight, flew nonstop from New York to Germany.

Skywriting was a common sight, especially over the beaches in the summer, spelling out "I. J. Fox for Fine Furs" and "Griffin All-White for All White Shoes." Occasionally I would see one of the majestic airships float overhead, so large and so smoothly silent. I remember the *Graf Zeppelin*, the *Hindenburg*, and either the *Akron* or the *Macon*, with the tiny Sparrowhawk fighters that it carried in its vast interior swarming around it.

Aviation movies were popular and exciting, and I faithfully attended every one that I could as many times as possible. In fact, the first movie that I remember is *Wings*, the 1928 Academy Award winner. Others that particularly impressed me include *Hell's Angels*, *Dawn Patrol*, *Hell in the Heavens*, *Devildogs of the Air*, the comedy *Sky Devils*, and *The Eagle and the Hawk*, with its never-to-be-forgotten scene of the young observer (played by the baby-faced actor who was killed in every World War I film) falling out of the back cockpit, sans parachute, at the top of a loop. One of my most prized possessions was a book based on the screenplay of *Wings* illustrated with stills from the film. My uncle gave it to me when I was quite young, and I read it dozens of times.

The aviation pulp magazines of the day were frowned on by adults but were highly prized in my set. Most of them featured stories of air fighting in World War I; some featured fighting in other, usually improbable, locales. The magazine titles alone were exciting: *G-8 and His Battle Aces*, *Battle Birds*, *The Lone Eagle* (not Lindbergh in this case), *Sky Fighters*, *Dare-Devil Aces*, *Flying Aces*, *Aces*, *Contact*, *War Birds*, and *Wings*.

The pilots had names that went well with the stories and the writing styles: G-8, the master spy who could in a few seconds, using only a small flesh-colored makeup kit taped to his thigh, impersonate a German general or a little old Hausfrau to perfection; Nippy Weston, the Terrier Ace; Bull Martin; Smoke Wade and his Pinto Spad; Kerry Keen, the Griffon, with his amphibian the Black Bullet; the Red Falcon, with his hybrid fighter and his giant Senegalese gunner; and the ineffable Phineas Pinkham, the practical jokester who spent his time in every issue of *Flying Aces* hornswoggling the Heinies, swindling the Squareheads, bamboozling the Boche, and outgunning and out-punning both friend and foe. To Phineas there were no British and French, only Limeys and Frogs. One pilot, Coffin Kirk, even had a gunner that was a trained ape named Tank, masquerading as a strong, silent mechanic.

In recent years I have reread some of the pulp magazines and found almost all of them to be miserably written and highly romantic, not to mention totally inaccurate. The Phineas Pinkham stories, on the other hand, held up well, partly because they were never intended to be other than farcical and partly because I was better able to understand the puns with which the stories were rife. Some titles of Pinkham stories were "Sky Finance," "Eclipse of the Hun," and "Zoom Like It Hot."

I've often wondered how much effect the aviation pulp magazines had on predisposing me and others of my generation toward a "natural" enmity for the Germans and the Japanese. The residue of hatred for Germans remaining from World War I was apparent in all of the stories based on that war. There was little subtlety. All the Germans were bad and all the Allies were good, with the possible exception of a few brass hats. In the mid-thirties, as Japanese power increased and Manchuria and China were attacked, more and more stories used contemporary settings with either Japanese or thinly disguised Japanese as villains. They were always portrayed as vicious, treacherous, and cruel, and they were invariably shot down by American secret agents or soldiers of fortune and even, occasionally, by an ape. By the time we actually went to war with the Axis powers it seemed perfectly in order to want to kill the Germans and Japanese.

I had my first flight in an airplane when I was about seven years old. My father, mother, brother Carl, and I drove to Canarsie Shore, about a mile from our home, where William "Buster" Warner, a friend of the family, was hopping passengers in an open-cockpit Waco biplane. There was no airport; he was flying off the sand beach. My mother and I rode together in the front cockpit, and I remember seeing my uncle waving a bedsheet in the front yard as we flew over. I was not frightened at all and would happily have gone up again if given the opportunity. It seemed quite natural to be looking down at the world.

Buster Warner later became a pilot for Ericson and Remmert, a Waco agency at Floyd Bennett Field. He flew photographers for the *New York Daily Mirror* and was grounded for a short period for flying too close to the burning cruise ship *Morro Castle*. He also flew a Vultee in the 1936 Bendix Trophy Race, won that year by Louise Thaden and Blanche Noyes.

On weekends he usually hopped passengers at Floyd Bennett Field in a cabin Waco. Often, on weekends, my family drove to Floyd Bennett to watch the airplanes. I invariably stood by the fence opposite Warner's Waco, looking as wistfully eager or eagerly wistful as possible. The Waco could carry three passengers, so when only two people wanted to fly, he gave me a nod and I jumped in for a free flight. Sometimes, when my parents didn't want to drive to the airfield, I would ride there on my bike and repeat my performance. Warner was naturally one of my heroes, and I acquired a certain amount of prestige through flying with him.

A Navy Reserve squadron of Curtiss Helldivers was based at Floyd Bennett. Often, if I begged hard enough or ran errands, the sailors on duty let me sit in the cockpits. The simplicity of the controls and the fixed landing gear made it a much safer operation than it would have been in more modern aircraft, but it was still a big thrill for me.

Many years later I paid tribute to those sailors who let me into the cockpit of the Helldiver. In the early fifties I landed a North American B-25 Mitchell, a medium bomber widely used in World War II, at the civilian airport in Mankato, Minnesota. I stayed with the airplane while the other pilot attended to some business in town. A group of young boys crowded up to the fence, getting as close as they could to the B-25. Remembering how much it had meant to me, I brought them into the cockpit by twos, against all Air Force regulations, and let them sit in the pilot and copilot seats. I explained how the controls worked, while keeping one hand on the landing-gear retraction handle. I hope at least one of them became a pilot and that his visit to the B-25 played a small part in his decision.

In 1937, Buster Warner stopped hopping passengers to concentrate on charter flying, so I could no longer scrounge rides. I didn't know it then, but my flying had ended for the time being.

In 1939 we moved to Tampa, Florida, and lived a long way from the nearest civilian airport, but my avid interest in aviation continued, expressed now only through reading.

With the start of World War II, my interest in flying, especially in flying fighters, increased. The papers, the magazines, and the newsreels were full of stories and photos of the various aircraft in combat. The Battle of Britain particularly impressed me, and I resolved that some-day I would fly a Spitfire—an ambition that was never fulfilled, to my great regret. Although I often thought about going to Canada and joining the Royal Canadian Air Force, I never considered it seriously, since I was only sixteen years old at the time.

At about that time two Army airfields were built in Tampa, MacDill just south of the city and Drew in the north of the city not far from where I lived. MacDill was a bomber training base and Drew a fighter base equipped with P-39s. Since my house was on the edge of the fighter traffic pattern, the P-39s regularly passed overhead in vertical banks as they turned toward the runway. The Bell P-39 Airacobra (a fighter with the engine behind the pilot and a 37-millimeter cannon in the nose) is a beautiful airplane in a vertical bank, and I still remember the thrill of watching them. I vowed that someday I would fly one of the Airacobras, and I was able to keep that vow a few years later.

In June 1941 I was graduated from Hillsborough County High School. The next September I entered the University of Tampa as an engineering student, little dreaming that the United States would be in the war within a few short months. I became a member of the first crew at the university and rowed many a mile on the Hillsborough River. Crew was the only sport in which I was able to make the varsity, since it was the only sport in the school that allowed me to participate sitting down. I was not a fast enough runner to make any of the other teams.

I learned that freshmen were allowed to participate in the Civilian Pilot Training Program (CPTP). This program was established in universities and colleges all around the country to create a large group of trained pilots who would be available in the event of war. I applied, passed the physical, and entered the program along with my good friend Harold Williamson, who at six foot four was at the high end of the height restrictions.

The ground school was taught at night at the university, while the flying was done at Peter O. Knight Airport on Tampa's Davis Island. Ludwig Flying Service was the contractor for the flight training. Piper J-3 Cubs were used in the primary phase and Waco UPF-7s in the secondary phase.

I was well into the ground school but had not yet started flying when, on December 7, 1941, the Japanese bombed Pearl Harbor. A few days later, like many other Americans, I went to the recruiting station in the main post office to try to enroll in the Army Air Forces aviation cadet program. The officer who interviewed me said that I could sign up then if I wanted to, but he thought I would be better off finishing my first year of college and completing my CPTP primary flying course. The Air Forces cadet program was so overloaded with students that I would have had to stay at an Army post, essentially killing time, until there was room in the cadet program in about six months. That seemed like good advice, so I took it and continued in school.

In a few weeks we started the flying phase of the program and were assigned to our instructors. Mine was Billy Chancey, the son of a former mayor of Tampa. He was a good pilot, a good instructor who was at ease in the air. Unlike many instructors (whose inner panic is often manifested by raging and screaming at the student), Chancey and his pleasant, relaxed manner made learning to fly much easier than it might otherwise have been, as I was to learn in Army Primary Flying School in the not too distant future.

Our practice flying area was along the shoreline of Tampa Bay, over a deserted area of sand and swamp. The aircraft were orange Piper J-3 Cubs, the first airplane of many pilots. After a few flights in which we practiced air work (level flight, turns, climbs, glides, and stalls), I made my first takeoff and felt the airplane come alive in my hands as it approached flying speed and the controls took hold. It was a thrill that I never tired of, no matter how many times I experienced it.

We continued with our air work, adding steep turns, eights on pylons, and spins to our repertoire, but most of our practice consisted of takeoffs and landings. On one occasion Harold Williamson and I were embarrassed when my instructor spotted us installing small flags in our practice flying area. When we were given a simulated forced landing in training, we had to land into the wind. Since our practice area was rather barren, it was sometimes difficult to determine the wind direction. Being enterprising young engineering students, we thought to solve that problem by installing the flags. We saw a Cub overhead while thus engaged but hid behind a dune until it left. Bill Chancey, however, recognized the car parked nearby. The next day he chewed us out in front of the other students and sent us back to retrieve the flags. He said, among other remarks, "What the hell will you do if you have to make a forced landing where there are no flags?" So much for preflight planning.

Finally, after the requisite eight hours of dual instruction, Chancey climbed out of the plane after a landing and I soloed. Since I kept no logbook at that time, I don't remember the date, but it was early in 1942. I do remember being surprised at how light the Cub felt and how quickly it lifted off the ground. I shouldn't have been surprised, as the instructor's weight was an appreciable part of the Cub's total weight. It was an awesome feeling to be up in an airplane alone, in complete control, but I loved it and never have lost the joy of it.

The rest of the flying course was uneventful, except for an occasional thrill when a flight of Martin B-26 Marauder bombers blasted through our practice area at low altitude. We usually didn't see them until they were quite close. I think the pilots were trying to scare us; if so, they succeeded. I finished the required thirty-five hours, filled in all the squares in the course syllabus, and was scheduled for a flight check with the local Civil Aeronautics Administration (CAA) inspector, a Mr. Vavarina. Although I was scared to death at the prospect of flying with such an illustrious person, I passed the check with no difficulty and was granted my student pilot certificate. Forty flying hours and a cross-country flight were required for a private license, but that was not included in the CPTP course.

On May 8, 1942, I could wait no longer, so I enlisted. I passed the written examination and the physical and was sworn into the Army as a private in the enlisted reserve to await an opening in the aviation cadet program, which was still overloaded. The lieutenant who swore a group of us (Harold Williamson included) into the Army, said at the conclusion of the ceremony, "I'm sure there will be at least one Distinguished Flying Cross in this bunch." I vowed that I would be the one to get it, and I was.

I had signed up for the CPTP secondary training course but did not start it as I did not return to college the next semester. I did, however, manage to scrounge a few flights in a Waco UPF-7 from one of the instructors that I knew.

I spent the rest of the summer working in the meat department of the A&P to earn money to continue my flying. Every Sunday, I would drive to the airport and rent one of the Cubs for half an hour of flying. I practiced spins and loops and an occasional extra landing and finally amassed the forty hours needed for my license. I was saving up for my cross-country, which required several hours, when I received my notice to report for active duty.

On the evening of September 3, 1942, I said good-bye to my mother, brothers, and several friends and boarded a train in Tampa's Union Station, along with an acquaintance from Tampa University, Dick Ferguson, en route to the Army Air Forces Southeast Training Command's Cadet Classification Center in Nashville, Tennessee. It was, incidentally, my first ride on a train.

3

WINGS FOR A FUTURE FIGHTER

"You'll be sorreee!" was the cry that echoed and reechoed in my ears during my first weeks in the U.S. Army Air Forces. Soon after we boarded the train from Tampa to Nashville, the porter prepared the berths and I crawled in and went to sleep. During the night the train stopped at Lakeland, Florida, site of an Army primary flying school, and a group of washed-out cadets boarded, en route to Nashville to be reclassified as navigators and bombardiers.

There were three of these aircrew classification centers: one at Nashville, one in San Antonio, Texas, and one in Santa Ana, California. They served as processing and classifying units for the massive flying training program established by the Army Air Forces in 1942. Candidates were given rigorous physical exams as well as psychological and aptitude tests. They were also issued uniforms and given rudimentary military training before being sent to the preflight schools.

In the morning, Dick Ferguson and I were walking into the dining car when these cadets spotted us. For some reason, although we were in civilian clothes, they assumed that we were new cadets and immediately began the "you'll be sorry" routine. We ignored them and joined a few other new cadets from Tampa whom we knew. For the remainder of the trip, until we arrived in Nashville late in the afternoon, whenever we passed any of them or they passed us the now familiar and increasingly irritating cry rang out.

We got off the train at the smoky and rather run-down Nashville station and assembled under a sign that read, "Incoming Cadets." There a sergeant told us that a truck would pick us up in about an hour and a half and that we could get something to eat if we wished. At about the same time two more groups of new cadets arrived, one from New York State and one from North Carolina. As we all started off to find a place to eat we introduced ourselves, and I met Dick Jones from Lewiston, New York, and Jesse Gray from Stokes, North Carolina, who were to become two of my best friends. Dick and I are still close. He served as my best man and I served as his, and although we now live a continent apart, we have always kept in touch and see each other whenever possible.

Later, as we entered the Army Classification Center for the Southeast Flying Training Command in the back of a six-by-six Army truck, we were assailed from all sides by "You'll be sorreee!" We were each issued two blankets and a pillow, told where the mess hall and the latrine were, and were dumped in an empty barracks containing about forty cots with rolled-up mattresses that I think were manufactured by Ugly-Rest, from the looks of them. For two days we wandered around in our civilian clothes with nothing to do but listen to the cry and wonder what was going on. On the third day we were taken in hand by a sergeant who led us to Supply, where we were issued two pairs of coveralls, a flight cap, shoes, and socks. We were told to wear these from now on and to send our civilian clothes home.

Later we were sitting on the steps of our barracks when an officer walked past. Jesse Gray had heard that you were supposed to salute officers, so he twisted around to face the officer and saluted from a sitting position. The officer returned the salute with a strange expression, somewhere between amusement and dismay, and went on his way.

That afternoon we were taken in hand by the sergeant, instructed in the rudiments of military courtesy and drill, and told that we would now march in formation everywhere we went. The week-long classification process then began in earnest. It consisted of a stringent physical exam, some written exams, and a psychological interview that included a large number of questions that were variations on "Do you like girls?" I was going to answer, "Yes, do you have any?" but thought better of it and settled for a properly enthusiastic affirmative. Smart asses were no more popular then than now.

Those exams were followed by a long battery of tests designed to measure coordination, reaction time, and resistance to stress. In one I manipulated a stick and rudder to cause a green light to follow a randomly moving yellow light in both the vertical and horizontal planes. In another, I held an electric stylus at arm's length in the center of a small hole in a metal plate while I was bombarded with sudden loud noises and flashing lights. Each time I touched the plate it was recorded on a counter. In a third test, I was given a large board full of square pegs painted white on one half and black on the other. I had to rotate as many pegs as possible through 180 degrees in a given time period. We had heard rumors that candidates who did well on this dexterity test would be made bombardiers, so we debated throwing the test to escape that horrible fate. In the end we decided to perform as well as possible and not try to outwit the system. That was evidently the right move; everyone in my group was classified as pilot.

During this period we were issued the rest of our uniforms, learned more about military customs and courtesies, were taught the rudiments of drill, and were nauseated by the sex hygiene lectures. Also, in what seemed to be typical Army fashion, we were given the myriad shots of the inoculation program and then, while we were suffering from a combined touch of all the diseases known to man, started our calisthenics program.

While at Nashville, I served my only tour of KP duty and decided that once per career was an acceptable frequency. The night before KP, I knotted a towel around the foot of my bed so that the orderly would know I was to be awakened at 4 a.m. I dressed and went to the mess hall, and the sergeant assigned me, along with several others, to preparing oatmeal. We mixed it in several large, deep pots and had to stir it for an interminable period while it cooked. We then carried the pots to the serving line and served the oatmeal to the cadets. Following breakfast we spent several hours cleaning the pots, the dishes, and the kitchen. My hands and wrists got so limp from submersion in dishwater that I couldn't have saluted if my life depended on it. I was lucky that I didn't have to take the psychological exam that day.

My next assignment was to slice several crates of tomatoes for lunch. When I applied the knife to the first tomato, it was so dull that instead of cutting, it crushed the tomato. Since I had spent about five months working as a butcher before I was called to active duty, I was quite adept at knife sharpening. I found a steel and put such an edge on the knife that when I pointed it at a tomato, the tomato immediately waved a small white flag and fell into slices. Unfortunately, the mess sergeant had been watching, and I was removed from the tomato detail and given all the knives in the kitchen to sharpen, a task that took me the rest of the day.

A few days later several hundred of us were ordered to preflight school at Maxwell Field, Alabama. We marched to a convoy of trucks and climbed in to be driven to the railroad to entrain for Maxwell. As we rode through the center for the last time, our ears were once again assailed from all sides by "You'll be sorreee," but you know, I never was.

After an all-night trip in an ancient train (there were still some arrows stuck in the sides of the cars), we arrived in Montgomery and were trucked out to Maxwell. Maxwell Field was a permanent Army installation, with well-built barracks and attractive landscaping. We were assigned to squadrons and to barracks rooms within the squadron alphabetically, four to a room. My three roommates were all twenty-five or twenty-six years old, six or seven years older than I, and all had been in the Army for at least two years. We had little in common, and I must admit I felt a bit homesick that first night at Maxwell. Fortune smiled, however, and the next day the powers-that-be decided to put five cadets in each room, and I was moved. My new roommates included Jack Beddingfield (a friend from Tampa who had attended CPTP ground school with me), Jay Downing and John Allison (two cadets who had finished two years of college), and Atkinson, a former P-40 crew chief from Hawaii, who said he wanted to become a pilot because he had barely been able to resist the temptation to try to fly the P-40 when he was taxiing it to the flight line. John Allison, in addition to having a great sense of humor, had been at the Citadel, the military college in Charleston, South Carolina, for two years and was a tremendous help in briefing us on military procedure and on how to get by with as little effort as possible.

During our two months at preflight, we were on duty five and a half days a week, with Saturday afternoons and Sundays off. After the first month we became upperclassmen and were allowed to leave the post during our time off. The privilege was called open post.

Half of each day was spent in the classroom studying such subjects as military customs and courtesies, theory of flight, navigation, aircraft engines, code, military justice, and aircraft recognition. We used the WEFT system of aircraft recognition, learning the appearance at different angles of the various types of wings, engines, fuselages, and tails. All aircraft used some discrete combination of these types, and through the use of models, photographs, and silhouettes we learned to identify them. We were tested by identifying aircraft projected on a screen by a tachistoscope for periods as short as one seventy-fifth of a second. This program, continued throughout our training, was very effective. I never had any trouble identifying aircraft, enemy or otherwise, in combat, where a delay of only a few seconds or a misidentification can be costly.

The rest of the day was spent in outdoor activities, including drill, physical training, and weapons qualification with the .45-caliber automatic, carbine, rifle, and Thompson submachine gun. A highlight of physical training was the obstacle course known as the Burma Road, a two-mile run over rough terrain. Fortunately I was in good condition from my rowing and had no trouble negotiating the course.

Two events from my time at preflight stand out in my memory. The first took place during the regular Saturday morning inspection. The inspecting officer was the universally feared Capt. "Jungle Jim" Turner, our group tactical officer. Less than five minutes before he was due to appear, Atkinson dropped a bottle of Dyanshine liquid shoe polish on the concrete floor, where it spattered and formed a three-foot reddish brown circular spot. If Lady MacBeth thought she had spot trouble, she should have seen this one. Inspired by the greatest motivator of all, terror, we cleaned up the glass and took our inspection positions just before being called to attention as Jungle Jim entered the barracks. The tension mounted as we heard the inspection party proceeding through the barracks toward our room. It peaked as he entered the room and fixed his glare on the damned spot. He roared, "What in the hell is that spot," to Atkinson, who was nearest the door. Atkinson, the old soldier, said with a perfectly straight face, "What spot, sir?" To our surprise and relief, Jungle Jim burst out laughing, turned around, and left the room, still laughing. We heard no more about the spot, although it still showed faintly when we left Maxwell.

The second occurred while we were engaged in calisthenics in the usual area adjoining the airfield. We heard some aircraft approaching the field in a dive but couldn't see them because they were behind us and we couldn't turn around. The PT instructor, a sergeant with a big heart, stopped the workout, ordered about face, and then put us at ease. Three P-40s appeared, painted in the pinkish desert camouflage, circled the field once, and then peeled off to land. I will never forget the thrill I got from that sight. They looked so fast, skittish, and beautiful. I'm sure the other cadets shared my combined sense of questioning whether I could ever fly such a plane and the increased determination to do just that.

From preflight at Maxwell I was transferred to primary flying school at Union City, Tennessee. This was a new school; we were only the second class there. It was a civilian-run contract school, as were all primary schools, operated by Embry-Riddle, which also operated a number of similar schools in Florida. The only military personnel there, aside from the cadets, were the commanding officer, two check pilots, the commandant of cadets, the physical training officer, and the flight surgeon. All the flying instructors, ground school instructors, and maintenance and service personnel were civilians. The barracks and other buildings were new and comfortable.

The regular schedule called for flying for half the day and ground school, physical training, and military training for the other half. The upper class flew while we did our ground training and vice versa. We were on duty six days a week and were usually granted open post on Sundays. When the weather was bad on afternoons when flying was scheduled, especially Saturday afternoons, we were sometimes given open post. This led to the coining of a term for heavy clouds, "Cumulus Openus Postus." We often sent messages to the heavens on Saturdays by chanting, "Send it down, Dave!" I never found out who Dave was, but he wasn't very accommodating.

After a few days of general orientation we were assigned to flight instructors in groups of five. My instructor, Sid Bennett, was a good-looking, prototypical pilot with a pleasant manner. We were initially quite pleased with the luck of the draw. Little did we know.

Since I had some flying experience, I was chosen to fly first. He let me make the takeoff and initial climb in the Fairchild PT-19. Although heavier and more powerful than the Piper Cub, it was an easy airplane to fly, and I thought I was doing well, that is, until he started screaming at me through the Gosport tubes, a one-way, instructor to student, communications system. I soon learned that he was afflicted with some kind of altichronophobia. The higher we climbed and the longer we flew, the madder he became, and I use the word "mad" in lieu of "angry" advisedly.

He ranted and raved throughout the flight, occasionally quieting down to demonstrate a technique or maneuver. Much to our dismay, we found this was his standard operating procedure (or the SOB's SOP), and it got worse as the day progressed. Strangely enough, when we met to discuss the day's flying both before and after, he was soft-spoken and pleasant and explained the good and bad points quite rationally. We dreaded flying with him, especially as the last student of the day, when his freakiness peaked. We implored Dave to see what he could do about getting us a different instructor.

Although he was a good pilot himself, I think he was terrified with a cadet at the controls, and his fear was manifested by rage at the student. He may have had a bad experience with a student at one time or even several times. Many years later, when I was an experienced pilot, I began to understand that some of what he must have felt was justified. I always felt some apprehension in an airplane with someone else at the controls, unless I knew the pilot well and had confidence in his skill. I could well imagine that going up with five novice pilots of varying abilities every day could be nerve-racking, but it seemed to affect him much more than most; all my subsequent instructors, although subject to the same stress, were much more relaxed. Perhaps the experience with Sid Bennett was valuable in that it helped prepare me for the many stressful situations that I was to encounter as a pilot.

It was bitterly cold in those open cockpits in the northern Tennessee winter, but the thrill of flying what seemed at the time to be powerful airplanes provided an inner warmth that more than compensated. Also, the warmth in my ears, from the heated words emanating from the front cockpit, spread through my body and helped me to forget the cold. It didn't seem right to complain about the cold when we were reading every day about the Soviet encirclement of Stalingrad in below-zero weather.

I had no trouble with the flying and soloed on schedule after about eight hours of dual instruction. It was a great relief to be able to fly, at least part of the time, without Mr. Bennett, and no doubt he welcomed it too. Of course, I still had to fly with him occasionally, as about half of our training flying was dual instruction. Despite my steadily increasing skill, he still went berserk at the slightest provocation.

Once when we were returning to the main field to land at the end of a flight, he said he would demonstrate a full-flap landing. We normally landed with half flaps. On the final approach he called for full flaps, and I moved the manual control handle into the full-flap detent. About ten seconds later the cable snapped, the flaps came to full up, and we plunged toward the ground. Instead of correcting the airplane's attitude, he changed his attitude from his normal angry to furious. He turned around in his seat and almost stood while screaming at me. Since I could see the ground rushing up, I gave serious thought to screaming, too. I was just about to grab the stick when he turned around, leveled out, and landed as though nothing had happened. After we parked and the crew chief told him that the cable had broken, he made no comment and never mentioned the incident again. I imagine that if I had touched the stick he would have killed me or, even worse, tried to wash me out.

About a week later we were practicing spins, and he told me to do a two-turn spin to the left. I banked to clear the area below me, pulled the nose up, and when the airplane stalled applied full left rudder to start the spin. After a turn and a half I applied full right rudder to stop the rotation, but we kept spinning for three more turns before the rotation stopped. I popped the stick forward to break the stall and pulled out of the resulting dive. Although he should have seen that my actions were correct for spin recovery, he yelled, "Damn it, when I say a two-turn spin I don't mean a five-turn spin!" We were much lower than the prescribed height for spins, but he grabbed the controls and started another spin to the left. He started his recovery at one and a half turns, but we did another five-turn spin, recovering below 1,000 feet.

After landing, the airplane was checked, but the crew could find nothing wrong. Two days later, however, all the PT-19s were grounded because two of them had spun in at the primary school just south of us at Jackson, Tennessee, killing two students and an instructor. The investigation revealed a rigging problem in some PT-19s that made it impossible to apply full right rudder even with the pedal fully depressed. The problem was corrected, and we went back to the PT-19s after starting to switch to the Stearman PT-17s that our upperclassmen flew.

Fortune then grinned broadly on the three remaining of the original five in Sid Bennett's flight (the others had been washed out). Our fervent supplications to Dave were finally answered when Mr. Bennett received his long-awaited commission in the Ferry Command, and we were assigned to a new instructor, Roald E. Boen, a soft-spoken gentleman both on the ground and in the air, the complete antithesis of his predecessor. He and his brother ran a small airfield and flying school in nearby Milan, Tennessee, and commuted to Union City daily in a Piper Cub.

I was the first to fly with him, and he told me later that Bennett had given me a backhanded compliment by saying that I would be the least likely of his students to kill him. After I had flown for most of the period, shooting landings and practicing other maneuvers under his direction, he asked if I minded if he took the controls, as he had never flown a Fairchild; his previous training had been in Stearmans.

Aerobatic training was by far the most enjoyable flying I had done. I particularly liked snap rolls and vertical reverses, a half snap starting from a vertical bank in one direction and ending in a vertical bank in the opposite direction. The first vertical reverse I did, after the instructor demonstrated it, was so good that he accused me of practicing them on my own. I hadn't, but only because I'd never heard of them. Thereafter I practiced them on every flight.

He and I got along famously, and I looked forward to flying with him. Sometimes, on the coldest days in January, we took off and, instead of going to the practice flying area, flew on the deck directly to his airport at Milan, landed, and taxied into his hangar to be met by his sister with hot chocolate and homemade cookies, a real treat after the mess hall chow. Warmed and refreshed, we took off, completed our mission, and returned to Union City. Mr. Boen suggested that if we were reported, I should say with my most innocent demeanor that he was demonstrating strange field landings. Fortunately, we were never reported. That was the first time I experienced the joy of mildly bending the rules.

When we became upperclassmen we bent the rules far beyond the breaking point. Every morning we had to get up to meet reveille formation at six, return to the barracks, put everything in inspection order, and then march to breakfast. When we were underclassmen the upper class monitored the formation and took the roll, but we took charge when they left. After the first few days we noticed that none of the officers, who all lived in town, came to the reveille formation, since they would have had to rise half an hour before the cadets to make it. We decided to skip the formation entirely, so both upper and lower classes made breakfast the first formation, thus avoiding standing for about fifteen minutes in the cold, rain, and snow while we went through the rigma-roll call.

This happy situation continued for three weeks of our month as upperclassmen, but as all things must, it came abruptly to an end one morning when the commandant of cadets made a surprise visit to what he thought would be the reveille formation. He got all the cadets out of the barracks and into formation, chewed us out royally, and confined us to the post for the rest of our stay. Since that was only one week, we felt that we had come out way ahead on the deal. I think that he chose not to make too much of it since an officer was supposed to be present at all the reveille formations.

I passed all of my flight checks without difficulty, including the dreaded final check with the Army check pilot. Incidentally, it was my first flight with a military pilot, which made me feel more a part of the Army Air Forces and a step closer to my goal. Our class, 43E, having completed primary, was transferred to Newport, Arkansas, to a new basic flying school.

After an all-day trip our train pulled into the town of Newport in the late afternoon. We had only a brief glimpse of the railroad station since trucks were waiting to carry us to the base. It was to be our only look at Newport, except from the air, until we returned to the station two months later to leave for advanced flying school. There was an epidemic of undulant fever in the area, and we were restricted to the base for our entire two-month stay.

Newport and the Army airfield were in a low, flat, rice-growing section of the state, and from the looks of the base when we arrived, it was wet and muddy enough to grow rice. It was a new, hastily constructed base of the type being thrown up all over the country to meet the demand for pilots. The wood and tar-paper buildings were heated by coal stoves in the rooms, and the latrines and showers were in a separate building. The furnishings were GI cots and primitive bare-wood furniture. Wooden sidewalks were laid between the buildings, and if one of us had the misfortune to step off into the mud, he developed an intimate relationship with his shoeshine kit, rather than the intimate relationship of his dreams. All in all, it was quite a letdown after the comparative luxury of Union City.

The mess hall was an aesthetic and gastronomic disaster, appropriately known to the cadets as Chez Barf. At Union City we had been served at tables by waitresses. At Newport, we carried metal trays along a GI chow line and were served by prisoners from the stockade, who had little use for cadets and made no secret of it.

The flight line was a different story. The hangars, concrete ramps, and runways were all new and in excellent condition. We were warned not to let a wheel go off the runway because it would sink into the mud and probably flip the airplane onto its back. Despite the warning, that happened twice during our course, fortunately without injuring anything but the pilot's pride.

My instructor was Lieutenant Davidson, a small, wiry Texan who was both a fine pilot and a fine instructor, which was not always the case. He introduced me to the basic trainer, the Vultee BT-13 Valiant, known far and wide as the Vultee Vibrator. I didn't think it vibrated much in the air, but it certainly vibrated windows for miles around during takeoffs when the propeller was in low pitch and whenever the propeller was changed from high to low pitch prior to landing. It was considerably larger than the PT-19 and had about twice the power, as well as a two-speed propeller.

It was an easy airplane to fly, with no bad habits, and in it I was introduced to the mysteries of formation, instrument, night, and cross-country flying, all important tools of the trade. Formation flying was particularly interesting because until then we had been strictly enjoined to stay away from other aircraft. Once I learned the secret of good formation flying—that is, not to worry about being too close but to worry about not being close enough—I had no trouble and enjoyed it thoroughly. After the war I put this skill to good use flying tight formation in jets in airshows.

After I completed a little more than eight hours in the BT, Lieutenant Davidson scheduled me for my twenty-hour check with the flight commander, Lieutenant Kurtz. While returning to the field after the check ride, which had gone well, Lieutenant Kurtz suddenly did a violent snap roll. The hand microphone (which was hanging on its hook on the side of the cockpit instead of in the clip where it was placed for aerobatics) flipped through the air and slammed down on my watch, smashing the crystal, hands, face, and most of the innards. It was an expensive Swiss chronometer that had arrived just a few days before, a Christmas present from my uncle. I never mentioned the incident to Lieutenant Kurtz or to my uncle, but from then on, I always wore the standard-issue pilot's hack watch, and I always wore it on the inside of my wrist, a practice I follow to this day.

Everything went smoothly throughout basic, and near the end of the training we were required to choose single-engine or twin-engine advanced. I chose single-engine because of my intense desire to become a fighter pilot. At the end of basic I was delighted to learn that I would go into single-engine advanced training at Craig Army Air Field, Selma, Alabama.

We traveled to Selma by train via Memphis, where we were given four hours of leave between trains, our first time off base in more than two months. Only the certainty of punishment and the prospect of being commissioned in the near future restrained my more exuberant classmates from running amok. As a nondrinker, it fell to me to help many of the heavier drinkers back to the train, establishing me as a nineteen-year-old father figure.

Obviously there hadn't been many cadets in Memphis. As we walked through town we received many quizzical glances and hesitant salutes from enlisted men who, confused by the resemblance between cadet uniforms and officer uniforms, weren't sure what we were, but they weren't taking any chances.

Craig Field was an old established base with paved roads, grass, and stucco and concrete barracks, the antithesis of Newport. The barracks were uncrowded, with only three to a room. I was delighted to find that Dick Jones and Jesse Gray, whom I had met on the train platform at Nashville, were in the same barracks. In fact, Dick was in the next room, thanks to the alphabetical method of room assignment. They had gone to different primary and basic schools but had requested single-engine training and so were sent to Craig.

We cadets were rather relaxed in advanced flying school. We were only two months from graduation, and we were all confident of our ability as pilots. About 40 percent of the class had washed out in primary and about 5 percent more in basic, but we had all heard that it was almost impossible to wash out in advanced, as so much time, money, and effort had been invested in getting us that far. Like most rumors it contained some truth, but many cadets found, to their sorrow, that it was not completely accurate.

We flew the North American AT-6 Texan, a handsome airplane with retractable gear, a constant-speed propeller, and 200 horsepower more than the BT-13. In advanced we were to hone our skills in aerobatics, formation, instrument, and night flying and would be introduced to aerial gunnery. It was a joy to fly and seemed to us to be almost a fighter. It required close attention on landing or it would ground loop violently.

Dick Jones and I were assigned to the same flight but to different instructors. My instructor was Pilot Officer Richard Harry of the RAF, one of a large contingent of British cadets who had been trained at Craig and one of the few who had been retained as instructors. He was fair, clean-cut, and looked young even to me at nineteen. In fact, he looked like the young RAF pilot who was killed in every World War I aviation movie. Sad to say, he was to be killed later in combat over Europe. He was a fine pilot and a good, patient instructor who was well liked by all his students.

It was at Craig that I first met Dick Mullineaux, someone whose misadventures I would observe with awe in the year to come, when he was assigned to my flight. He had started out in Class 43C, but while at preflight at Maxwell he had decided, rightly, that it was difficult to tell a cadet from an officer in a bathing suit and had been taking advantage of that fact to swim at the officer's club pool every weekend. He learned, much to his regret, that it was easy to tell a cadet from an officer when the cadet dives into the shallow end of the pool and breaks his arm and nose. He gained a reprimand and lost two classes while recuperating. That was the way things went for Mullineaux.

After some classroom training we were taken to the skeet range and introduced to that fine sport. It was believed that skeet shooting would teach us to estimate quickly the lead required to hit a moving target, which is the essence of aerial gunnery. After being checked out, we shot several rounds of skeet almost every day. It came naturally to me, and I rarely broke fewer than twenty-two of the twenty-five targets. We also learned to field strip and reassemble the .30-caliber Browning machine gun.

In the air we started out using gun cameras on both ground and towed aerial targets, since actual gunnery could not be practiced at Craig. The film was reviewed and assessed by the gunnery instructor before the next mission. I found that I had a knack for aerial gunnery and was able, instinctively, to lead the target by the proper amount even at high angles off the target.

We then flew our aircraft, in flights of five, to Field 3 at Eglin Army Air Field, on Florida's gulf coast, for actual gunnery training. (I would later spend six years at Eglin as a test pilot after the war.) We fired at individual targets on the ground with our single machine gun, and we fired bullets dipped in various colors of paint at towed sleeve targets. To be rated an expert aerial gunner a pilot had to score 50 percent in air-to-ground shots and 30 percent in air-to-air. I scored more than 70 percent and 50 percent respectively and helped our flight to win the pool for the highest gunnery score. We gave the money to our instructor, who had been promoted a few days earlier and was now Flying Officer Harry.

One evening at Eglin all the cadets and officers were assembled in a hangar to see a film that was classified secret. We all knew that Lt. Col. Jimmy Doolittle had led a group of B-25s that bombed Japan on April 18, 1942. Japan was far beyond the range that any B-25 could reach from any known airfield, and President Roosevelt had announced that the bombers had flown from Shangri-La. The film we saw showed the B-25s being launched from the deck of the carrier *Hornet*, as well as some of the training of the pilots for the mission. It was a thrill for us to learn how it was done, especially since the pilots were trained at the very field we were flying off.

After the war we learned that the eight Doolittle raiders that had been captured were tortured, starved, and sentenced to death by the Japanese. Three were executed, one died of disease, and the other four survived. The Japanese high command, who had promised the people that no bombs would fall on their homeland, was so infuriated by the loss of face that some 250,000 Chinese men, women, and children who lived in the area where the B-25s had come down were slaughtered by Japanese soldiers.

Much later, in my position as assistant director for aeronautics at the National Air and Space Museum, I was privileged to meet and work with Jimmy Doolittle. Never was anyone less appropriately named. He did far more in his lifetime than most. He was a test pilot with a doctoral degree in aeronautical engineering from MIT, one of the greatest air race pilots (the only one to win all three of the major trophies, the Thompson, Bendix, and Schneider), and the wartime leader of the Eighth Air Force.

Returning to Craig with some three weeks left to graduation, we were all confident as the final fittings were made on our officer's uniforms, when suddenly the Gestapo struck. In every squadron ready room, at any time of the day, three instructors from another squadron would walk in and select three cadets, seemingly at random, for a formation check ride. Invariably one and often two of the three would be washed out. Panic and rumor swept through the class. We heard that the operational units were dissatisfied with the flying ability of the graduated cadets and had asked the advanced schools to toughen their requirements (this was true) and that 50 percent of the class would be washed out (this was not true). The three-instructor groups were immediately nicknamed "the Gestapo," and cadets went to any extreme to avoid them. Some spent many extra hours in the Link instrument trainers, while others stayed on the flight line acting as wing walkers for the taxiing planes. Others climbed into their lockers and hid whenever a strange officer approached the ready room.

Many years later, while serving in the Pentagon, I met the former commander of the training squadron at Craig. He told me that the selection of the cadets was not random at all. Only the cadets rated by their instructors as marginal were washed out. We discussed the effectiveness of the flying training and agreed that as good as it was, it could not deliver top-notch combat pilots. There is no substitute for actual combat. More flying experience made a pilot better able to absorb the lessons of combat, but it could not substitute for them.

Fortunately I didn't have to sweat this out too long. About a week after the first Gestapo raid, I was selected as one of a small group of cadets to fly for ten hours in the P-40 prior to graduation. We were transferred to the P-40 squadron and spent the first day in ground school and in cockpit familiarity checks. The next morning we made five backseat landings in the AT-6 and were pronounced ready for the mighty Warhawk, the P-40F.

I will never forget the mixture of elation, awe, and apprehension I felt as I climbed into the cockpit for the first time. The P-40 was twice as fast, had about twice the horsepower, and seemed, although it wasn't, twice as big as the AT-6. The nose extended so far in front of the cockpit and loomed so high that I could see nothing ahead. I remember having a vague hope that the engine would fail to start, but it caught on the first quarter turn of the prop, so there was no turning back. I taxied to the end of the runway, checked the mags, and got tower clearance for takeoff. I advanced the throttle all the way and started down the runway. It was fortunate that the runway was so wide, or I would have run off both sides of it. First the powerful torque turned me to the left, then I overcorrected and swerved to the right, and was finally getting it straightened out when I lifted off. After a few flights I learned the secret of straight takeoff in the P-40. The pilot had to demonstrate immediately that he was in charge by kicking hard right rudder at the start of the takeoff run. An experienced P-40 pilot can easily be recognized by his muscular right leg.

It was much easier to handle in the air. I retracted the gear as I climbed to 10,000 feet over the practice area and did a series of turns, climbs, gentle dives, and stalls to get the feel of the airplane. Becoming more confident, I did some steep turns and a few loops and decided to try a snap roll. It snapped so violently that I banged my head on the side of the canopy, but I learned quickly and was able to perform several snap rolls and vertical reverses without further head damage. After a few practice landings on a cloud I returned to the field and made a reasonably good landing. As I taxied in, I realized that some twelve years after my first airplane ride with Buster Warner, I was at last a fighter pilot. Walking in to the operations building, I glanced back at the sturdy P-40, the plane that would be my dependable companion on almost one hundred combat missions.

One great thrill remained before graduation. I was one of eighty-five cadets selected to fly in an aerial review before President Franklin D. Roosevelt over nearby Maxwell Field, Alabama. Actually the planes were flown by instructors with cadets in the rear seats. We flew in seventeen flights of five-plane vees in trail, and I was in the last flight. We were stacked down slightly to stay out of the turbulent air generated by the propellers of the planes ahead, but it was still quite rough for us at the rear of the formation.

On the day of the review we took off from Craig early in the morning, formed up, and flew to Maxwell Field, where we landed. The AT-6s were lined up with mathematical precision in three long rows on the ramp. Lined up next to us were the same number of BT-13s from Gunter Field on the other side of Montgomery from Maxwell. The propellers were aligned by hand in the horizontal position, and the crews of the airplane in the front row and of the two behind it stood at parade rest in front of their airplanes. When the president's open car came into view, we came to attention and saluted. He drove past slowly, quite close to us, and I could see clearly his cape, fedora, and famous smile. He looked rather weary and drawn, clearly reflecting the strain of wartime leadership.

After he had passed, the tower flashed a light signal and we ran to the cockpits, climbed in, and turned on the radios. At the command "energize," the pilots of all the aircraft hit the energizer switches, and the inertia starters began winding up with their distinctive whines. At the command "engage," 170 propellers started turning at precisely the same instant. This must have been an impressive sight to the hundreds of spectators, and I wish that I could have seen it from a better vantage point.

We then took off, made a long, slow circle to get into formation, and passed in review over the runway twice at about 500 feet before returning to Craig. After the formation loosened up a bit, the instructor let me fly it most of the way back. Leaving the airplane, I realized how privileged I had been to participate in a ceremony before the commander in chief. It was a fitting end to my long period of training and a fitting start to my role as a fighter pilot.

A few days later, on May 28, 1943, we were graduated, and I received my wings, my commission, and my expert aerial gunner badge. My mother and father, who had recently been divorced, both made the difficult trip to Selma for the impressive and long-awaited graduation ceremony.

The class of 43E, immaculate in freshly pressed and heavily starched khaki uniforms, stood at attention in the warm sun in front of the outdoor stage. As the names were called, each cadet marched proudly across the platform to receive his certificate of commission from Colonel Anderson, the commander, and his wings from Lieutenant Colonel Burke, the director of flying. Following that, we returned to the formation, and Colonel Anderson administered the oath, formally commissioning us as Army Air Force officers. The formation was dismissed, and we dispersed to join our families and friends. My mother pinned on my wings as my father stood proudly by.

I was now a second lieutenant in the Army Air Forces and a rated pilot with orders to participate in "regular and frequent aerial flights," a duty I looked forward to with great anticipation.

Some thirty years later I realized what a minuscule part of the flying training program I had experienced. As chairman of the Aeronautics Department at the Smithsonian's National Air and Space Museum, I was gathering statistical material on the World War II training program for an exhibit. The Army Air Forces had graduated 193,440 pilots between July 1, 1939, and August 31, 1945; during that same period more than 124,000 pilot trainees had failed to complete the course for various reasons. At the peak of the program, in December 1943, 74,000 cadets were in pilot training at 106 bases throughout the country. Those numbers are impressive enough in themselves, but add to them the training of other air and ground crew members, the combat training, the actual fighting of the air war, and the training programs of the other services, and it becomes clear that no country but the United States, galvanized by the sneak attack on Pearl Harbor into an all-out effort, could have carried out such a prodigious program.

4

THE SCHOOL
OF RAT RACING

After graduation my father went back to New York and my mother and I went by bus back to Tampa, where I would spend my ten-day leave before reporting to the Third Fighter Command pilot pool at Dale Mabry Field in Tallahassee, Florida. Tallahassee, the capital of Florida, has one of the distinctive Indian names found in that part of the state.

My leave went by quickly, and though I enjoyed it, I was anxious to get into the war. I felt a sense of urgency to develop my new-found skills as a pilot and to put them to use against the enemy. Today the enemies are not so clearly defined, but at that time in World War II, Nazi Germany and the Japanese empire were roundly hated by most Americans. We were itching to make the Japanese pay for Pearl Harbor, the Bataan Death March, and other atrocities. Perhaps some of my dedication could be attributed to my entering manhood. Despite my chronological age of nineteen, I had proven that I could fly a high-performance fighter as well as any, and better than most. I was confident that I would do well in combat.

I saw most of my old friends who were not yet in the service and a few who were home on leave. Harold Williamson, who had learned to fly, joined the Air Force, and rowed on the crew with me, was now an instructor at the Twin-Engine Advanced Flying School at Valdosta, Georgia. He came home for the weekend, and we went out to the airfield where we had learned to fly to visit our former instructors and to show off our wings to the junior birdmen who were still flying Cubs. They were duly impressed.

However, I lost a bit of the face I had made at the airport when I later tried to show off my new uniform and long-coveted silver wings to a girlfriend. I borrowed my brother's bike one evening (remember, there was a war on and gasoline was rationed) to ride to her house. I was both embarrassed and chagrined when she mistook me for a Western Union boy delivering a telegram. Perhaps my entry into manhood wasn't as apparent as I had thought.

The ten days were soon over, which was fine with me, as I couldn't wait to get back into the air. I went by bus to Tallahassee—an uneventful trip, except that a small boy in the seat in front of me spent most of the 250 miles leaning over the back of his seat and saying, "Can you drive an airplane, mister?" even though I had assured him I could any number of times. I didn't mind because I'm sure I would have done the same in his situation.

After reporting in at Tallahassee and being assigned to a bed in a long dormitorylike barracks, I was happy to see that many of my good friends from Craig Field were in the same barracks, including Jones, Gray, and Mullineaux. Many other new pilots from other flying schools were there also, some of whom would become my close friends.

Except for receiving some shots and some physiological training in the low-pressure chamber where high-altitude flight was simulated, there wasn't much to do but await our assignments. We were able to go into town often and found Tallahassee a pleasant city, much different from the southern Florida cities to which I was accustomed. It was hilly, instead of flat, and filled with large oaks and other shade trees. The capitol and the campus of Florida State College for Women, now Florida State University, were quite beautiful. Unfortunately, the women were home for the summer vacation.

Jones, Gray, Mullineaux, and I, along with several of the group that I was beginning to know well, were assigned to the 337th Fighter Group at Sarasota, Florida, a fighter replacement training unit (FRTU). The Third Fighter Command, in the southeast United States, was responsible for the training of most of the single-engine fighter pilots after they had been graduated from flying school. There were thirty-four bases like Sarasota in the command, plus sixteen auxiliary fields. More than 35,000 day-fighter pilots were trained in FRTUs from December 1942 through the end of the war.

To my dismay, I learned that we would be flying P-40s; I had been hoping for P-51s or P-38s. After flying P-40s for about a month, however, I swore by them and became one of their strongest supporters. This is de rigueur with fighter pilots. The plane they are flying regularly is always the best. I am convinced that if a pilot were assigned to fly a manhole cover, he would soon swear that it was the best flying machine around.

Leaving Tallahassee, a large group of us went to Sarasota by commercial bus, arriving at just about dark. We were met at the depot by a lieutenant, who had arranged for us to eat and sleep at a downtown hotel. We were to be picked up by trucks in the morning and taken to the airfield. Before the war I had been to Sarasota many times as copilot on an Armour meat truck.

In the morning we were grouped in front of the hotel waiting to be picked up when a large flatbed truck drove slowly past us carrying a P-40, broken into small pieces and piled in a heap. In fact, only the distinctive tail section, which was relatively intact, identified it as a P-40—a real morale builder. I learned later that the oxygen system had failed, causing the pilot to pass out at about 30,000 feet and dive straight into the ground.

The trucks arrived and took us to the field, which was about halfway between Sarasota and Bradenton. There were two fighter squadrons, the 98th and the 303rd. Jones, Gray, Mullineaux, and I all went to the 98th. Our quarters for the first six weeks, while awaiting the completion of the bachelor officer's quarters, were the worst I ever lived in, including those in China. We lived in wooden hutments, about twenty feet wide by forty feet long. The top halves of the walls were screen, which could be covered by wooden shutters that doubled as awnings when open—and we had to keep them open because of the high temperature and humidity of the Florida summer. They were crowded, with twenty officers to a hutment, and totally bare of furniture except for the twenty cots. All of our belongings were piled on the floor by our cots, making us wonder why there was so much emphasis on neatness during training. Fortunately, we wore flying suits most of the time, so most of our uniforms could remain packed. Our preflight tactical officer, Jungle Jim Turner, could not have survived an inspection of these quarters. If the quarters went this far downhill from aviation cadet to second lieutenant, I certainly wasn't looking forward to being promoted.

The 98th was equipped with new P-40Ns, a lightweight model powered by the Allison V-1710, a V-twelve liquid-cooled engine of 1,250 horsepower. After a short briefing by the squadron commander, Captain Chapman, we were given some cockpit time to learn the layout of the controls and instruments. Following that, after individual cockpit checks by the instructors, none of whom had combat experience, we made several orientation flights, getting the feel of the airplane and becoming familiar with the local flying area, which included the beautiful beaches and keylike islands of the Gulf Coast. We made three touch-and-go landings at the end of each flight that were graded by an instructor in a jeep at the end of the runway. Once they were satisfied that we could handle the P-40, our training began in earnest. Some of the pilots who had not flown P-40s in advanced had problems, and three were sent back to Tallahassee for reassignment. I was sorry for them, since they were most likely sent to bombers.

The training syllabus included instrument flying in a BT-14 (a two-seat, fixed-gear basic trainer built by North American) as well as in the P-40, formation flying, air-to-air and air-to-ground gunnery, night flying, minimum-altitude flying, and combat tactics. All flights started and ended in tight formation. At some point in almost every flight we had a rat race, a game of aerial follow the leader, a children's game raised to the ultimate level. The instructor would put the formation in echelon, then peel off with the rest of the flight following in close trail. After about five minutes of diving, rolling, looping, and zooming, the leader would circle, rocking his wings, and we would rejoin the formation. Depending on the amount of fuel remaining, we would have another rat race or return to the field to land. It was great sport, and it seemed unfair to be paid for it.

The 98th CO believed that you had to fly on the edge of danger— or as they say now, on the edge of the performance envelope—to learn to be a good fighter pilot. When we peeled off to land, out of our echelon formation at 1,000 feet, we had to execute a tight vertical bank and were fined if we did not pull streamers with our wing tips. Streamers are white trails of water vapor, like contrails, that are formed off a plane's wing tips in high-g turns. It usually required about 4 g to generate them. In contrast, the 303rd squadron fined the pilots who pulled streamers on the landing break because too tight a turn could result in a high-speed stall, followed by a spin with insufficient altitude to recover. That happened to one of our pilots, but the fatal accident did not cause the 98th to change its policy. Although we were not fined, it was considered poor technique to have to add power once the pilot had chopped the throttle on the break. We were supposed to be able to glide through the entire 360-degree turn to a full-stall landing. Although Tom Wolfe had not yet coined the term "the right stuff," the ability to make a tight 360-degree approach without touching the throttle was one of the first steps up the fighter pilot's ziggurat.

At Sarasota I met for the first time Lt. Sam Brown, one of the wildest characters I have ever known. Sam was of average height, with unruly black hair and piercing wild eyes. He was a bundle of energy, with quick jerky moves, and he almost shouted when he spoke. He had arrived at Sarasota several months earlier, completed his training, and been retained as an instructor. While instructing his first group of pilots, he led them in an unauthorized minimum-altitude training flight during which he made a sudden tight turn, forcing the wingman on the inside of the turn so low that he hit a tree. The airplane was severely damaged, but the pilot managed to climb high enough to bail out safely.

As a result of that incident, Sam was court-martialed, fined, and assigned to go overseas with our class. In the meantime, he was to continue as an instructor. My first contact with him was when he burst into our flight's ready room and loudly announced that if he made any head-on passes at us in simulated combat we had better turn, because he never did. Fortunately, I was never attacked from head on by Sam, but as described earlier, I did run into one of his Japanese cousins flying an Oscar.

Another of Sam's misadventures took place one weekend at the Lido Beach Club near Sarasota. After a refreshing swim, we went into the snack bar for lunch. Sam had gone in a bit earlier and obviously had had a few drinks. He started complaining loudly (he did everything loudly) that it was too hot in the snack bar. Announcing that he was going to find the main ventilation fan and put it into low pitch, he went to the fan room, forced open the door, and, still in his wet bathing suit, started fooling with the controls. Suddenly there was a bright electrical flash. We rushed in and found Sam sprawled on the floor, unconscious. We dragged him out and were relieved to find that he was still breathing. After a few minutes, his eyelids fluttered, then opened, and he started moving; then he got up and yelled that he had fixed the fan. He soon was his old screaming self again, so we assumed that the shock had done no further damage to his brain. If some of these antics appear sophomoric, consider that many of the participants were sophomores or even freshmen in age. A squadron can stand a few Sams, but fortunately Jones, Gray, and most of the others, while fine, eager fighter pilots, were much more stable.

Simulated combat training was great sport and the start of what we all looked forward to. On the scheduled missions we were briefed to attack or be attacked under varying conditions of altitude, location, and situation. For instance, two flights would take off, fly to the target (concentric circles marked on a deserted islet just off the beach), and while one flight dive-bombed, the other would provide top cover. At some point during the mission the flights would be attacked by two or more flights from the other squadron. The importance of seeing the enemy first became apparent from the results of the combat. Once the flights were engaged, they would mix it up in a dogfight for several minutes until the instructors called halt. Leader-wingman coordination was stressed, with instructors acting as one or the other. This was drilled into us, and it proved invaluable in combat. The results were hotly disputed on the ground, with both sides claiming victory. It really didn't matter; the experience was what counted.

During that period we could get away with things that would have brought a court-martial after the war. We regularly flew down the main streets of Bradenton and Palmetto just above the housetops when returning to the base. When we found large herds of cattle being rounded up, we would dive on them, causing them to scatter wildly. I'm sure the cowboys would have preferred Indians to P-40s. One of our instructors, called On the Deck Beck, insisted that we fly low enough to leave a wake when practicing low-altitude navigation over some of the Florida lakes.

It was also the practice in the 98th to attack any flight that was spotted after the formal part of a mission was completed. This included attacking aircraft from other bases flying P-51s, P-39s, and B-26s, as well as P-40s. There were no P-47 squadrons within our range. Once when we bounced some P-39s from Venice Army Air Field, one of them stalled in a tight turn and went into a flat spin. Fortunately, the pilot baled out safely, but we soon received orders not to attack P-39s as they were susceptible to flat spins when they had expended their ammunition. This aggressive attitude, inculcated in us by the commander, led to a fine esprit de corps and pride in being part of the 98th.

One feeling that stayed with me in varying degrees throughout my Air Force career was the sense of awe that I was really flying a powerful fighter in the middle of a formation, watching and correcting for the jiggles and slight changes of position that occur constantly in formation flying but are not visible from the ground. The same feeling occurred while flying alone sometimes. It was dreamlike and wonderfully satisfying.

One technique I used, taught to me by Sam Brown, when I couldn't shake another fighter from my tail was to climb vertically until my airplane stalled and fell back toward the one behind me. He would have to break off to avoid a collision, and I often ended up on his tail. That would have been useless in combat using real guns, but it was effective in simulated combat. In retrospect I realize I was lucky to survive Sam's School of Stupid Strategy.

Night flying was hairy in the P-40 because of the flames from the stacks of the in-line engine. They were so bright that they destroyed a pilot's night vision as soon as he advanced the throttle for takeoff. I could see the lights along the runway, but everything went black when I passed the field boundary. Once I reduced power, the flame pattern became much smaller and my vision gradually returned. One of our pilots evidently did not regain his vision in time, because he dived straight into the Gulf after takeoff and was killed. Landing was an even greater problem. With the throttle cut back to idle the engine backfired continually, causing large bursts of flame that were directly in line with the normal landing field of vision, making it extremely difficult to judge the plane's height above the runway. Fortunately, I never had to make a night landing in combat without runway lights, although I made many night takeoffs.

Mullineaux's first night landing was memorable, to say the least. He ran off the side of the runway on takeoff but managed to haul the P-40 into the air before hitting anything. Somewhat flustered, he forgot to return the landing gear handle to the neutral position after retraction. When it was time to land, he put the handle in neutral, instead of down, held the stick trigger for the prescribed length of time, and then checked the hand pump to see if the pressure was up. It was, because the gear was locked in the up position. The P-40N had no cockpit gear position indicator; instead pegs on each wing extended when the gear was down. Unfortunately, the pegs were not visible in the dark. Blinded by the flames, he lined up improperly and landed off the runway to the right on the belly. He noticed immediately that he was off the runway because there were two rows of lights to his left, so he cut his engine with the mixture control and the ignition switch. He swore later that he didn't know his wheels were up until he got out and jumped off the wing and found it only three inches to the ground. He had attributed the roughness to being off the runway.

After the war, if a pilot damaged an aircraft in that way, he would have been grounded until he met an accident board. At the least he would have received an official reprimand. In this instance though, the operations officer said to Mullineaux, "Well, do we land with our wheels up?" and Mullineaux replied, "Yes, sir, I guess we do." That was the end of it, and Mullineaux climbed into another plane and made the prescribed number of successful landings.

All in all, the hours I spent rat racing above central Florida were some of the most enjoyable of my life, especially among the cumulus clouds that usually formed in the afternoons. Diving, in trail, into the dark valleys between the clouds and then zooming up over the bright, sunlit, towering hills, only to roll inverted to hurtle down the other side, was pure joy, and I wished it could go on forever. When I was between the sun and the cloud, the shadow of my airplane racing along the white, puffy surface was surrounded by a brilliant circular rainbow, called the pilot's halo. I felt sorry for the poor earthbound folk who could not experience this exhilaration.

One weekend in August, near the end of my stay at Sarasota, I went home to Tampa. By chance, Harold Williamson had flown a Beechcraft AT-10 trainer to Drew Army Air Field in Tampa that weekend. That Saturday afternoon we drove to Drew, and on the pretext of a test flight, he took me for a short flight, my first in a twin-engine aircraft. It convinced me that I had been correct in choosing single-engine. We agreed to meet over his house in Tampa at 1,000 feet early on Monday, when he would be leaving to fly back to Valdosta, Georgia.

Bright and early on Monday I talked our operations officer into letting me have a P-40 for an hour. I took off and made a beeline for Tampa, where I found Harold circling. I slowed way down to his speed of about 150 mph and joined up on his left wing. We let down to about 500 feet and cruised over our neighborhood, where all our friends had been alerted. I saw the A&P where only ten months earlier I had been grinding 19-cents-a-pound hamburger for 35 cents an hour. We then waved good-bye and went our separate ways. That was the last time I saw Harold until after the war in Europe had ended. Talk about a class act—our families and friends talked about it for years. Western Union boy, indeed.

That aerial rendezvous would be impossible today, what with air traffic control radar, noise abatement regulations, and air traffic congestion. I understand why it can't be allowed today, but I wish today's pilots could get away with what we did during the war.

Just for the record, following his instructor duty Harold went to Italy and flew weather reconnaissance missions in P-38s. After the war he went back to school and became a fine orthopedic surgeon. His practice is in Tampa, and for many years he satisfied his need for adventure by driving racing cars, culminating in a win at the Daytona 24-hour race.

Suddenly our two months of training was over. I realized that in addition to the formal goals of the course, we had learned, in varying degrees, the one vital skill that gave a pilot a fighting chance to survive in combat: the ability to fly by instinct. That was the real goal of the innumerable rat races and dogfights. At some time, near the midpoint of the program, the student became one with the airplane. The pilot, not his airplane, followed the plane ahead through any and all maneuvers without conscious attention to the controls. He could devote his mind to planning his next move or anticipating the other pilot's, without worrying about flying the plane. His eyes automatically scanned the instrument panel every few seconds and any improper reading would jump out. We felt as ready for combat as we could be without actual combat experience.

The deaths of some of our squadron mates in training had no noticeable effect on the rest of us. I believed, and I'm sure most of the others did also, that the ones killed had not been quite good enough, and that I would be able to handle any emergency or combat situation that I found myself in. None of my close friends was killed, so I don't know how that would have affected me.

We packed our belongings, said our good-byes, heard the ritual "Get one for me" from the instructors, and boarded the bus for Tallahassee, where we would receive our assignments to combat squadrons overseas. If nothing else, the living conditions there would be better.

All through our training we kept up with the war news, both through official military information and from the newspapers and radio. A great deal had occurred during the two months at Sarasota, from mid-June to mid-August of 1943. Sicily had been invaded and captured, Mussolini had been driven from power, the Soviet forces had stopped a major German advance in the Kursk area, Army Air Force B-24s had attacked the Rumanian oil refineries at Ploesti (putting 40 percent of the plant out of action but losing fifty-four aircraft), and in the Pacific the Allies were advancing in the Solomons and New Guinea. Although the tide of war had clearly turned in favor of the Allies, there was no doubt that there would be more than enough war left for us.

5

FLYING TIGER
TACTICS

Back in Tallahassee we were assigned to the same barracks as before, with the same dull routine—little to do but speculate on which theater of war we would be sent to. Actually, we were more interested in what we would fly than where we would be flying. Although we had trained in P-40s, we still hoped for P-51s because P-40s were being phased out. Obviously the medics knew where we were going, because they immediately started a whole new round of inoculations that included typhoid, typhus, yellow fever, and cholera. That, along with the installation of jungle kits (a back pad containing a folding machete, hard chocolate bar, fishing gear, and some other odds and ends) on our parachutes convinced us that we were a cinch for the Aleutians or Alaska.

Our luggage was stenciled with a destination code, and we were told that we could carry only a B-4 bag for our clothes and a parachute bag for our flying gear. Typically, Mullineaux wasted a lot of time trying to break the code. All other belongings were placed in footlockers that would be shipped to our destination. I packed about twenty Schick Injector cartridges of ten blades each in my footlocker, anticipating a long stay overseas. (The footlockers, true to footlocker tradition, did not catch up with us for eight or nine months. Some of the other pilots were inconvenienced, but I had shaved only about three times in the interim and was still using the Tallahassee blade in my razor.)

A few days later we boarded a train and left the oak-shaded streets of Tallahassee for the royal palm–lined boulevards of Miami Beach, where we were billeted in one of the oceanfront hotels taken over by the Army. Although most of the more luxurious furnishings had been removed, it was far nicer than any other place we had been thus far. We still didn't know our final destination but had narrowed it down to the Caribbean, Mediterranean, or China-Burma-India theaters. I hoped it would be the CBI because I had recently read *God Is My Copilot*, by Col. Robert L. Scott, and was a great admirer of Gen. Claire L. Chennault and the Flying Tigers.

In *God Is My Copilot*, Colonel Scott tells of joining General Chennault's American Volunteer Group (AVG), the Flying Tigers, to fly with them and learn the tactics that were so successful against the Japanese. They had destroyed 299 Japanese aircraft in the air and lost only 8 AVG aircraft. Colonel Scott became the first commanding officer of the 23rd Fighter Group formed from the AVG when it was disbanded on July 4, 1942. He remained in command until January 9, 1943. Two of the AVG aces, David Lee "Tex" Hill and Ed Rector, transferred to the 23rd as squadron commanders, and they figured prominently in the story. Later I was to serve under both of these, to me, legendary figures, who fully lived up to my expectations. I'm proud to claim them as good friends to this day.

The five days in Miami were essentially, but not officially, a short leave before departing the ZI (Zone of the Interior, which is what the Army for some reason called the United States) for overseas. Hoping to ring some southern belles, four of us—Mullineaux, Jones, Gray, and I—rented a 1940 Plymouth convertible for three days, for something like $5 a day plus a small mileage charge, and cruised around Miami Beach and Miami. We tried to minimize the mileage charge by jacking up the rear wheels and running the car in reverse, but the gear ratio was so low that it wasn't worth the effort. There were so many officers and officer candidates in Miami Beach that the city was almost solid khaki, and it was nearly impossible to meet an unattached girl. I guess the girls figured a paddlefoot (nonflying officer) in the hand was worth two fighter pilots in the bush. In our case, even with the convertible, it turned out to be a dead loss. None of them was interested in second lieutenants who would be there for only a few days at best. That was hard for us to understand, because in the movies, beautiful girls were always chasing the dashing young warriors flying away to save the world.

Our only duties were to check the hotel bulletin board twice a day to see if we had been alerted to leave, and finally, on September 7, 1943, we were delighted to find the names "Jones," "Mullineaux," "Gray," "Kaiser," "McEnteer," and "Lopez" on the list with instructions to be packed and ready to leave at eight the next morning. I felt that at last the preliminaries were over and the great adventure was about to begin.

The next morning we were taken by Army bus to Miami's Thirty-sixth Street airport (now Miami International) and unloaded at the Air Transport Command Terminal. After a short wait we were called along with many higher-ranking officers—there were none lower—and we carried our bags out to a C-54 on the ramp. We all stood around on the ramp for about fifteen minutes until a staff car with a U.S. flag on the fender pulled up. We were called to attention as two colonels and a civilian in khakis got out and boarded the plane. I was intrigued that one of the colonels had a briefcase chained to his wrist. A major who was waiting to board told us that the civilian was Ambassador Clarence Gauss, who was on the way to his post in China. One did not have to be a Sherlock Holmes to deduce that we might be going to the same place.

As the lowest in rank, our group of second lieutenants was the last to board. We sat together in the rear of the cabin, which because of the ambassador had airline seats instead of the customary military bucket seats. We were the only flying officers on the plane, as the crew was from Pan American Airways.

The first leg of our flight carried us to Borinquen Field in Puerto Rico, where the plane was refueled and we had lunch. We heard the surprising news that Italy had surrendered. The ambassador said that the surrender should shorten the war considerably, but as it turned out, the Germans fought tenaciously for every inch of Italian soil for almost another year. Next we flew to Georgetown, British Guiana, where we spent the night, or in Army Air Forces terminology, we R.O.N.'d (remain overnight). After dinner in the RAF Officer's Club, we went into the bar. There, for the only time in my life, I hit the jackpot on the slot machine and won a pocketful of shillings, which I was unable to spend for some time but took as a good omen for the future.

Our next stop was Belém, in Brazil, and then another R.O.N. at Natal, on the eastern bulge of Brazil. This was the jumping-off place for flights across the South Atlantic. Both flights that day were above the impenetrable rain forests of Brazil. It was almost useless to search for planes that crashed in that area, as they were swallowed up by the jungle. The chances of survival were much better in a crash at sea. I was amazed by the width of the Amazon River, which we crossed near its mouth. It took about fifteen minutes to fly across. My horizons were broadening at a rapid pace.

In Natal each of us pilots bought a pair of the coveted Natal boots, midcalf boots that were beloved by flying officers, as they helped to distinguish us from lesser mortals. Ambassador Gauss was not feeling too well, so we didn't take off until late morning. I learned later that he hated flying, which probably explained the hostile stares he gave us whenever we passed him. Perhaps that was standard ambassadorial behavior, but since he was the first ambassador I'd seen, I had no way to judge.

After flying over miles and miles of ocean that confirmed the wisdom of my decision not to become a Navy pilot, we landed on that minuscule dot in the middle of the South Atlantic called Ascension Island. This tiny volcanic island had a few barracks, a mess hall, and a long runway cut between two mountains. The airport was called Wideawake Field, after the wideawake birds, the local name for sooty terns, that infested the area. A major problem on Ascension was keeping the bird population down and away from the runway, where they were a hazard to aircraft. My memories of this island were refreshed some forty years later when the British used it as a staging area during the Falklands war.

Jones, Gray, and I did some exploring of the island during the few hours of daylight left and, much to our chagrin, cut our shiny new boots to shreds on the sharp lava stones that formed the base of the mountains.

Early in the evening, an RAF ferry crew joined us in the visiting officer's quarters, the navigator still gibbering to the pilot about the landing. They were landing in their Martin Maryland bomber when the flaps failed, snapping to the full up position on the final approach. The navigator, sitting in the glass nose, had a terrifying view of the runway rushing up to meet him. The pilot partially recovered, and the plane hit hard on its main landing gear. Fortunately, only the navigator's morale had been damaged, and his next destination, Africa, was somewhat larger than Ascension.

From there we flew to Accra, on the western bulge of Africa, in what was then called the Gold Coast. We refueled and flew, once again across a jungle, to Maiduguri, just south of Lake Chad in French Equatorial Africa. It was difficult for me to believe that I was really in Africa. I was a bit disappointed not to see any of the lost cities in the jungle that I had come to expect from my avid reading of the Tarzan series.

Maiduguri was a large native village surrounded by cultivated fields. We caught a glimpse of it from the air as we approached the single runway that had been hacked out of the jungle a few miles from the town. The steward told us that we would spend the night at the airport, so we six second lieutenants rented horses from a local entrepreneur for a guided tour of the village. We were not accomplished riders, and the horses seemed to sense it, so they did whatever they pleased. The village was fascinating, with thatched huts right out of *National Geographic* and natives wearing loincloths. The guide stopped at one of the huts, but our horses kept going, since "whoa" evidently had a different meaning in their language. We had become completely lost when the horses suddenly took off at a gallop, heading for what we hoped was the airfield. I hung on for dear life until, while turning a corner at high speed, the cinch on my saddle snapped and the saddle fell off with me on it. Fortunately, the horse wasn't very tall, and I was uninjured. It would have been ironic to be wiped out on a horse before even reaching combat. The others stopped their horses by brute force, came back, and helped me tie the saddle cinch back together. Darkness was approaching, and we were more than ready to return. We decided to let the horses find the way back, but not at the speed they had in mind. I found out that I could control the pace by twisting the horse's ears. The harder I twisted, the slower it went. I passed this useful information on to the others, and we made it back under control.

Arriving at the airport, we found to our dismay that the ambassador had decided to continue the trip that evening, and the plane had been held up waiting for us. The engines were running and the steps had been rolled away as we hurried toward the plane. The door opened and a knotted rope was lowered for us to scramble up. We slunk quietly to our seats, trying to be unobtrusive despite the many high-ranking glares aimed our way. The steward, who seemed to enjoy the discomfiture of the ambassador and his entourage, was kind enough to give us some sandwiches to make up for the meal we had missed.

One of the engines did not check out properly on the runup, so we taxied back in to the ramp and waited about four hours while the engine was repaired. Wearied from our long day in the saddle, we were glad finally to take off shortly after midnight and get some needed sleep. We arrived over Khartoum, Anglo-Egyptian Sudan, in the early light. While we circled before landing, I asked the steward to point out the adjoining town of Omdurman, where Winston Churchill, as a young officer of the 21st Lancers, had participated in the last British cavalry charge. He was part of Kitchener's expedition against the Mahdi and his Dervishes who had killed General "Chinese" Gordon. This had taken place forty-five years earlier, in 1898. Now Churchill was prime minister, and I was flying above the site of the battle at more than 200 miles per hour.

After refueling, we flew across the Red Sea and landed at Aden, Arabia. My only memories of Aden are the desert, the terrific heat, and the worst Coke I had ever tasted; it had so much chlorine in it that despite my thirst, I couldn't drink it. A few hours later we took off and flew up the south end of the Arabian Peninsula and across the Arabian Sea to Karachi, India (now Pakistan). We landed at Karachi Air Base, or KAB, as it was known. It was distinguished by a giant hangar that had been built to accommodate the ill-fated R-101, the British dirigible that had crashed in France at the start of its planned flight to India.

When we went into the terminal, a modern building filled with Americans and British in uniform and Indians in native dress, we were told that this was the destination of our group, although the airplane was going on to China. Collecting our belongings, we reported to a captain behind a counter marked "Incoming Officers." He checked our orders, directed us to the visiting officer's quarters in the same building, and told us to report to him at eight the next morning. It was hard to believe that in just four days we had traveled halfway around the world.

The next morning the captain told us that we would be going to the China Burma India Fighter Replacement Training Unit at Landhi Field, about fifteen miles to the east. Disappointed at the thought of still more training, we climbed into the back of the ubiquitous GI six-by-six truck and headed for Landhi. The country was flat and dry and got more so as we entered the edge of the Sind Desert. This part of India looked much as I had envisioned it from reading Kipling, except that there were no mountains nearby.

Landhi Field comprised a group of widely separated, low, flat buildings on a sunbaked expanse of sand. The airfield, with a control tower and alert shack, was about half a mile away. A baseball backstop and a volleyball court marked it as an American base, even without the flag in front of the headquarters.

Landhi was the site for a sound training plan. Fighter pilots from China and Burma who had finished their combat tours would spend about six weeks there on the way home, passing on their hard-won experience to the replacement pilots en route to combat in that theater.

The new pilots would thus be exposed to the most up-to-date tactics and techniques. The system worked well. The only disappointment was the war-weary old P-40s allotted to the training mission. Most were P-40Es that had been in Africa and China before coming to Landhi. There were even a few earlier models.

The concrete barracks were clean and airy. Mullineaux, Ray Kaiser, Jones, and I shared a room, and Jesse Gray was in the next room. We had Indian room boys, actually young men, to do all the cleaning and other odds and ends. They were all specialists. There were dhobi wallahs to do the laundry, panay wallahs to bring water, and various other wallahs to sweep the floor and make the beds. They must have had a strong union. Although it was hot, the humidity was low and there was almost always a breeze, so it was quite comfortable in our spacious rooms.

At lunch we met the rest of the trainee pilots and were glad to find that they had all been at Sarasota or at St. Petersburg, where the other two squadrons of the 337th Fighter Group were based. They were from my class or my upper class, and I knew many of them at least by sight, which gave me an immediate sense of belonging. Several of them were to become as close as brothers to me, with that special camaraderie generated in combat by the unspoken, but understood, commitment to risk our lives for each other. Two of them, in addition to Dick Jones and Jesse Gray, were Oswin H. "Moose" Elker and Wiltz P. "Flash" Segura. We served together in the 75th Fighter Squadron and still stay in contact.

Moose and Flash were totally dissimilar in appearance and manner but were both first-class pilots and natural leaders. Moose was of German descent and came from Surrey, North Dakota. He was of medium height, powerfully built, and balding, but with a magnificent red mustache that measured eleven inches from tip to tip. Although quiet and unassuming, he had a great sense of humor.

Flash was of French and Spanish descent and came from New Iberia, Louisiana. Handsome, with thick curly black hair and a slight Cajun accent, he was the ringleader in every gag and practical joke in our group. He was, and is, one of the funniest men I've ever met, with an irrepressible natural wit. One never knew when to take him seriously. He had ivory handles installed on his service .45 automatic, and all of his spare ammunition had been highly polished with a Blitz cloth and placed in a western gunbelt. He regularly wore British-style khaki shorts and a sun helmet, although neither was authorized for U.S. Army wear. They were, however, very practical in India's sunny clime.

While at Landhi, Flash outdid himself in military fashion design when he had a uniform made based on the then infamous zoot suit. The waistline of the trousers, which were twenty-four inches in diameter at the knees but tight at the ankle cuffs, was just under the armpits. The jacket had padded shoulders and a wide skirt that went down almost to the knees. The crowning touches were an oversize pair of pilot wings that could be flapped by pulling a string in the pocket and a five-foot gold-colored watch chain. He was the hit of the base. Fortunately, no member of the Air Force board that years later was to promote Flash to brigadier general saw his version of combat garb.

Both Moose and Flash exuded the confidence and sensible boldness, the courage without foolhardiness, the proper guts-to-brains ratio, that presaged leadership ability, and in both cases the prediction was proven correct in combat.

Flying ability is a major factor in leadership in a fighter squadron. Every fighter pilot wants to be led by someone he feels is almost as good a pilot as he is. It is safe to say that while not every good fighter pilot is a good leader, every good leader is a good fighter pilot. Outstanding leaders like Tex Hill, Ed Rector, John Alison, Hub Zemke, Don Blakeslee, and Gabby Gabreski were also outstanding fighter pilots.

Most of our time at Landhi was spent in flying or at the flight line talking to the instructors about their combat experiences. No time was spent in checking us out; it was assumed that we knew how to handle a P-40. We went out in flights with an instructor to learn the area, but after that every flight was simulated air combat, practice gunnery, both air and ground, or practice bombing. The area around Karachi had a stark beauty from the air, with the Sind Desert stretching to the north and east and miles of deserted beaches along the Arabian Sea. The many deserted areas for bombing and gunnery practice and cloudless skies practically every day made it an ideal place for combat training. In addition to dive-bombing and skip-bombing, we were introduced to parafrags, which we were often to use in combat.

Parafrags were accurate and deadly antipersonnel weapons. Each of the bombs weighed about sixty pounds and consisted of a cast coil spring filled with explosive, with a small parachute on one end and a long striker on the other. We usually released them at about fifty feet above the target just as it disappeared beneath the wing. The parachute stopped the bomb's forward motion, and the bomb dropped rapidly and exploded about a foot above the ground when the striker touched.

The spring broke into small fragments that were blasted with tremendous velocity over a circular area of several hundred feet. A P-40 could carry a cluster of three parafrags under each wing.

We were also introduced to shadow gunnery at Landhi. I had never heard of it before, nor have I heard of it since. An airplane flew over the deserted beach area at about 1,000 feet so that its shadow ran along the sand. The other fighters took turns diving and shooting at the shadow. It couldn't be scored too accurately, but the instructor could get a general idea of how the pilot was doing. As far as I know, the technique was developed at Landhi. Whether it was or not, it was an ingenious and effective method of practicing aerial gunnery.

We visited the city of Karachi whenever we were free, usually in the evenings or on Sunday, on a truck provided for that purpose. The main section of Karachi was clean and modern, but there were areas of unbelievable squalor and poverty surrounding the downtown, and they were off-limits to military personnel. The British Officer's Club was open to us and was an oasis of tranquillity and elegance. The building's architecture, antique furniture, and general ambience were similar to those of an exclusive London men's club, except for the turbaned Indian staff. At least part of its attraction was its contrast with the bare concrete rooms and GI furniture that we returned to every night. Equally impressive was the delicious and inexpensive food. The first time I went there, one of the British officers said that the prawn were excellent, so I ordered them even though I didn't know what they were. I was delighted to learn that prawn were large local shrimp and that they were, in fact, delicious.

We were warned not to eat anywhere except at the Officer's Club or the better hotels, since the local water was not safe to drink and there were germs and parasites in abundance. After one or two visits to the city, we confined our dining to the club.

Usually we stayed at Landhi and went to the evening movies, which were generally American B pictures or worse. My first night at Landhi I saw, written on a mess hall blackboard, "Tonight's movie, Hoot Gibson in 'HOOF HEARTED.'" I glanced at it casually and was surprised that a different movie was shown. After the sign remained there for three nights with no Hoot, I finally read it aloud and got the message.

Visiting the city was an unpleasant experience. Everywhere we went we were besieged by beggars of all ages, shapes, and descriptions. Most of them were so dirty that we hated to be near them, and many were horribly deformed and so grotesque that revulsion overcame pity.

We were told that parents often maimed their children to prepare them for begging. Frequently gangs of youths would chase a man, wanting to shine his shoes. If he ignored them they threw mud and horse manure on his shoes so he would need a shine. Once when a group of us were besieged by such a mob, a British Army captain approached. We saluted him, and he asked if they were bothering us. We said they certainly were, so he whacked one in the face with his riding crop and shouted something in Hindi. Whatever he said was effective. They took off at high speed and didn't bother us again.

Some of the beggars were imaginative and amusing in their pleas. In addition to the standard "Baksheesh Sahib, no mama, no papa, no food, baksheesh," they often added, "No flying pay, no per diem!" While certainly a true statement, it usually brought a laugh and perhaps a rupee (worth 33 cents at that time).

My distaste for India was shared by most of the Americans. Once we arrived in China we thought even less of the Indians. The Chinese peasants, who were at least as poor as the Indians, were clean and hardworking. I can't recall ever seeing a beggar in China.

One afternoon I was playing volleyball when a P-40, practicing dive-bombing nearby, pulled out too hard, stalled, and snapped into a spin. He had more than enough height to recover, but when he broke the spin he tried to pull up too soon and went into another spin. He did this three times before he hit the ground about 200 yards away. Since he had hit rather flat and didn't explode, we thought he might have survived. We ran to the crash, but the pilot had been thrown out and killed by the impact. He was the first dead person I had ever seen, and although I hadn't known him well, it was a sobering experience. The death of another pilot is easier to take if you don't have to see the body.

Two of the permanent staff at Landhi, Greg Carpenter and P.W., were involved in a weird incident. Greg had been shot down in a P-40 and crash-landed in Japanese territory but had escaped with the aid of some Chinese guerrillas (who at great personal risk played an invaluable role in rescuing and returning shot-down American air crews). Since he had left his parachute with his name on it in his airplane, he was not allowed to fly in combat again. The reasoning was that if he were shot down again, the Japanese would know that he had escaped from the first crash and might force him to identify the guerrillas.

Greg was an accomplished magician and often entertained and baffled us with his feats of prestidigitation, to say nothing of legerdemain. It was much appreciated, as entertainment was generally limited to what could be concocted by the limitless imaginations in our group. I don't remember P.W.'s real name. "P.W." stood for "Perfect Wingman," a name he had earned by staying in perfect formation with his flight leader, whose engine had failed at liftoff, as he crash-landed.

P.W. wanted some in-flight pictures of himself to send to his girl-friend. Greg volunteered to shoot them in the AT-16, an export version of the AT-6. He borrowed the base commander's large Speed Graphic camera for the flight. The plan was for Greg, in the front seat, to turn completely around and, with both front and back canopies open, photograph P.W. in the back seat with the ground showing behind him. They were flying at a very low airspeed with the gear and flaps down to reduce the wind force on the camera when Greg told P.W. to pull the nose up so that more ground would be in the picture. He kept signaling P.W. to raise the nose higher until suddenly the airplane stalled, P.W. instinctively popped the stick forward to recover, and Greg was catapulted out of the cockpit. He said his only thought was to save the base commander's camera. He was able to open his chute, but his foot caught in the lines, and for a while he was descending head first. He managed to get untangled, but he landed in a giant clump of cactus that scratched him up quite a bit. The camera, to his great relief, was intact. It also was unused. He hadn't taken a single picture. Greg always was a good magician, but we hadn't dreamed he could make himself disappear from an airplane in flight.

Our change of venue hadn't done anything for Sam Brown's stability. One day we were all standing around the mess hall waiting for it to open when Sam joined the group. He was wearing his .45 automatic because he was officer of the day. All was well until some birds landed near the feet of one of the pilots. Sam immediately drew his gun and fired at one of the birds about six inches from the pilot's feet. Angered, the pilot made a threatening remark to Sam, and Sam responded by chasing him around the building, firing behind his feet and shouting, "Dance, dance." Unfortunately for Sam, his gun held a finite number of rounds, and when he had fired the last one, the dancer turned around and became a puncher. I think he might have killed Sam if we hadn't intervened. Although we all considered it a great idea, the Army is pretty sticky about beating up the officer of the day, regardless of the provocation.

Landhi was about fifteen miles from Karachi and about fifty miles from Hyderabad. A well-worn camel trail between the two cities ran by Landhi's main gate. Six or eight long caravans of camels loaded with trade goods would plod along this trail every night, as it was quite hot during the day. Usually the lead camel had a rider, and the others were linked to each other by ropes. Segura and another lieutenant named Band noticed that the camel drivers were invariably asleep when they passed Landhi, so they came up with the idea of turning the caravans around and heading them back toward the city they had left. We began doing this on a regular basis. It was simple: one person just grabbed the lead camel's reins up by its nose and led it into a gentle 180-degree turn to the opposite side of the trail. The rest of the caravan followed docilely, and they slowly disappeared back in the direction from which they had appeared. I'm sure there was mass confusion when the drivers awakened to find themselves at the wrong end of the trail. It was a dirty trick that I'm not proud of now, but in the arrogance of youth, it seemed like a great way to spend a boring evening.

Landhi was the scene of one of the greatest buzz jobs I have ever seen. Buzzing is unauthorized low flying, called flat hatting in the Navy. It all began innocently enough when about ten Stinson L-5 liaison planes, destined for the U.S. Army Ground Forces in Burma, were delivered by ship to Karachi. After they were assembled, the powers-that-be decided that they would use pilots from Landhi who had finished their training to ferry the L-5s to Burma.

Ten pilots were selected, including Moose Elker, Walter Daniels (better known as Danny), and William F. X. Band, and ordered to report to Karachi Air Base to be checked out in the L-5s. After their checkout rides they were told to make another familiarization flight and to practice the loose formation they would use for the flight to Burma. Lieutenant Colonel Amen, the operations officer at KAB, warned them in no uncertain terms that he would not tolerate any buzzing. Completely unfazed by his warning, they took off at about noon and made a beeline for Landhi, arriving just as most of the officers were leaving either the barracks or the flight line for the mess hall. Suddenly the area, which was completely flat with widely spaced buildings, was a-swarm with buzzing L-5s. They came in from all angles, below the roof lines of the low buildings, some literally rolling their wheels on the sunbaked sand of the barracks area. People who were caught in the open had to lie prone to avoid having their hair trimmed by a propeller. Some of the planes came around the corners of buildings in vertical banks with the wing tips just clearing the ground. Moose came by the porch of my barracks rolling his wheels on the ground, pulled up over the volleyball net, ducked under the telephone lines, and immediately zoomed to clear the softball backstop. He must have enjoyed it as much as we did, because he repeated the performance several times. Miraculously, there were no midair collisions, although one could hardly call where they were flying midair, and after about ten wild minutes they left and flew back to KAB. This was, without a doubt, the high point (or from another perspective, the low point) of our self-generated entertainment at Landhi, exceeding by a wide margin camel caravan rerouting, Greg Carpenter's mystic feat, and even turning over sailboats with propwash, an invention of who else but Sam Brown.

Colonel Amen was furious when they landed, since the Landhi adjutant, who was not a pilot and therefore hadn't appreciated the artistry demonstrated by the L-5 pilots, had called him and reported the buzzing. Instead of an official reprimand or a court-martial, the colonel gave them what he considered stiffer punishment. He sent them all to combat units in China. They felt like Br'er Rabbit when Br'er Fox threw him into the brier patch. That was where they wanted to be anyway.

Finally, early in November, after about two months at Landhi, my group received orders transferring us to the Fourteenth Air Force in China, which delighted us all. We packed our gear and went to Karachi Air Base to seek transportation to China. Typically, in the rather informal CBI Theater, we were told to go to Operations and see if we could catch a ride to one of the Assam bases on the India side of the Hump (the Himalayas). It was strange that after more than a year of intensive training we had to bum a ride to the war. We saw a B-24 being refueled and found that it was going to Chabua in Assam, one of the main Air Transport Command bases for Hump traffic. I asked the pilot if he had room for five more, and he said he'd be glad to take us to Chabua. He was an older Ferry Command pilot, probably about thirty, and he was flying with just a flight engineer, no copilot. Jones, Gray, Mullineaux, Kaiser, and I found seats in the flight deck area and strapped in. After a lumbering takeoff and climb to altitude, the pilot asked me if I'd like to fly for a while. The autopilot was broken and he was tired.

I crawled into the right seat and took the controls, which the pilot didn't touch again until we started letting down to land at Chabua. I flew for four hours, and then Dick Jones took a turn. It was my first experience in a heavy multiengine plane, and at that time I hoped it would be my last. I could not believe how heavy and unresponsive the controls were. I thanked the fate that had directed me into fighters

(Dave was evidently still on the job). Later, in combat, I developed great respect for the pilots who flew those bombers unflinchingly into flak and fighters, although true to fighter-pilot tradition, I tried not to let that respect show.

Late in the afternoon we saw the impressive bulk of the mighty Himalayas looming ahead. Soon the pilot took over and started letting down for landing. From the air most of the area below looked like tropical or semitropical jungle. Once we had landed we found that was indeed the case. The buildings at Chabua, called bashas, were all made of bamboo with thatched roofs and open, screened sides. All the beds were enclosed by mosquito netting, called mosquito bars, that were standard there and in China. Also we found that we had left indoor plumbing behind. From now on, with rare exceptions, we used outside latrines with eight to twelve holes. Very discommoding.

After checking in at Operations and learning that it would be at least two days before we would leave for China, we were assigned beds in the transient officer's quarters. We spent most of the next two days in pickup volleyball games that were invariably won by the team that included a Hamilton Standard Propellers technical representative named Ted Fisher. Ted was about six foot six and was an excellent volleyball player. He regularly embedded the ball and one or two opponents into the turf with his powerful spikes.

Fortunately we escaped without serious injury, and on the third day we were notified that we would leave that afternoon. We went to the flight line and, along with some twenty other passengers, boarded a C-87 (transport version of the B-24). In due course we took off and headed east toward the legendary Hump and China.

6

HITCHHIKERS
TO WAR

As the C-87 slowly climbed above the foothills, I was excited at the prospect of crossing the mighty Himalayas, an almost mythical mountain range to me. Less than 1,000 miles to the west lay Everest, the highest of Earth's mountains. My experience with mountains was limited to a month in the Catskills when I was about seven years old, and the Catskills are better known for puns and comics than for peaks and canyons.

As we gained altitude the mountains became higher so that we maintained a ground clearance of 1,000 to 2,000 feet. The terrain became much more rugged as we flew east. One of the sergeants on the crew told us we had leveled off at 19,000 feet and that since there was no oxygen supply at the passenger positions, he would administer oxygen from a portable unit to anyone who needed it. It was quite cold in the cabin and we all could have used some heat, but only a few passengers were bothered by hypoxia and requested a short burst of oxygen.

The weather was good except to the north, and we could see the terrain below clearly. It was the most desolate and foreboding region imaginable. The chances of getting out alive even if you survived a bailout were close to zero, especially during the winter. The pilots and aircrews of the Air Transport Command (ATC) carried all of the fuel, ammunition, and other supplies used by the Fourteenth Air Force in China. The courage and skill of these men kept this vital supply line going under some of the worst flying conditions in the world using only the most primitive radio aids. Since it required six gallons of fuel in the transports to deliver one gallon to the Fourteenth, high cargo priority was assigned only to fuel, ammunition, parts, mail, and passengers.

More than 650,000 tons of cargo was flown across the Hump to China, but at a heavy cost. More than a thousand men were killed and almost six hundred planes were lost. In one month, January 1944, three men died for every 1,000 tons of cargo delivered to China.

About a year later I met a couple of classmates who were flying the Hump with the ATC, and they told me a story that may be apocryphal, but they swore it was true. They said Madame Chiang, the wife of the Generalissimo, had brought a load of expensive antique furniture, including a grand piano, from the States for her home in Chungking. Because of her influence it was given a number-one priority and immediately loaded on a C-46 to be flown to China. The pilot, evidently a clear thinker, was irritated because he knew how badly supplies were needed in China, so when he approached the halfway point he radioed that he was losing power on one engine and then jettisoned the entire load, ostensibly so that he could maintain altitude. This action was entirely within his rights as an aircraft commander, but he feathered an engine before landing to play it safe. I have always relished the thought of that piano ricocheting down the side of one of those rugged peaks, and not only because I spent endless hours practicing before washing out of piano lessons at an early age.

I told that story during a lecture at the Smithsonian in the eighties, and following the talk a pair of twin brothers, about my age, told me that they had served in the ATC squadron in Chabua in 1943 and had helped to load the furniture onto the C-46. They said they had also loaded two large trunks full of Bergdorf Goodman clothes. That information helped to explain the reports that later in 1943 the Abominable Snowman was observed on a number of occasions in drag, very stylish drag.

Somewhere along the route we crossed, without fanfare or even knowledge, into China, and after about three hours we began letting down to land at Kunming, the China terminus of the Hump. Since the elevation at Kunming was about 6,000 feet, the letdown didn't take long. As we circled over Kunming the terrain appeared checkered; as we lost altitude I could see that the checkers were rice paddies in various stages of cultivation. Men, women, children, and water buffalo became visible, all hard at work with primitive tools, straining to eke out a living from their small plots. I would see many more rice paddies before I left China, since the country was intensely cultivated and rice was the primary crop.

After landing we taxied to the ATC area and parked. We gathered our gear and stepped, for the first time, onto the soil of China. My ideas about China had come from reading books, mostly by missionaries, about our friends the Chinese and from the film version of Pearl Buck's book *The Good Earth*. They were pretty much on the mark. The peasants looked and dressed much as they did in the film, in loose overblouses, loose trousers, straw coolie hats, and sandals. Chinese workers were everywhere, repairing the runway, taxiways, and roads with crushed stone and mud. The stones, broken by women using small hammers, were carried off by men in baskets on the ends of yo-yo poles. Despite the hard, tedious labor, they always seemed to be in good spirits and invariably greeted Americans with a grin, a thumbs-up, and "Ding hao," Chinese for "very good." Even while working in mud and dirt, they always managed to look clean and energetic.

Our baggage was loaded into trucks, and I, along with the other officers, was taken to the transient hostel and assigned a room. In China, all the U.S. military personnel lived in hostels owned and operated by a Chinese government agency, the War Area Service Corps (WASC). Since Hump tonnage was so precious almost none was allotted to food, and the WASC supplied all our food as well.

The next morning we reported to Fourteenth Headquarters, where Jones, Gray, Mullineaux, and I were assigned to the 23rd Fighter Group, based at Kweilin, about 450 miles east of Kunming. This famous group had been formed directly from the AVG, when it was disbanded in July 1942. Its first commander was God's first pilot, Col. Robert L. Scott. We were thrilled to be joining it and even more thrilled when we learned that its commander was the famous Flying Tiger Lt. Col. David Lee "Tex" Hill. Normally, we would have been introduced to General Chennault, but he was away, so his deputy General Glenn said a few words of welcome. I met General Chennault a few months later at Hengyang.

We were given a short briefing by an intelligence officer on the general combat situation in China. Surprisingly, at Landhi we had been taught only combat tactics, nothing of the overall situation. Perhaps second lieutenants don't need to know the big picture.

The Japanese held most of north China down to the southern shore of Tungting Lake as well as the major southern coastal cities, including

Hong Kong and Canton and their environs. The Japanese were holding China as a source of rice and raw materials as well as to keep the Allies out of any territory from which the mainland of Japan could be bombed. There were more than 800,000 Japanese troops in China that could have been used to good advantage in the Pacific Theater, and a major goal of the United States was to keep China in the war and thus keep the Japanese troops in China.

The mission of the Fourteenth Air Force was to protect its bases, provide support for the Chinese Army, and attack Japanese troops and airfields and all methods of transport within China. The B-25 twin-engine medium bombers and the B-24 four-engine heavy bombers regularly attacked Japanese shipping in the South China Sea, the Gulf of Tonkin, and the Formosa Strait that had been driven close to shore by American submarines.

Jones and Mullineaux left by C-47 for Kweilin the next day, but Gray and I were delighted to learn that we were assigned to fly two P-40s to Kweilin a day later. The weather turned bad and prevented our leaving for several days. We had to remain on the flight line, however, to man our planes in case of a Japanese air raid. Finally it cleared and we took off for Kweilin, led by an experienced pilot who was returning to the group. The country between Kunming and Kweilin was rough, mountainous, and sparsely inhabited, with few distinguishing features to aid in navigation. Later I was to learn that the maps were not accurate except for major features such as lakes, rivers, and the larger cities.

Jesse Gray and I alertly searched the sky for Zeros throughout the flight, although the leader had told us it was highly unlikely that any would appear. After about two hours some peculiar, inverted–ice cream cone mountains came into view ahead, running north and south in a rather thin line. As we came closer the beautiful Li River came into view, running serenely between the crags. We turned and followed the river south for about fifty miles until we started to run out of those mountains, then the leader surprised us by turning 180 degrees and flying north for about eighty miles, until we reached Kweilin and landed at its main airfield, Yang Tong. It turned out that our leader had planned to hit the mountains to the north of Kweilin, then fly south until we reached Yang Tong. Instead, because the wind was more northerly than predicted, we were south of Kweilin when we reached the mountains, and when we turned south we were heading away from our destination. We had plenty of fuel, but if it had been low we could have continued south and landed at Nanning.

After checking in at the hostel we reported to the headquarters of the 23rd Fighter Group, which had been formed on July 4, 1942. I was told to report to the commanding officer, the legendary Tex Hill. A squadron leader in the AVG and one of its leading aces, he had accepted an Army commission and command of the 75th Fighter Squadron in the 23rd Group. After completing a tour he had returned to the States and had just recently come back to China as the group commander.

I had read about Tex Hill in *God Is My Copilot* and he was one of my heroes, so I was somewhat overawed at the prospect of meeting him. He put me at ease immediately. I entered his office, came to attention in front of his desk, and had started to salute when a long arm snaked out, grabbed my hand, and shook it before I could complete the salute. He was a tall, lean man who looked like a Texan. His office was stark, with two chairs, a desk, an in-basket, and an out-basket. There were no papers in sight; the in-basket was full of peanuts and the out-basket full of empty shells. China was a most informal theater. Tex Hill was obviously one who led by example and not by the trappings of military rank or by paperwork.

He briefed me on the group and, while showing me a map of the area and the locations of the three squadrons of the 23rd (the 74th, 75th, and 76th), gave me a brief rundown on combat tactics, reminding me never to try to turn with a Zero. I was excited when he told me I would be assigned to his old squadron, the 75th, that it was an outstanding squadron and he was sure that I would help to keep it that way. His air of quiet confidence was infectious, and I left with even more respect for him and full of determination to make him glad he had assigned me to the 75th.

Jesse had much the same experience with Colonel Hill, and he too was assigned to the 75th, which was based about 200 miles to the north at Hengyang. We were glad to be assigned to the same squadron, especially when we learned that Dick Jones, Flash Segura, Moose Elker, and several other pilots we knew well were in the 75th.

We made arrangements to fly to Hengyang the next morning on the C-47 run, and one of the operations staff offered to show us the base. The runway at Yang Tong was right in among the mountains, which looked even more distinctive from the ground than from the air. They were steep cones of gray rock rising 800 feet above the terrain, and they took on many different colors as the light varied. I later learned that the area around Kweilin is considered one of the most beautiful in China and is celebrated in literature and art.

The runway was about 5,000 feet long and wide enough for four fighters to take off abreast. Like all runways in China, it was made of crushed rock and was always in good condition because of the constant maintenance done by the Chinese. When a plane landed on the runways the wheels would throw rocks against the flaps on touchdown. This made a loud and initially disconcerting noise but didn't seem to damage the flaps. In very dry weather the mud used to cement the rocks would turn to dust and the aircraft would raise great, blinding clouds on takeoff.

On the far side of a ridge of mountains was another runway called the fighter strip. It was only a mile or so by road from the main runway area. The strip was so narrow that when two fighters took off in formation, as was standard practice, part of the outer wings of both aircraft extended beyond the runway edges. The 74th Fighter Squadron of the 23rd Group was based on the fighter strip.

We also visited the Cave. I had read about it in *God Is My Copilot*, so I was eager to see it. It was in a cluster of mountains not too far from 23rd Group Headquarters and served as the headquarters during bombing raids. The Cave was large and deep, well lighted, and full of desks, telephones, and other communications equipment. It looked like a natural cave that had been enlarged by the Chinese. It also was the terminus of the net.

The net was a system devised by General Chennault to provide early warning of Japanese air attacks since we had no radar, which would have been ineffective in the mountainous terrain anyway. It was a network of telephones set up in small villages throughout China. The Chinese lookouts in each town would report aircraft that flew overhead or within earshot. A typical report would be "Heavy engine noise over Changsha, heading Hengyang." If they could see the aircraft they would report the numbers, heading, and whether they were bombers or fighters. They were dedicated, diligent, and quite accurate within their limitations. We never were surprised by an air attack, except much later, when the Japanese had taken most of the territory to the north. The lookouts, especially those close to Japanese territory, operated at considerable personal risk. If they had been caught, they would have been summarily executed. To avoid unnecessary alerts, our pilots reported in by radio over specified points when returning from missions.

The net had another important function. If a pilot was lost, he could circle a village at low altitude and fire his guns. The lookout would report it to the nearest base, and the pilot would be given his location and a heading to the base by radio. This simple but effective system was very helpful, since navigation was so difficult in China with the inaccurate maps and little or no wind information.

The hostels at Kweilin were well interspersed among the mountains so they were not good bombing targets. They were typical of the WASC hostels at all of the bases. Each hostel included two clusters of buildings, one for officers and the other for enlisted men. The buildings were long one-story wooden structures divided into six or eight rooms, with a washroom at one end. Each room had eight to twelve bunks, most double decked, with crisscrossed heavy cord supporting mattresses filled with some kind of straw. The pillows were filled with rice husks and rice and were quite hard, but I suppose if we were cut off from food supplies we could always eat the pillows. Each bunk had a mosquito net, called a mosquito bar, that was tucked in on all four sides. There were a few chairs and tables and some built-in shelves for storage. The rooms were heated with charcoal stoves and had electric lights. It was often difficult to read at night, since the generators did not run smoothly and the lights dimmed and brightened continuously.

The buildings were covered with adobe on the outside and were sometimes painted. The interiors and all the furniture were unpainted raw wood. There were usually two or three ceramic water jugs, full of lin kai shwai (cool boiled water), and matching glasses. As you can imagine, it was not safe to drink unboiled water. The mess hall was in a separate building, and there were outside latrines, eight- to twelve-holers, nearby for the officers and the enlisted men.

Surprisingly, despite the unsavory atmosphere, the latrines became social centers of a sort. All of us had dysentery in some form or other for varying periods during our stay in China. We therefore spent a lot of time in the latrines and had many long and interesting discussions in those unlikely settings. Jesse and I, after the tour, visited the 74th alert shack and hostel and had dinner with some classmates and others we had trained with. They told us how-it-was-in-combat in great and lurid and, alas, inaccurate detail. We returned to the transient hostel for the night and the next morning boarded a C-47 for the flight to Hengyang. Our long, thirteen-month odyssey, from the Army Air Forces Classification Center in Nashville, Tennessee, to a combat squadron in Hengyang, China, was nearly over. We were about to join the war.

7

FIRST COMBAT

Flying generally north, we soon left the distinctive mountains of Kweilin. We followed the course of the Siang River and after about forty minutes flew over the airfield at Lingling, used only as an auxiliary field at that time. Typically, it had only one crushed-rock runway that appeared to be well under 5,000 feet long. Continuing northward for about an hour, we came in sight of Hengyang, first the city and then, a few miles farther and on the opposite side of the river, the airfield that was to be my home for the next seven months.

As we circled before landing, I looked over the area, trying to identify landmarks that might help me find the field in an emergency. The country around Hengyang was generally flat with low rolling hills. Almost all the land was covered with rice paddies, small water-filled plots divided by earthen dikes. The nearby river, running north and south roughly parallel to the runway, was to be a valuable aid to navigation. Directly across the river from the field was a tall stone pagoda, a constant reminder, if one were needed, that we were in China.

We landed and parked near the center of the field, where we were met by a truck for the cargo and a jeep that we thought was for us, but the driver was much more interested in the mail sacks than in a pair of new second lieutenants. He loaded the sacks on the jeep and drove off, shouting that he would come back for us in about half an hour. Upon his return, Jesse and I threw our bags in the jeep, climbed aboard, and were driven to the hostel, about a mile from the runway.

I was unprepared for the appearance of the hostel, which was quite different from the standard WASC hostels in China. Instead of the long one-story building I expected, the 75th lived in a U-shaped, two-story stone and wood building that had been a private girl's school before the war. Both stories had wide porches or balconies around the inside of the U, and there was a tennis court in the central area, as well as a theater complete with stage in one of the wings. These were the best lodgings I'd seen since Miami Beach.

All of the more than 200 men in the squadron, officers and enlisted, plus the Chinese room boys, cooks, and waiters, lived in the hostel. In addition there were two separate mess halls (one for officers and the other for the enlisted men), the squadron offices, and indoor latrines with, wonder of wonders, flush toilets and hot showers. To my sorrow I soon found that the hostel's inhabitants included a more than ample supply of hot and cold running rats. More on them later.

We reported to the adjutant, Lt. Myron Levy, who assigned us to a room and told us to report back to his office right after dark to meet the CO when he returned from the flight line. Jesse and I went to our room on the second floor and found that we would be rooming with Dick Jones, Earl Green, and Duff McEnteer. They had been there for about a week and had already flown several missions. After impressing upon us that they were now experienced combat pilots, they said that Moose Elker, Flash Segura, and Danny Daniels—who had been at Landhi Field with us—were also in the squadron. The system of training all incoming pilots at Landhi, in addition to its other merits, made it certain that you would know a number of the pilots in your squadron when you joined it and that you would know a number of pilots in the other fighter squadrons in the theater as well. It removed much of the trauma of being a new kid on the block.

Later we returned to the headquarters office and reported to the CO, Maj. Elmer Richardson, a short, no-nonsense type, an experienced fighter pilot, and an ace. Jones and Green had told us that he was a fine CO, well liked and highly respected, and I soon came to share their opinion. He said that we would be put on the flying schedule immediately and that there would be no orientation or practice flights because we couldn't spare the fuel. He then introduced us to the operations officer, Capt. Bill (pronounced Beel for reasons unknown to me, unless it had something to do with his prior service in Panama) Grosvenor.

Grosvenor briefed us on the operating procedures of the 75th and on the combat situation. Every evening the operations officer would

WHITE ABLE	WHITE BAKER	WHITE CHARLIE
172 Maj. Richardson	155 Capt. Glover	163 Lt. Long
177 Lt. Jones	188 Lt. Segura	159 Lt. Green
166 Lt. Tanner	186 Lt. Casey	172 Lt. Folmar
187 Lt. Vurgaropoulos	191 Lt. Lopez	195 Lt. Elker

WHITE DOG	WHITE XRAY	WHITE ZEBRA
151 Lt. Scoville	183 Capt. Grosvenor	175 Lt. Anning
167 Lt. Armstrong	189 Lt. Oswald	
157 Lt. Aylesworth	193 Lt. Howard	
171 Lt. Gray	154 Lt. Balderson	

Figure 1

post the flying schedule for the following day based on the number of available aircraft. The squadron was supposed to have twenty-five P-40s and about thirty-five pilots but was usually a few short of both. There were always more pilots than planes, so each pilot did not fly every day. The three squadrons of the 23rd Fighter Group had the call signs Red (74th), White (75th), and Blue (76th). The propeller spinners were painted to match the call signs. Aircraft tail numbers ran from 100 to 149 in the 74th, from 150 to 199 in the 75th, and from 200 to 250 in the 76th. The flights were designated by the color of the squadron followed by Able, Baker, Charlie, etc. A typical flight schedule would look like Figure 1. Regardless of how many flights went on the offensive missions, Xray and Zebra flights always remained on alert for base defense. The only flying allowed, other than combat missions, was engineering test flights to check aircraft that had been repaired.

Most of our missions would be flown in the area 150 miles north around Tungting Lake, fed by the mighty Yangtze River. The two main Japanese air bases in that area were at Yochow and Hankow, about 170 miles and 270 miles away respectively. The Chinese had just harvested the rice crop in the area known as the rice bowl of China, near Changteh, on the west side of the lake. The Japanese ground troops had moved in to confiscate the crop, as they did every year, both to feed the occupation forces and to ship back to Japan. The 75th was flying strafing missions in the Changteh area, as often as the weather permitted, to attack their boats and trucks engaged in removing the rice. We also were to attack the troops who had a Chinese garrison trapped in the town of Changteh.

The standard procedure on strafing missions was for the three or four flights to fly to the target area together. The first two flights would then drop down to about 500 feet above the ground to locate and strafe targets of opportunity while in a loose trail formation. The planes essed along the road or river so that they would not be hit by ricochets from the following plane. Normally, they would be flying back toward the home base while strafing in order to be as far as possible from the enemy when low on ammunition and fuel.

The other flight or flights stayed at 3,000 or 4,000 feet to provide top cover for the strafers. The flight leader kept his eyes glued on the low planes so as to remain above them while the rest of the pilots watched for enemy aircraft. When the low flights had expended most of their ammunition, the high and low flights exchanged positions and missions. It was left to the judgment of the low flight leader to determine when his flights were low enough on ammunition to make the switchover, since the P-40 had no ammunition counters. Each plane carried 250 rounds per gun, enough for about twenty-five seconds of firing, 12 or 13 two-second bursts. When the second group of strafers had expended its ammunition, it climbed up and joined the top cover and returned to base.

At dinner that evening I met the other pilots. Most of the flight leaders had served together in Panama before coming to China and had a great deal of P-40 experience. The dinner consisted of bean sprouts and rice along with some fatty, strange cuts of pork that looked as though a pig had been thrown into a propeller (we called them prop-chops). Little did I know that would be our fare virtually every night. None of the food was American, since there was insufficient cargo capacity over the Hump for food. I noticed that many of the pilots took a few bites, then shouted, "Eggis," and in a few minutes the waiters brought them huge omelets. There seemed to be an unlimited supply of eggs in Hengyang, but we were never served chicken nor did I ever even see one.

Because all supplies had to be flown into China, the United States had contracted with China to provide all housing, food, roads, and other construction. The United States paid for it all, so the Chinese economy, which was badly inflated, received much-needed dollars.

The housing and the construction were more than adequate and well maintained, but the food was bad and monotonous. The eggs were our salvation, but if we had known about cholesterol then we might have thought twice about eating four- or five-egg omelets for three meals a day.

Although I was not on the flying schedule for the next day, I got up when the room boy, a twenty-year-old student from Shanghai who spoke English well, came in before dawn to wake up Jones and Green, who would be flying. We washed up (fortunately, I needed to shave only once every other month or so), dressed, and went down to breakfast. We had a choice of eggs, any style, or pancakes. The pancakes were passable, but the syrup was made from fermented sugar, so I stuck to the eggs.

At first light we drove in jeeps and a weapons carrier to the airfield, where we could hear the P-40s being warmed up and taxied by the crew chiefs to the flight line from their night dispersal locations. When we arrived at the alert shack the aircraft were parked in a line next to it in the flight order directed by the schedule. Each pilot took his own chute and helmet from the rack and went to his assigned airplane, where he placed the chute in the seat and the helmet on the stick, then got into the cockpit and made sure that the seat and rudder pedals were adjusted properly and that his radio headset was connected. These preparations would allow him to take off in the minimum possible time in the event of a scramble to repulse an enemy air raid.

There was nothing for most of the pilots to do until the first mission went out, except to be available. Many went back to sleep in the alert shack, some played cards or read, and later in the morning there was a volleyball game on the court between the alert shack for the pilots and the one for the ground crew. Paperback books were in great demand because there was so much time to kill. When new books arrived, either to an individual or, most often, the wonderful Armed Services Editions that came through Special Services, they went through the squadron as rapidly as dysentery.

At midmorning and again in midafternoon a truck came down from the mess hall with tea and sandwiches. The sugar for the tea was fermented and the sandwiches were gummy and filled with an unrecognizable substance, but we ate them since there was no other choice. I'm sure P. G. Wodehouse would have said they tasted like wet blotting paper, but I didn't think they were that good. At noon everyone except for one flight that stayed on alert went to the mess hall for the usual eggs. However, if a mission was out we waited until it landed before going to lunch.

Almost all the pilots came to the flight line when a mission was due back, both to hear the debriefing and to watch the planes land. Pilots are highly critical of each other's landings, so there was more than the usual incentive to try to grease them in (make a smooth landing) with the entire squadron watching. One pilot regularly forgot to turn off his gun switch before landing, and when he pulled the stick hard back to land he squeezed the trigger and fired his guns, scaring hell out of him and us. After the third episode the CO chewed him out so royally that he never forgot again.

That evening I was happy to see my name on the schedule for the next day. Almost a year had passed since I made my first flight in a U.S. Army Air Forces aircraft, a PT-19 in Union City, Tennessee, but it seemed as though I had been in training forever. At last, I was about to put my training to use in combat. As it turned out, the miserable weather made me wait for two more days, with such low ceilings and rain that no missions could be flown. My excitement and anticipation mounted until the third day, when the weather broke and I rose into the heavens, no irreverence intended, and became a combat pilot.

On that first mission we were briefed to fly to the area of Changteh and strafe any vehicles or boats we came across. The intelligence officer told us that any boats in that vicinity were either carrying rice out or returning for another load. I was to fly as number four in White Baker flight with Capt. Don Glover as flight leader and Lt. Bob Casey as element leader.

We climbed into the cockpits at about nine o'clock and, with the aid of the crew chiefs, strapped on our chutes and safety belts and plugged in our helmet radio leads and throat mikes. At Glover's signal we started our engines and warmed them up at idle power until it was our turn to taxi to takeoff position. The alert shack was on the south end of the runway, and we always took off to the north to minimize taxiing. It saved fuel and kept the engines from overheating.

As Glover and his wingman lined up for takeoff, Casey and I swung our P-40s into position just off the runway with our noses about 45 degrees from the takeoff heading, ran up our engines, and checked our magnetos to see that both were functioning properly. As soon as Glover's element started rolling, we taxied into takeoff position with Casey on the left. I set my cowl flaps for takeoff, and when Casey nodded his head sharply I opened the throttle to hold my position to the right of and slightly behind his plane. The runway was quite narrow, but I had long since mastered the art of keeping a P-40 straight on takeoff. As soon as I lifted off I moved the gear handle into the up position and pulled the trigger on the stick that activated the hydraulic motor. As we rolled into a climbing left turn to join up with the flight leader, I set the cowl flaps for climb and switched the fuel selector from the fuselage tank to the 75-gallon belly tank. The belly tanks would be jettisoned if we ran into enemy aircraft, and we wanted to use as much of their fuel as possible first. As we climbed I rolled the canopy shut, set climbing rpm, and adjusted the throttle to maintain formation.

My element joined up with the flight leader's and climbed on course toward the target area. As soon as we were out of sight of the field the leader's wingman slid over to his left side and we spread out into the combat finger formation. We were the second of three flights on this mission. We leveled off at about 10,000 feet and throttled back to cruise power. The flight leader maintained his position relative to the lead flight, while the rest of us kept a constant lookout for enemy aircraft.

I don't remember feeling any apprehension, only exhilaration, on that first mission. I was eager to get into combat and never gave any thought to being shot down. I was totally at home in the airplane and completely confident of my ability. I had flown so many practice missions similar to this first actual mission that it seemed almost routine.

After about an hour, Tungting Lake came into view, and the first two flights started descending while the third flight stayed above us for top cover. We leveled out at about 1,000 feet, and I increased the rpm, turned on the gunsight, and gun arming switch. As we approached the west end of the lake we spotted a large number of sampans and some larger boats. They had evidently seen or heard us, as they were all heading for shore. The squadron leader peeled off and dived to attack them, and we followed in trail with me bringing up the rear.

As I picked out a target and dived on it I could see that several of the boats had been set on fire by the other planes. I could also see soldiers on the boats firing at us with rifles. When I came into range I squeezed the trigger and six lines of tracers poured into the boat and crew. I saw several soldiers go down and others jump into the water. As I pulled up, I looked back and saw smoke pouring from the covered part of the deck. We continued attacking the boats, essing across them as we strafed until all the boats were burning or sinking and everyone on the decks appeared dead. It was awesome to realize that a slight pressure by my right forefinger was the difference between life and death for the soldiers on the boat. I felt no compunction, since I, along with the rest of the country, was totally convinced of the need to defeat Japan. These were, after all, the ones responsible for Pearl Harbor, the Bataan Death March, and numerous other atrocities that began, incidentally, here in China.

Killing from the air is impersonal. The pilot shoots at small moving figures several hundred yards away. Except for seeing them fall, like toy soldiers, there is none of the bloody evidence of death that one would see in close ground combat. Fighting other airplanes is just that: the pilot thinks about shooting down the airplane, not killing the opposing pilot or crew. He is even spared the trauma of seeing his friends die. In fighters pilots often see one of their planes go down, but it is rare that a badly shot up pilot brings his fighter back and either survives or dies. Once he augers in, his buddies just don't see him anymore. We never used the words "dead" or "killed" in connection with our pilots. We used euphemisms like "bought the farm," "augered in," or "bought it"—anything to avoid reality.

There were many boats on the lake, so we climbed up to take over the top cover role while the third flight came down to strafe. When they had exhausted their ammunition, they climbed to join us and we headed back to Hengyang. As we flew south we left the lake and followed the Siang River. About thirty miles south of Changsha a distinctive U-shaped bend in the river went around a small abandoned airfield in square DD-24 on the grid map. This was fifty or sixty miles north of Hengyang, and returning flights were required to call in over Dog Dog two-four so they would be identified as friendly.

Just before we came into sight of our home field, we abandoned our loose combat formation and went into tight right echelons by flight. As we passed the field the first flight made a diving left turn and approached the south end of the runway at an altitude of about thirty feet. As they crossed the runway they peeled up to the left and landed out of a 360-degree descending turn. All four aircraft could land in less than ninety seconds from the peelup. The second flight peeled up just as the last plane in the first flight touched down. Much of this was to put on a show for the ground crews and other pilots.

After we parked, the ground crews immediately began refueling and rearming while the pilots were debriefed by the intelligence officer. After that we were on our own until the next mission or until sundown. Just before dark we returned to the hostel, and the crew chiefs taxied the planes to their respective dispersal areas for the night.

I flew on several similar missions over the next few days, including two dive-bombing missions on the Japanese-occupied section of Changteh, and began to learn some of the landmarks. This was important, as the maps of the area were notoriously inaccurate. Fortunately, our location on the river was a great aid to navigation.

One morning as we arrived at the flight line I noticed that our metal belly tanks were being replaced by bamboo tanks. I knew our planes had once used bamboo tanks but thought our supply of metal tanks was in better shape than that. Prior to our mission the CO said that the Chinese garrison, surrounded in the town of Changteh, was running out of food. The bamboo tanks were filled with bags of rice that we were to drop in the town. We were not to do any strafing because there would not be enough fuel.

As we flew over Changteh we made our approach in trail, flying as low and slow as possible along the main street. I dropped mine at less than 120 mph from just above the roof tops. Although 120 mph is quite slow for a fighter, it is much faster than the average waiter delivers rice. I guess if you are near starvation even rice approaching at 120 mph looks good. Later we were gratified to learn that almost all of the rice was recovered and eaten and that the Chinese soldiers had survived the siege.

The following day the squadron escorted twelve B-25s to the Changteh area, where they were attacked by about ten Oscars. The P-40s drove them off before they got to the bombers but did not claim any victories. A few days later the movie comedian Joe E. Brown, along with a guitar player named Harry Barris, arrived on a USO tour. Brown said that he had been in the nose of one of the B-25s and was glad to meet the fighter pilots that had routed the attackers.

Brown was pleasant and natural and seemed genuinely glad to be with us. He had a son who was an Army Air Forces pilot. In his show, on the stage of our theater, he did a lot of old vaudeville bits as well as some scenes from his movies, and he was not fazed by the revelation that one of our pilots, Eddie Oswald, had a mouth bigger than his. I was a great fan of his and was delighted to see him in person. In 1959, when I was teaching at the Air Force Academy, Brown attended the first graduation ceremony. I chatted with him about the attack on the B-25s over Changteh and about the welcome entertainment he provided at Hengyang. He remembered the instances and was as pleasant to talk to as he had been in China sixteen years earlier.

We had been told that the enemy would attempt to bomb us on the anniversary of Pearl Harbor, since they had done so in 1942, and as that day approached we were keyed up for a raid, especially we newer pilots who had never been through one. The weather was bad for several days on and after December 7, so the raid did not materialize on schedule. It began clearing on the night of the ninth, so we went to bed expecting action on the tenth.

Shortly after midnight, the loud clanging of the jing bao gong woke us, and the Chinese station commander announced that heavy engine noise was over Changsha heading for Hengyang. Instead of going to the slit trenches as we should have, five of us thought that we would be going up after the bombers in the dark so we grabbed a jeep and headed for the alert shack. None of us—Tanner, Segura, Gray, Jones, and I—had been through a night bombing, and we didn't know that fighters were seldom sent up because of the extremely slim chance of finding the bomber and because we had no runway lights or navigation aids.

In blissful ignorance we drove down the long road to the runway and then down the runway to the alert shack. We were quite surprised to see that no one else was there and that none of the aircraft had been brought to the flight line. After a short discussion we decided to go back to the hostel and find out what to do. As we started back up the runway we heard a twin-engined airplane approaching. We stopped the jeep to hear it better and noticed that the props were unsynchronized, which gave it a distinct sound that we later found to be characteristic of Japanese bombers. The sound grew in intensity as the bomber started diving. We all suddenly realized how stupid it was to be parked on the runway with the lights on, turned off the lights, and drove off the runway as fast as possible, stopping behind a storage building about fifty yards away. We bailed out of the jeep and huddled against the wall of the buildings as the first bombs hit, fortunately on the opposite side of the runway. As the first bomber pulled up we heard others approaching.

The building we were using as a shelter was painted yellow and stood out pretty well even in the dim moonlight. It seemed a likely target for the next bomber, which was just starting its run, so we bolted for a slit trench bomb shelter some 100 feet from the building. It seemed as though we were racing the bomber as we leaped into the trench, landing on someone already huddled in the bottom whose only comment was a loud, agonized grunt. The bombs hit much closer than the first batch, so once again we took off, running wildly through the darkness as the third bomber dived. Suddenly, we tumbled over the edge of a high embankment into the edge of a rice paddy, which seemed so safe that we remained crouched there until the bombers departed. Except for some bomb craters near the runway, there was no damage.

Somewhat sheepishly we went back to the jeep, stopping by the slit trench to see who it was we had stomped, but he had gone, probably figuring even the runway was safer than that trench. We drove back to the hostel and went quietly to our rooms, telling no one about our fiasco.

Just before dawn the jing bao sounded again, and the WASC commander announced that a large force of bombers and fighters was headed our way. The pilots and ground crews all headed for the field in whatever transportation was available. It was hazy, and the airplanes were still parked in their dispersal areas, so the pilots just took the first airplane they came upon in order to get them all airborne in time. Planes were taxiing toward the runway with the pilots standing in the cockpit to see over the fogged windshield. On others the crew chief was sitting on the wing helping guide the pilot.

I reached my assigned P-40 just in time to see it being taxied away. I searched for another one but all the flyable planes were gone. By the time I got back to the alert shack all of our fighters had taken off despite the fogged canopies and generally poor visibility. We now knew enough to stay away from the runway area, so a group of us jumped into the ambulance with the flight surgeon and drove up into the hills to the east of the airfield, where the Chinese had a battery of 20-millimeter antiaircraft guns.

It seemed like a good place to watch the raid, as it overlooked the runway and was well equipped with slit trenches. We could hear our fighters struggling for altitude but couldn't see them through the haze. After about ten minutes the sound of Japanese radial engines blended with the familiar Allisons, followed by the rolling thunder of the P-40's six .50-caliber machine guns, interspersed with the slower firing and lighter sound of the enemy's machine guns and cannon. It was frustrating to hear the fight but not be able take part or even to see it.

Suddenly the 20-millimeter guns near us opened fire, and I saw in the north twelve Japanese bombers, in vees of three, approaching the runway at very low altitude. I recognized them immediately as Kawasaki Ki-48s (assigned the code name "Lily"). Although I had studied them in silhouette and model for the past year, seeing them in full scale, approaching with their bomb doors open, was quite a different thing. The dark and light green mottled camouflage and the enormous red ball insignia gave them an ominous beauty.

Slowly, almost majestically, they flew down the runway and began dropping their bombs. The antiaircraft guns near us were blasting away, but none of them used enough lead and the shells were passing well behind the bombers. The bomb explosions were walking down the runway with great bursts of flame and smoke as they tore large chunks of earth and gravel out of the runway. It was a helpless feeling to see these unopposed bombers beating hell out of our field while all our fighters were engaged at high altitude.

Suddenly, above the cacophony of engines, machine guns, cannon, and bombs, I heard a P-40 winding up in a dive, and Deacon Lewis came into view from the south in a head-on pass at the bombers with all guns blazing. I've never seen a more thrilling sight; we were all cheering like spectators at a sporting event, which in effect we were, as the lead Lily suddenly burst into flames, small at first and then engulfing both engines. With the Lily trailing an immense plume of black smoke, the pilot, true to Japanese kamikaze tradition, pulled up in a right wingover and tried to dive into our hostel. Fortunately he hit about 200 yards short. The tremendous explosion sent pressure waves through the building, breaking some of the windows, and terror waves through the occupants of the nearby slit trenches.

Lewis and the bombers disappeared into the haze in opposite directions. We could hear P-40s and Zeros diving, along with a lot of firing, but the sounds gradually faded away to the north. About fifteen minutes later, the all-clear sounded and we rushed down to inspect the damage.

The runway was full of large craters, and two B-25s parked nearby were hit by shrapnel, but fortunately the damage was slight, causing us to question the enemy's target selection, since the loss of two aircraft would have weakened us much more than a few holes in the runway that would be repaired within a few hours by our efficient force of coolies.

We later learned that one of our pilots had been killed by a bomb. While on the way to the runway for takeoff, he taxied over a piece of shrapnel from last night's raid and blew a tire, forcing him to abort. He took shelter in a small bomb crater that, against all probability, took another direct hit. He was never seen again.

During the latter stages of the raid I had seen, from my vantage point on the hill, what appeared to be a P-40 dive straight into the ground. I reported what I had seen, and later a search team found the wreckage and the body of Lieutenant Beauchamp wrapped in the shrouds of his partially opened parachute. He had evidently bailed out of his damaged plane at too low an altitude for his chute to open completely. The deaths removed any sense of participation in a sporting event but did nothing to diminish our commitment to combat and revenge.

In addition to the bomber that Lewis destroyed, Jesse Gray and Flash Segura each got one, and several Oscars were shot down as well, so the Japanese lost more than we did. A few of our planes managed to land next to the cratered runway but most went on to Lingling, about 100 miles to the south. Segura tried to make it but ran out of fuel and was forced to land on a small road. He got down safely but couldn't stop and the plane nosed over. We soon learned that he was safe, and once again one of our pilots returned from a mission by train. While on the train, after vainly trying to converse with a Chinese seatmate in a mixture of English and Chinese, they had a long conversation in French.

The industrious Chinese had the runway repaired by late afternoon, and the rest of the planes flew back from Lingling. Major Richardson told us that evening that in the future we would keep at least one flight low in order to guard against a similar attack, since the Japanese often used the same tactics over and over.

The battle was refought in the hostel that night as the pilots told and retold their versions of the action. I was sorry to have missed it but was looking forward to getting a shot at the enemy on their next raid. Two days later I got my wish.

8

PADDLEFOOT
PILOTS

After the bombing raid on December 12 (described in Chapter 1), the monsoon season began in earnest, and the squadron was able to fly only three or four days a month through most of April. There was light rain or heavy, thick mist almost all the time, with an occasional heavy rainstorm, but we rarely had the violent thunderstorms that were so frequent in the United States, especially in the South. Since it was obvious that neither we nor the Japanese could fly, we rarely had to stand alert. Most of our supplies, including that most important commodity, mail, were flown in, so there were long periods with virtually no communication with the outside world. All in all, it was a depressing period with little to do.

The weather was described quite graphically by our flight surgeon, Capt. Jones C. Laughlin of Eagle Lake, Texas, in his informal medical history of the 75th during his tenure.

We flew from Kunming to Kweilin in the soup and from CA3 (Kweilin) to AX2 (Lingling) up the valleys under the soup. From AX2 to SM5 (Hengyang), the transport flew about 200 feet above the river and about the same distance below the soup, which was a solid overcast. For the next month the soup hung on the chimneys or lay on the ground or it rained. During the first part of the month we ran out of powdered milk for coffee for breakfast (we had coffee only one meal a day), and later in the month we had no coffee. We received mail only once, and it was by train from

Kweilin. The weather was so bad that the birds could not see to fly in the soup, which constantly precipitated and slowly dropped in a fine spray or more like descending fog. The birds sat under the bushes on the ground and hopped around and caught bugs and worms. The temperature was low, and the air was so wet that all body heat was quickly lost. It was necessary to wear a leather jacket and wool pants, overshoes, and an umbrella to keep warm and dry. The green mold grew on all the bricks except those walked on. Shoes were covered with green mold in a few days' time, and the zippers on the fleece-lined winter flying suits corroded quickly. This type of melancholia prevailed the atmosphere, and sick call was 20 to 30 men each morning out of the 150 enlisted men. This type of weather persisted all month. The visibility was limited to a few hundred yards, and it was dark inside the buildings during the day.

Entertainment of any type was at a premium, and books continued to be circulated through the squadron at a rapid pace. Most of us received books from home, and fortunately we had purchased a lot of books in India and brought them with us to China. The Perry Mason books were so popular that there was a sign-up list for them. My *Life* magazines, though several months out of date, were also in great demand. I could have entertained myself with books alone, since I had always been, and still am, a voracious reader.

Movies were shown in the auditorium several nights a week, depending on their availability. The large auditorium had wooden benches on the stone floor, and there was no heat. We bundled up in our fleece-lined winter flying suits and boots to watch the films. The suits were never used for flying, since they were much too bulky for the P-40 cockpit, and the boots greatly reduced our feel of the rudders. They were perfect, however, for our theater in the winter. No one ever missed a movie, although we got a lot of low-, or almost no-, budget pictures. There were so many pictures starring Richard Arlen with Andy Devine as his sidekick that we were surprised that neither of them was considered for an Academy Award. Andy Devine's gravelly voice was not as funny to the pilots as it was to others, since everyone sounded like him on our aircraft radios.

In addition to the squadron personnel, all the Chinese workers attended every film. Although few of them could understand English, they seemed to enjoy them as much as or more than we did. In many of those films not understanding English would have been a distinct advantage.

Since our films were flown in from Kunming by transport, the monsoon season often caused long delays between film showings. We often had to show the same film many times. I remember seeing one film, *Reveille with Beverly*, with Ann Miller, about five times in a row. The dance scenes were particularly popular with the girl-starved audience, and often the projectionist ran them by several times. Surprisingly, although we saw some war films, I don't recall seeing any aviation films. They were probably saved for the infantry.

A second USO tour group, of Paulette Goddard, William Gargan, and Keenan Wynn, visited us during this period; Joe E. Brown had been the first. I didn't know it at the time, but it was to be the last to visit our squadron. A few other groups made it to China, but none made it to the forward areas where we were based.

They put on an entertaining show in the theater and were very congenial. They all looked much as they did on the screen, but I was surprised to see that Paulette Goddard had reddish hair and freckles. I had seen her only in black and white films, and I thought her hair was dark. She looked great in any case. They had to stay over an extra day because of the weather, and we chatted with them quite a bit. Keenan Wynn sat with Jesse Gray, Dick Jones, Earl Green, and me at dinner and told us a lot about film-making in Hollywood. We had seen him fire a .30-caliber aircraft machine gun in his bare hands in a film, and he assured us that he had actually done it, using blanks of course.

The extra night the group spent with us in Hengyang proved to be the undoing of our flight surgeon. Since there were no women's quarters on the base, Paulette Goddard was given a room in the hospital. I guess the flight surgeon thought that gave him some territorial rights, because late at night, following some heavy drinking, he forced his way into her room by breaking down the door and had to be dragged away from her. The next day, after sobering up, he came up with what I thought was an inspired defense. He said that he was a gynecologist in private practice and just wanted to keep his hand in.

He was transferred soon afterward and replaced by Dr. Laughlin. We heard that he was court-martialed as a result of the incident but never found out for sure. It is more likely that he was transferred because, as a major, he was one grade too high for a squadron flight surgeon.

Another source of entertainment and education for me came about because of my status as a very junior officer. Officers were allowed to censor their own mail; their signatures on the envelope certified that no classified or other sensitive material was in their letters. The mail of the enlisted men, however, had to be censored by an officer. This duty fell to the junior officers in the squadron. Two or three evenings a week we would go to the orderly room and read through all the outgoing mail. Although they knew the letters had to be read by a squadron officer, most of the writers were completely uninhibited in their discussions of the local Chinese women and in what they were going to do with or to their girlfriends or wives when they got home. Some were quite touching as they discussed family problems engendered by too little money and too much distance. Many of the men had been overseas for more than two years and had little hope of getting home soon. At that time everyone thought the war would last much longer than it did. "The Golden Gate in Forty-eight" was a familiar rallying cry. I think that I learned more about life during my three or four months as a censor than I had in the previous nineteen years.

Jesse Gray, my roommate from Stokes, North Carolina, got into big trouble during this period because of the self-censoring of letters by officers. Jesse, the son of a terrible-tempered tobacco farmer, had inherited most of his father's temper. He said that as a boy he and his brothers fought to keep from sitting next to his father at meals because invariably one of them would be knocked from his chair by his father for some minor infraction. Once his father was operating an expensive piece of tobacco planting equipment when it broke down more than a mile from the barn. His father got off the machine, walked to the barn, got a big, sharp ax, walked calmly back to the machine, and methodically chopped it to bits.

Jesse had graduated from East Carolina Teacher's College, or ECTC as he called it, when he was twenty and was teaching school and working on the family tobacco farm when he joined the Army. I could get a backache just by listening to Jesse's tales of "breakin' bacca" in the fields of North Carolina. He said he was not sure what he would do after the war, but he was sure it wouldn't be tobacco farming.

Anyway, to get back to censoring, Jesse insisted that he could say whatever he wanted to his family in letters home because they weren't spies. No matter what we argued, he could not be convinced that the problem was not that his family might be infiltrated by spies but that his letters might be intercepted. Even though there was little we knew that could help the enemy, we were certifying by our signatures that there was no improper information in the letters. Jesse was adamant, and "by damn," he'd tell his family whatever he damn pleased!

Our letters were evidently spot-checked by the mail service censors, because about a month later Jesse got a letter from his mother that contained one of the letters he had sent home. It looked like a stencil mat for Morse code, with dots and dashes cut out all over. Jesse was furious and ranted and raved for days. He took it not as a warning but as a challenge and from then on included not only whatever location and other material he chose but also profane notes to the censors warning them to stop cutting information out of his letters. He also told them that bunch of "noncombatant mail weenies" shouldn't be interfering with the mail of combat pilots. For the censors that was the last straw; they could accept profanity more easily than truth. After receiving and ignoring several warning letters from the censors to cease and desist, he was notified by the adjutant that 23rd Group Headquarters was going to court-martial him for continued deliberate breaches of security as well as insubordination. That, finally, got Jesse's attention. He agreed, through our CO, to accept squadron punishment in lieu of court-martial. He was fined $75 a month (one-third of his pay) for six months, and his promotion to first lieutenant was held up for three months. Jesse never was convinced that he had done anything wrong and continued to rail against the censors, but no longer in writing.

Bill Carlton, a funny extrovert who lived on Peachtree Street, no less, in Atlanta, spent a lot of time with Moose Elker and Flash Segura answering magazine ads and writing outrageous responses to published letters in magazines and then reading the replies to the rest of the squadron. They began a fruitful correspondence with a Mr. Elmer of New Orleans, who owned Elmer's Candy Company, manufacturer of Elmer's Gold Bricks. Moose told him that he had received a box of Gold Bricks from home and that they were so good that he had been beaten severely about the head and body by his squadron mates and robbed of the Gold Bricks. This missive must have struck Mr. Elmer's fancy, because he began a continuing and amusing correspondence with Moose, Bill, and Flash. We all appreciated the humor, but not nearly as much as we appreciated the large boxes of Gold Bricks that accompanied every letter.

About that time Moose received a delayed Christmas package that included a small book, *Ladies Night at a Turkish Bath*. When the book was opened a spring was released that exploded a small cap. After milking it for as many laughs as possible, Moose and I decided to use the large supply of spare caps to better advantage.

Recently someone in one of the other squadrons had been killed when a .45 pistol, being cleaned by another officer, had fired. We carefully removed all the rounds from my .45 and placed about four folded caps in the groove where the hammer hit the firing pin. I pulled the trigger and got a satisfactory, loud explosion. I went back to my room and sat on my bunk and ostentatiously began cleaning my gun. This, incidentally, was common practice. Pilots were always sitting around cleaning their guns, although they were rarely fired. A few minutes later Moose wandered in and stood in the center of the room shooting the breeze with Jesse and Dick. During an appropriate lull in the conversation, I pulled the trigger with the gun aimed at Moose. He clutched at his chest, staggered, and started to fall but was caught and lowered gently to the nearest bunk by a visibly shaken Jesse, who yelled for Dick to get the doc. Moose, however, couldn't keep from laughing, and when Jesse caught on I thought for a minute that both Moose and I might really need a doctor. Fortunately, Jesse's relief and his sense of humor prevailed, and he thought it was a great joke to play on others. We decided that Moose hunting season had opened.

For the rest of the afternoon and evening we lured other pilots into the room on one pretext or another and shot Moose. I was the designated shooter, Moose the shootee, and Jesse the catcher and gentle lowerer. We fooled everyone until Moose began putting on such elaborate death scenes—staggering around the room moaning and running into things, making the death scene from *Camille* look like a comedy—that Jesse and I started laughing and gave away the show. Fortunately, we were nearly out of caps by then, and Moose was becoming so proficient at acting that he might have given up flying for the stage, and he was too good a pilot to lose.

A favorite form of entertainment was to kid Moose, Danny Daniels, and Bill Carlton about being so old. They were all twenty-seven or twenty-eight, while most of the pilots in our part of the building, the more recent arrivals, were in their early twenties. We expected age in the CO, who must have been about the same age, but thought they were ancient for second lieutenants. They had all entered as cadets at the maximum allowable age of twenty-six. We told the room boys to check them every morning to see whether to wake them up or cover them up, and we often put glasses of water by their beds for their teeth. I guess you have to be twenty to think that twenty-seven is old.

Quite often, we would either walk or, if we could scrounge a jeep, ride into Hengyang. It was a town of some 25,000, with narrow streets paved with stones. Though somewhat primitive, the town was quite clean, and the people were friendly. We visited only the downtown area, where most of the streets were lined by narrow wooden stores with the merchants usually displaying their wares on tables in the front. There were many stores selling bolts of silk cloth and garments made of silk. Others sold brass and beautifully carved objects of jade and ivory. Being young, inexperienced, and a bachelor, I had little interest in collecting objets d'art. I quite likely missed the opportunity to buy some beautiful and valuable pieces. We were expected to bargain with the Chinese and never to accept the first price. The Chinese money used dollars as the denomination, and it was called CN, for China National. When I first arrived in China, $1 U.S., referred to as "gold" by the Americans, was worth $60 CN. The rate of inflation kept increasing, and by late 1944 the rate was more than $5,000 CN to $1 U.S.

Almost everyone had a camera, and essentially everything was recorded on film. Copies of good photos were in demand, and negatives were borrowed regularly for copying. Because of this the photography shop in Hengyang did a booming business. The shop sold, developed, and printed film and shot studio photos as well. Almost all the pilots posed for photos in their leather jackets, which came out well, except that the photographer retouched them so much, removing blemishes and darkening lips and eyes, that we all looked like the silent-movie star Rudolph Valentino. I was intrigued by the teacup that the photographer used as a lens cover for his large studio camera.

If we walked to town, something over a mile, we took a sampan across the river, but if we drove we had to take the ferry. The sampans were low wooden boats about thirty feet long and six feet wide, with a small bamboo shelter in the center. They were propelled by poling or rowing, depending on the depth of the water. Hundreds of sampans were tied up on the riverbank on the Hengyang side, and they were occupied by families who spent most of their lives onboard. On the Hengyang side of the river we would be met by a swarm of rickshaws pulled by coolies clamoring for our business. At times we organized rickshaw races and paid a bonus to the winning coolie. There was always a hassle when we paid the drivers. They always wanted more than we gave them, although we probably paid five times what a Chinese customer would pay for the same ride. They screamed and ranted and threw down our money until they saw that was all they would get. Then they bowed, gave the universal thumbs up, said "Ding hao" (very good) several times, and left.

Buckshot Smedley (who at six foot one and more than 200 pounds was by far the biggest pilot in the squadron) invented a game that only he could play called coolie launching. Rickshaws were pulled by means of two long wooden shafts under the coolie's arms. Smedley would come up behind a rickshaw and jump on the two springs, one on each of the wheels, that protruded behind the rickshaw, propelling the coolie like a rocket into the air. Pretty soon the word must have gotten around among the coolies, because they quickly got out from between the shafts when they saw the big red-headed Smedley approaching. However, the launchee didn't seem to mind it at the time, and the other coolies thought it was hilarious.

Whenever we had a jeep in town, a tremendous crowd gathered around it wherever we parked. There were few motorized vehicles in that part of China, and the locals were fascinated by them. Segura and Carlton took advantage of this to campaign for Segura's election as mayor of Hengyang. Carlton, as campaign manager, and Flash would make impassioned speeches from the hood of the jeep, during which the crowds would clap or cheer wildly on cue. The crowds would remain as long as they were willing to talk, and Flash was indefatigable. Segura's platform was simple but appealing: a chicken in every pot and an Allison engine in every sampan. If Segura had been able to speak Chinese he would have been a shoo-in for mandarin.

Christmas 1943 came and went without fanfare. It was just another day, and we had the same greasy pork chops for dinner that we had every night. The weather was marginal, so we kept three flights on alert at the flight line. We did have a short church service that evening in the mess hall. None of the Christmas presents and fruitcakes from home arrived until late January.

A few days after Christmas the citizens of Hengyang gave a big banquet for the squadron. It was held in a large dining room of a restaurant in town. The mayor, Segura's rival, and many high officials from Hengyang and from Hunan Province were the hosts. We sat with Americans and Chinese interspersed at separate round tables for ten. We had some kind of soup served individually, but the main course, if you could call it that, was a big bowl heaped with unrecognizable chunks of meat and vegetables and large chunks of pure fat. Some of the meat was our usual pork cut into new shapes. We also had individual bowls of rice. I had been expecting chop suey or chow mein or something that I knew as Chinese food in the States. No Chinese restaurant in the States would stay in business five minutes with this kind of food.

We had been warned by the doc not to eat anything that wasn't cooked and not to drink any water. The only other beverage served was the potent Chinese rice wine. I didn't drink any, but many of the pilots were bombed much more effectively than they had been during the enemy bombing raids.

I ate little but rice because the food looked so unappetizing and because I hadn't yet been checked out on chopsticks, the only utensils available. I was fascinated by the appearance and eating habits of the Chinese gentleman sitting next to me. He nodded to me when I sat down but didn't say a word. He was obese and dressed in colorful and expensive Chinese robes. When the soup was served, he put the bowl almost up to his mouth and used the spoon as a viaduct to slurp the soup into his mouth; he seemed to inhale it, with accompanying sound effects. When the main bowl was placed on the table, he began grabbing all the pieces of fat with his chopsticks and wolfing them down. He was a passed master with the chopsticks, and I believe he could have threaded a needle with them. He would probably be appalled at the recent news from China that chopsticks may be banned because they spread germs. None of the Americans wanted the fat, and the other Chinese seemed to defer to him. When the meal was over and we stood up to leave, I was completely surprised when he said to me in perfect English, "It was a pleasure having you with us." It seems that he was the water commissioner of Hunan Province and had a master's degree in civil engineering from Cornell. Had I known sooner, it would have been a marvelous opportunity to learn more about China and its people. I think he didn't speak before because he didn't want to be diverted from big eating by small talk.

When we were leaving the building each pilot was presented with a six-foot, parachute-silk scarf with a beautifully embroidered 75th Squadron insignia, a tiger shark with six machine guns firing from its elongated fins, on one end. In 1976 I donated it, along with my flight jacket, to the National Air and Space Museum of the Smithsonian Institution, where it is part of a Flying Tiger exhibit.

Another form of entertainment at Hengyang—especially during the monsoon season, when we slept a lot in the day and thus could stay up at night—was rat hunting. The hostel was infested with large and bold rats, so bold that I'm sure they believed that the hostel was infested with humans.

My first encounter with a rat took place only a few days after I moved into the hostel. I had gone to sleep but evidently hadn't tucked my mosquito bar in very well. I was awakened by something walking on my blanket. Dick or Jesse had fallen asleep without turning off the light, and I could see that it was a large, dirty brown rat, about the size of a small cat, strolling on the blanket over my leg. I quickly ducked my head under the covers and started kicking and yelling. The rat, slowly and with some dignity, left the bed and disappeared under it.

We all jumped up, grabbed flashlights, GI shoes, and pokers and searched for it without success. The next day we tried to rat-proof our room by nailing boards over all the rat holes. This wasn't effective, as the building was honeycombed with rat holes and the wood was so flimsy or rotten along the baseboards that the rats could gnaw through in almost no time.

So as the monsoon set in we went after the rats in earnest. Guns were the only weapons that were taboo. One of the other squadrons had some near-accidents caused by shooting at rats. The heavy .45 slugs had gone through the walls and hit occupied beds and chairs, but miraculously had not injured anyone. Major Richardson said he would have the ass of anyone who fired a gun in the hostel, and Major Richardson was not one for idle threats.

The eight rooms on one side of the center of the hostel were occupied by the more junior pilots in the squadron, those from the last three or four classes from India. We organized and coordinated our rat hunting efforts as diligently as we planned our combat missions. The Ratbusters' first step was to locate the rat holes. About six or eight of us would go into a room, move all the furniture into the center, and block all the rat holes that were behind furniture or under the beds. The more visible holes we either covered with glass, hoping the rats would run into it, or lined with razor blades set at an angle so that the rats could enter the room between them but would be cut by the blades when they tried to leave. Ingenious but ineffective, I'm afraid. A few rats ran into the glass, but it didn't seem to faze them. Others were momentarily deterred by the razor blades, but none was injured as far as we could tell. So back to the drawing board.

Our most successful tactic was the search and destroy mission. We kept bricks and rocks in each room, and when anyone heard or saw a rat he immediately blocked the known holes with them and sent someone to alert the other rooms that a rat jing bao was on. Three or four of us would scramble to the room to intercept the enemy, eager for the kill. Then, using flashlights along with the room lights, we tracked down the rat and killed it with shoes, pokers, shovels, or whatever came to hand. We became quite adept at cornering the rats while staying far enough away to keep from being bitten. God knows what diseases they were carrying.

On our night rat missions we used the same terminology that was used on air raid alarms. A typical message would be "Heavy engine noise in [room] 203. I think it's a bomber; a recce [reconnaissance plane] was in earlier." One night when there was heavier than normal rat activity, we were racing up and down the porch passing messages back and forth. Room 204 had been occupied by two pilots who had been killed in December, and it was still empty. Unbeknownst to us, two infantry officers, a lieutenant colonel and a major, advisers to the Chinese, had moved in that night to wait for an airplane to fly them to Kunming. They were awakened by all the activity on the porch and, thinking we were talking about a real air raid, they piled into their clothes and came out onto the porch wearing, in Moose's words, enough equipment to fight a guerrilla war for two years. The foot soldiers seemed to find the incident much less amusing than we hardened Ratbusters did, and I'm sure it did much to confirm their suspicions that fighter pilots were not quite right.

The rats were not always totally defeated. One evening the final score was one rat confirmed, one pilot probable. Eddie Oswald, or Ozzie as he was known, had called an alert since there was a heavy bomber in his room. Dick Jones and I grabbed a poker and a shovel and ran down to his room. Dick Long, an Allison engine tech rep with the squadron (who was deathly afraid of rats), was on the top bunk manning the flashlight. Ozzie said that he had spotted the rat climbing into one of the dresser drawers and had quickly slammed it closed, trapping the rat inside. The strategy was that Dick and I would each stand on one side of the drawer, and when Ozzie opened it we would clobber the rat. Standing in our underwear shorts, with weapons poised, we awaited the count of three. As Ozzie jerked open the drawer, the rat leaped right onto his bare chest and then onto the floor. Simultaneously, Dick and I hit Ozzie on the chest with the poker and shovel with all our strength. He fell to the floor with a thud, the wind knocked out of him. Undaunted, Dick and I chased the rat around the room, finally cornering it and, figuratively at least, shooting it down in flames. During the monsoon season, a dead rat was rated as an aerial victory. Despite Ozzie's questionable condition, Dick Long refused to leave his bunk to help him until we had carried the rat out of the room. We were surprised that we hadn't broken any of his ribs, but he had some tremendous bruises, which had just about faded away when he was killed in a crash about a month later.

After a long, hard winter campaign, the search and destroy missions, along with a strict rule on keeping edibles in sealed metal containers, ended most of the rat incursions into our rooms. There were still plenty of rats in the hostel, but they stayed away from our rooms. Little did the rats suspect that some six months later I would run the ultimate search and destroy mission against them.

Dick Jones had passed some of the monsoon season by carving an excellent model of a Japanese Tojo fighter out of hardwood. He also made a cigarette lighter from a Japanese 12.7-millimeter round, after disarming the explosive head. Dick was a perfectionist who, like my father, seemed to be able to do anything and do it well. Besides being an excellent flier, he was a top-notch bowler, a fine softball catcher, and a good golfer. He also did all his own automobile repairs and in recent years has built an outstanding recreation room and bar in his basement, doing all the cabinetmaking, carpentry, wiring, and plumbing.

I was surprised, but pleased, to learn that despite our remote location there were two groups of American missionaries in and around Hengyang. A group of Methodists lived in a compound in town, and there was a small Catholic mission north of the town, just across the river from the airfield. Both groups of missionaries, the Catholics and the Methodists, seemed to be well liked and well respected by the Chinese.

The missionary families in the town of Hengyang ran a small church and hospital for the Chinese and were helpful in doing what they could to make life more pleasant for us. The group comprised two ministers, a doctor, and one who was both; he took care of both the body and the soul or, in today's parlance, the hardware and the software.

One of the ministers came out to the base every Sunday and conducted a nondenominational church service complete with hymns to the accompaniment of a small pump organ. After the service he often stayed for a while to teach us a few useful phrases in Chinese, in which he was fluent. At the end of one such session he asked if we had any phrases we would like translated. Jesse held up his hand and, to our embarrassment, asked the minister, "How do you say, `Kiss my ass'?" The preacher thought a while and then said, "You don't say, `Kiss my ass.' If you want to insult someone you call him a turtle, which is believed to be sexless, or you can call him a wearer of a green hat." Jesse was delighted and quickly memorized both phrases. After that we seldom had any contact with the Chinese when Jesse didn't call one of them a turtle or at least a green-hat wearer. It never seemed to evoke any response, so either the preacher was wrong or Jesse was mispronouncing it. Probably the latter, because we often had trouble understanding Jesse in English. For instance, he pronounced "ass" "ace."

We spent many pleasant evenings at the home of Reverend and Mrs. Blackstone, learning a lot about China and the Chinese. One of the missionary doctors had been a pilot in World War I. He had never been to combat, but he regaled us with stories about his flight training in Jennies and Spads at Arcadia, Florida. He was delighted that most of us had done our fighter training at Sarasota and had flown over his old field at Arcadia. I think that they were interested in hearing as much as possible of home and wanted descriptions of where we lived and what was going on in the States. We brought them magazines and newspapers from home when the squadron was through with them, and they gave us a sense of calm and dignity in the strange world in which we found ourselves.

The Blackstones had three children, a boy and two girls who were all less than ten years old. They enjoyed walking out to the base with us on nonflying days and sitting in the cockpits of the P-40s. The parents, too, were quite interested in the airplanes and enjoyed climbing up on the wings to look into the cockpits.

The Catholic priests also visited us regularly and celebrated mass for the Catholics. They were knowledgeable and interesting and had been in China for more than ten years. Since Jesse, Dick, and I did not smoke, we endeared ourselves to the priests by giving them our monthly cigarette rations, even though none of us was Catholic.

The weather started improving as we got into April, and it looked as though we soon would be back flying against the Japanese full time. We were all bored by the forced inactivity of the monsoon season and were more than ready to get back to the excitement of combat flying.

9

SEARCH-AND-DESTROY MISSIONS

The United States had now entered the third year of the war; the Allies had taken the initiative, and there was no doubt that they would ultimately be victorious, although much hard fighting remained. Our forces were advancing in Italy and the Pacific, and the Soviets had stopped the German drive and were advancing. In England the U.S. Eighth Air Force and the Royal Air Force Bomber Command were raining bombs on Germany around the clock, the U.S. by day and the RAF by night. In China we were holding our own, but there were rumors that in the spring the Japanese would try to drive us from our bases to stop our attacks on their transportation.

The key to the Allies' success was their great production capacity. The Soviet factories had been moved beyond the Urals and were producing at a high rate. In 1943 the United States made prodigious strides, producing 85,000 aircraft, 148,000 tanks, 1.2 million trucks, 42,000 guns, and 27 million tons of shipping, and the rate of production was still increasing.

In February I learned that a close friend, Fred Didier, had been one of the 1,000 Marines killed in taking the small Pacific island of Tarawa. More than 2,000 Marines were wounded in the battle, which had been fought from November 20 to 23, 1943. Fred was married, and his wife was pregnant with twins when he was killed.

Although flying was limited during the months of the monsoon season, we managed to fly a few missions. I had one in January, four in February, and four in March. Except for one on which we escorted B-25s, they were all strafing and dive-bombing missions up on the south shore of Tungting Lake near the city of Yochow. There was a large Japanese airfield (Pailuchi) at Yochow, but it was not occupied, since it was too close to the front lines.

Our strafing missions were to knock out boat and road traffic in the area east of the Yangtze River and Tungting Lake, where there was a great deal of Japanese activity. Except for some rumors, we did not know that the Japanese were preparing for a major drive to the south. Several times we caught truck convoys on the road and destroyed them. Many of the trucks undoubtedly carried fuel or ammunition, because they either burned or blew up in fine fashion. It is gratifying to leave a convoy in flames; it provides tangible evidence of a mission's efficiency.

Although I had always been a good shot, my skills increased with practice. I learned to use my ammunition to better effect by firing much shorter bursts and by aiming first for the engine and then for the cargo compartment. A few .50-caliber armor-piercing slugs would destroy an engine beyond repair by going right through the engine block. We always began by strafing the first and last trucks in a convoy, trying to immobilize the whole convoy so that we could make continued passes until it was destroyed. Not only was motor transportation at a premium for the Japanese but there were also few roads; blocking them with burned out trucks denied their use to the enemy for long periods. The sight of the wreckage didn't do much for the morale of other truck drivers, either.

The convoys usually comprised ten to twenty trucks, khaki colored, with canvas-topped cargo compartments. On the open road they were defended by light machine guns and rifles. Since we usually made repeated passes on the same target, we often picked up a few bullet holes from the ground fire. The damage was usually superficial, unless the coolant or oil system was hit. The coolant was the most vulnerable, since it had much more area. Even the small-caliber Japanese rifles could shoot down a fighter with one hit in the coolant system.

When a P-40 took a coolant hit it immediately began to leave a steamlike trail of ethylene glycol. The first pilot to spot such a trail would call the pilot of the damaged plane and tell him that he was hit in the coolant. From the time he was hit until the engine overheated and froze, the pilot had approximately three minutes. An early warning gave him time to climb high enough to bail out and to put a few miles between him and the troops that were being strafed. In this area the troops stayed pretty close to the main roads, so if a pilot could bail out five or six miles from the road, he had a good chance of being rescued by the ever-vigilant Chinese guerrillas.

On one memorable mission we took off with eight P-40s to escort six B-25s on a sweep of the Yangtze River, from near Hankow southeast to Kiukiang, a distance of some fifty miles. The B-25s were from the Eleventh Bomb Squadron, at that time the only B-25s in China. The Eleventh was a first-class outfit that flew excellent formation, bombed with accuracy, and pressed home its attacks regardless of the opposition.

The North American B-25 Mitchell was a versatile twin-engine medium bomber used effectively in the Pacific and Mediterranean theaters as well as in the CBI. In addition to the standard Plexiglas nose of the bomber version, it also came equipped with a solid nose with eight fixed machine guns for strafing. One model mounted a forward-firing 75-millimeter cannon in the nose.

The B-25s flew in vees of three in trail at 10,000 feet, and we essed back and forth 2,000 feet above them. The weather was generally clear except for some broken clouds at 15,000 feet. We were especially alert since Hankow was a major Japanese stronghold with several active airfields. About ten minutes from the target, fifteen Oscars popped out from behind some clouds and dived toward us. I spotted them first and yelled, "Zeros at two o'clock high!" We turned toward the Oscars as we jettisoned our belly tanks and opened our throttles all the way in order to get between them and the bombers. As they dived toward the bombers they passed in front of us, turning to the right. I fired as one passed in front of me and saw a few of the telltale flashes on the fuselage indicating hits. They pulled back up into the clouds and disappeared from view. We climbed after them but couldn't catch them because of the speed they had built up in the dive, so we resumed our position over the bombers with our eyes peeled for the next attack, which we expected momentarily.

None came, however, and the B-25s shifted into a loose trail formation and started letting down so as to be on the deck when they reached the river. We let down to about 10,000 feet and continued to weave over them. Our flight leader kept his eyes on the bombers while we searched the skies for enemy fighters. He had told us to take occasional glances at the bombers to make sure that we didn't lose sight of them. They were difficult to pick out from that altitude because their camouflage matched the terrain so well, but they showed up clearly against the river. I could see that there was a lot of traffic on the river. In addition to the omnipresent sampans, there were some small ships and a few gunboats.

The B-25s began their attacks, essing back and forth across the river. They strafed the sampans, but the ships and gunboats were strafed and skip-bombed (bombs dropped at very low altitude in level flight so that they skipped across the water into the target; delayed-action fuses were used to give the bomber time to get away before the explosion). They left a visible trail of death and destruction behind them. The river was covered with burning and sinking vessels. The wooden sampans burned furiously, and some of the smaller ships were blown out of the water by the bombs. Often there were secondary explosions as cargo blew up, and oil fires were pouring masses of black smoke. Up ahead the boats were scattering wildly to get out of the bombers' path. The gunboats were loaded with antiaircraft weapons, and they lit up like Christmas trees as the bombers approached.

After about ten minutes we were nearing Kiukiang, where the B-25s were to break off and head for home. We couldn't understand why the Japanese hadn't sent some fighters to attack the bombers, and I imagine that same thought occurred to those on the boats. Suddenly my exhilaration at the success of the mission was dampened. I was looking down as a B-25 made a run on a gunboat. As it neared the target it started trailing smoke, but it continued the run and released its bomb. The smoke turned to flame, and the B-25 started a climbing turn that became a rolling dive into the riverbank. There was a tremendous explosion as it hit; simultaneously the gunboat blew up and broke in half as the bomb exploded. The boat and the airplane had each avenged itself.

To me, seeing a bomber crash was much harder to take than seeing a fighter go in. A bomber, out of control, rolling and diving, looks unnatural and ungainly, but it is hard to tell that a fighter is out of control, except from close up, until it hits the ground. More important, bombers carried from five to ten men, only one of whom was flying the airplane with some measure of control over his destiny. The pilot would be trying to regain control and pull out up to the time of impact, while the others were helpless passengers, despite their important duties during the rest of the mission. In a fighter there is only the pilot, who always believes that he can escape until the last millisecond. Death must be easier to take without the period of anticipation between the airplane's mortal damage and the crash.

The remaining bombers pulled up from the river and reformed their formation as they climbed on course for home. We stayed above them until we were about fifty miles north of Hengyang, then our leader led us down into close formation where we could see that most of the bombers had been damaged by the heavy antiaircraft fire. The bomber pilots often told us that nothing was more comforting than an escort of fighters. As we approached Hengyang, we gave them the thumbs up, then broke away and went in to land. The B-25s continued on to their base at Kweilin; we knew that none had been seriously damaged and that no one was wounded or they would have landed at Hengyang. Another advantage to flying fighters is that the pilot who takes off in a fighter knows that if he returns, it will be in a fighter. A pilot who takes off in a bomber may return in a flying ambulance or hearse full of dead or wounded comrades.

We knew that the Japanese had radar in the Yochow and Hankow areas and that it had been used to direct the Zeros into perfect position for their attack when they broke out of the clouds. They had evidently returned to their base, as we saw no more of them that day. About six months later we used their radar to our advantage in several attacks on the Pailuchi airfield. Although radar is commonplace today, it was quite new to us then, and we knew little about it.

Two of my missions during that period were dive-bombing attacks on a railroad bridge that crossed a small river near where it entered the Yangtze to the northeast of Tungting Lake. The bridge, close to a village called Puchi, was only about 200 yards long, of steel truss construction set on concrete piers. It carried a single pair of tracks on widely spaced ties. Looking down at it from above, we did not see a substantial target, since it consisted mainly of open spaces. Destroying it would have stopped all rail traffic in that area from Hankow, the main Japanese base, to the south. We had never seen any rail traffic, but intelligence reported that it was used extensively at night. That type of intelligence came from Chinese guerrillas who worked in the area with a few American intelligence officers.

On these missions we carried two 500-pound general-purpose bombs, one on each wing rack, with instantaneous fuses. With the two bombs and our standard 75-gallon belly tanks, the P-40s climbed even more slowly than usual. We normally started our dives from about 8,000 feet, pulling out at about 1,000 feet, but it was possible to attack from lower if we had to stay under the clouds (although we could not establish much of a dive from below 5,000 feet). If there was heavy flak or other ground fire, we could start at 10,000 feet and pull out at 2,000 or 3,000 feet, but with some loss of accuracy.

Dive-bombing runs on bridges are always made along the length of the bridge, as errors in range (short or long) are always much greater than errors in azimuth (left or right). As the flights neared the target,

Able flight would shift into right-echelon formation while the other flights stayed in finger formation to provide top cover. When the leader came abreast of the bridge he peeled off to the left into a 70- to 80-degree dive, lining up on the target with his gunsight and then releasing his bombs as he started to pull out. The other three in the flight followed in trail, with all four in their dives before the leader had released his bombs. As Able flight zoomed back up, Baker flight echeloned and dived, followed by Charlie flight, and so on. On heavily defended targets, all the flights went into echelon at the same time and dived one after the other with no perceptible interval between flights. It was like some great game of follow the leader, but with much higher stakes than mere loss of face.

At this time the Puchi bridge was undefended, or at least we didn't see any evidence of ground fire. Despite the ideal dive-bombing conditions, we didn't damage the bridge much. Many of the bombs went through the bridge and exploded in the water, while others hit trusses or ties and exploded in the air. The greatest damage was done by bombs that hit on the approaches, blowing up the rails and ties and the earth underneath. Of course many of the bombs missed entirely. We learned through intelligence that after both missions the craters were filled and the bridge was repaired within a few hours by large teams of coolies. I believe the Puchi bridge was finally destroyed by a flight of B-24s some months later.

It took a fair amount of experience and muscle to dive-bomb with accuracy in a P-40. As in all Allied single-engine fighters, the vertical stabilizer was offset slightly to the left to counteract the torque (the tendency for the airplane to roll in the opposite direction from the rotation of the propeller). The offset was designed to require no rudder trim at cruising speed. This meant that the airplane needed right rudder and right rudder trim on takeoff and at low speeds and left rudder and left rudder trim at high speed. In practice the pilot set in some right rudder trim before takeoff and still needed a hell of a lot of right rudder to hold a straight line on the runway. In a dive it was just the opposite: it took more and more left rudder as the speed increased. The pilot could not add left rudder trim as he dived for two reasons: the trim didn't operate fast enough, and he needed his left hand to pull the manual bomb release cables. We had electric releases operated by a button on the top of the stick, but they were unreliable and no one used them.

The key factors in accurate dive-bombing were, for azimuth, to keep the ball of the turn-and-bank indicator centered throughout the dive, which meant that the plane was not skidding or slipping, and for range, to release the bombs at the proper instant. There was also the matter of experience and feel. If the pilot held the pipper of the gunsight on the aiming point on the ground and released the bombs before starting to pull through, the bombs would land short. He could either hold the pipper slightly forward of the target and release before pulling through or hold it on the target and release as he started to pull through. I used the latter method, pulling the release just as the target disappeared under the nose, with generally good results.

My dive-bombing technique was to crank in about 5 degrees of left rudder trim before starting the dive and compensate with right rudder until I was into the dive. As I rolled into the dive, I cut the power almost to idle to keep my speed down as much as possible. In addition to the reduced thrust, the propeller acted as a brake. As the speed picked up I concentrated on keeping the ball centered, by feel, not by watching the ball, and the pipper on the target. I usually fired a short burst or two from my guns during the dive to keep the anti-aircraft gunners' heads down. I had to be a bit of a contortionist, especially in the last stages of the dive. I was going almost straight down, standing on the left rudder and holding the stick forward to maintain the dive angle and to the right to keep from rolling to the left. I was making constant minute stick and rudder adjustments to stay on the target while holding the two bomb release cable T-handles, located on the floor behind and to the left of the seat—a most unusual fighting position, the left leg fully extended and exerting great pressure, the right arm pushing hard into the right forward corner of the cockpit, the left arm extended back to the left holding on to two cables, the body in a bit of a crouch to reach the bomb release, and the neck extended to keep a line of sight through the gunsight. None of the smaller pilots ever mentioned it, but I'm sure that some of them were hard put to carry out a good dive-bombing run.

On the pullout, after the bombs were released, I let the airplane skid a bit as it is much harder for ground gunners to hit a skidding plane. I usually pulled 4 or 5 g on the pullout, which caused my vision to dim for a few seconds, then I rolled on my side in the climb to see where my bombs hit. Once we leveled out again at altitude, I joined up in the standard finger formation. On the way back to the base the flights went down by turn to strafe targets of opportunity.

In early April Madame Chiang paid a visit to Hengyang and made a short speech in the auditorium thanking the United States for its long friendship with and support of China. Luckily there was no question-and-answer period, so Jesse wasn't able to ask about her piano. She was in the area to visit with the high officials of Hunan Province. I was on alert that day and had to stay in the cockpit during her stay on the base. We were afraid the Japanese might have learned of her visit and would bomb the airfield and city during her stay, but the ceiling was too low and no enemy aircraft came our way despite her presence. She made a queenly drive by the flight line when she arrived, waving to the pilots in the cockpits, but it was a closed car so I didn't see her clearly.

We did have to scramble twice to intercept inbound Japanese bombers, once in March and once in April. The first time we received ample warning and were in the cockpits for the two-ball alert when the third ball went up and we scrambled. We climbed at top speed to the north, but the Japanese turned back about fifty miles away, near Dog Dog two-four, and we never sighted them.

The next time, however, the warning net broke down for some reason, and we were in the alert shack when the three balls were hauled up and there was a mad clanging of the warning gong. We ran to our planes, jumped into the cockpits, started the engines, and took off as quickly as possible. We went in no prescribed order but took off as soon as we could taxi onto the runway. I put on my helmet as I started the engine so I would be in radio contact, but I didn't take the time to put on my parachute or fasten my seat belt. Our ground station announced that bombers and fighters had been spotted about fifty miles to the north, heading toward Hengyang. Contrary to our usual practice, I closed my canopy before taking off to give me a better feeling of security. My element leader and I got started together, so I took off on his wing. We climbed straight to the north to intercept the enemy as far from Hengyang as possible. As soon as I had my wheels up, I slid out into looser formation and struggled into my parachute and seat belt, no easy task. We spotted some dots at twelve o'clock high that were undoubtedly the enemy, but they had turned around and were climbing up into the clouds to safety. When they disappeared we continued north for about ten minutes in the hope of finding something to shoot at, but to no avail, so we returned to Hengyang and landed.

The Japanese ran these abortive raids periodically. We never found out if they turned back because they knew we had scrambled or if they were designed to make us waste our precious fuel. In any case, we did waste a lot of fuel on these scrambles, with twelve or more airplanes flying close to full throttle, even though the missions usually lasted only thirty to forty minutes.

Although I had to take off on scrambles several more times without fastening my parachute and seat belt, I never got used to it. It wasn't that I was afraid of falling out of the cockpit or of bouncing away from the controls; I just didn't feel like part of the airplane until my seat belt was fastened. I felt as though I was just along for the ride instead of being an integral part of the machine, or rather the machine being an integral part of me. Once I was strapped in I just went wherever I wished and the airplane went with me, without conscious effort on my part. I never thought about moving the airplane into closer formation, I just moved closer. I made the minute adjustments necessary to keep my sight on the target without any thought of flying the airplane. The feel of the seat belt was a vital part of that feeling of oneness with the machine, and I felt ill at ease without it. I feel the same way in a car and strongly approved the introduction of seat belts.

The fighters were just beginning to be equipped with shoulder harnesses to go along with the lap belt. These early harnesses did not have the inertia reels that automatically lock on impact, so we had to lock and unlock them manually. They were of little use when unlocked and much too restricting when locked, so nobody used them. We all thought it more important to be able to look behind you easily than to protect your head in a crash, especially since none of us thought we would ever crash.

Weather is a major factor in all flying, but it was a major deterrent in China, since we almost never flew on instruments in the P-40s. There were several good reasons: no radio aids, inaccurate maps, and mountainous terrain. Any one of them was sufficient, but the main reason was the lack of flight instruments in the P-40s. Some of the older P-40s had artificial horizons and directional gyros, but they were usually in poor operating condition at best. The P-40Ns were designed as lightweight models and had no flight instruments except a bank-and-turn indicator, or needle and ball, as it was called. The ball operated by mechanical forces, but the needle was electrical instead of vacuum driven. That in itself was not the problem. The problem was that it never worked. It indicated a single needle width turn to the left no matter what the pilot did. Later, when we were equipped with P-51s with good flight instruments, we were so out of practice that it took quite a while to get used to flying on instruments in the clouds.

To compensate for our inability to fly in the clouds in the P-40s, we learned every inch of the terrain over which we flew and became expert at flying up and down the river under low ceilings, both to attack targets to the north and to return to base if we were blocked by low clouds. That happened often, because the weather forecasting was very inaccurate. Our forecasters were competent but were handicapped by the lack of reporting stations.

10

COMBAT
INTERMISSION

April, when the monsoon finally folded its tent and silently stole away, was a good month, not only because the sun returned and our world dried out but also because on the fifteenth I learned that I had been promoted to first lieutenant, effective April 1. A few days later Major Richardson called Lieutenants Armstrong, Oswald, Gray, and me into his office and told us we were to ferry four of our old P-40s back to India and bring back new P-40Ns. Army Armstrong, who was about two months senior to us, was to lead us to Kweilin, where we would be joined by four pilots from the 74th Fighter Squadron, then on to Kunming, the China terminus of the Hump.

Ferry trips were highly prized and were assigned more or less by seniority. Jones and Green had gone on one earlier in April. We were excited by the opportunity and believed this would be a good time to go, since the weather was just starting to improve and we wouldn't miss too much combat.

There were several reasons why these ferry trips were so desirable. It was quite an experience flying a fighter all the way from China, across the Hump and the whole subcontinent of India, to Karachi, a distance of more than 3,000 miles. Also, the ferry pilot usually was assigned the airplane he flew back as his personal airplane, to fly on missions whenever he was on the schedule. Probably the most important reason, however, was the chance to eat some decent food for a change in the mess halls and restaurants in India. We also were scheduled to visit Calcutta for a few days, where we could buy state-side food in the commissary to fly back to China. Dick Jones and Earl Green had brought back a lot of canned food, a welcome supplement to our regular diet of bad pork and eggs.

In addition to loading up with as much food as possible, we wanted to buy a phonograph and some records if we could find them in Karachi or Calcutta. We missed the big-band music that was so popular at that time in the States, since there were no radio stations in China. On the squadron shortwave set, we occasionally were able to pick up Tokyo Rose, who played a lot of Glenn Miller, Artie Shaw, Benny Goodman, and other top bands. She didn't call herself Tokyo Rose—that was the GIs' name for her. She always identified herself as Orphan Annie. Her main theme was that it was too bad that we young Americans had to be at war in the Pacific and China while the draft dodgers and 4-Fs played fast and loose with our girlfriends and wives back home. No one paid any attention to her messages, but we did like the music. At least no one admitted that they were bothered by her messages.

Unable to leave on April 18 because of bad weather, we took off in the early afternoon of the next day, when the clouds lifted enough for us to get to Kweilin under them. All of our P-40s were war weary, with many hard hours on them. I was flying P-40K number 169, *The Deacon's Sad Sack*. This was the airplane that Deacon Lewis was flying when he shot down the Lily on a head-on pass over Hengyang on December 10. We circled the field in tight formation, then took up our course to Kweilin, loosening up the formation once we were out of sight of the field. Just before we reached Lingling Ozzie pulled up next to Army and signaled that he was going back to Hengyang. I don't know if his radio wasn't working or if he maintained radio silence out of habit. In any case he peeled off without a word and headed back. We continued on and landed at Kweilin about one hour and twenty minutes later. We didn't land at Yang Tong, the main airfield at Kweilin, but on the narrow fighter strip where the 74th was based. It was only a mile or so from Yang Tong, but there were a number of the distinctive Kweilin mountains in between.

Ozzie didn't arrive at Kweilin that night, so we were expecting him the next morning when we went down to the flight line. Just before noon Hengyang sent a message asking if Ozzie had arrived. They had received no arrival report through the net telephone system as they should have, since he had taken off more than two hours earlier. When, after two more hours, he had not arrived, we were sure that he was down somewhere. There was a good chance that he had either bailed out or belly landed somewhere, but the total lack of radio contact was ominous. Dismal weather prevented our continuing on to Kunming, but we waited at the 74th alert shack all day hoping for good news. Late the next morning we learned from group headquarters that he had crashed a short distance from Hengyang and his body was in the cockpit. We never learned the cause. He had dropped out of our flight because his engine was running rough. He had landed at Hengyang, where the malfunctioning spark plugs had been replaced. The engine had checked out okay on the ground and had sounded good on the takeoff. The weather was not a factor, so we could only surmise that he must have tried to land after his engine failed and didn't quite make it. Generally it was better to bail out if possible because most of the terrain was not suitable for a belly landing.

After sitting on alert for two depressing days waiting for the weather to clear, we took off for Kunming, landing two and a half hours later. They parked us on the 26th Fighter Squadron flight line, since two of its planes were to be ferried to India with us. The 26th was part of the 51st Fighter Group, at that time the only other American fighter group in China. In addition to the 26th, the 51st Group included the Sixteenth Squadron at Chengkung, across the lake from Kunming, and the 25th, the Assam Dragons, at Yunnanyi, to the west of Kunming.

Jesse and I went into the alert shack and found Ted Coakley and Pinky Mace, old friends from our training days at Craig Field and Sarasota. We also ran into the infamous Sam Brown, who had come to the 26th from Landhi. The 26th's mission was to defend the base at Kunming, the all-important China terminus of the Hump. Since the Japanese rarely attacked Kunming the 26th pilots had seen little action, so we, because of our tremendous combat experience, could needle them a bit. They had flown a few escort missions with the B-24s of the 308th Bomb Group, "The Liberators of China," down south to the Hainan Peninsula, but there was no air opposition. A few months later they moved east to Nanning and got all the combat they could hope for.

We planned to stay there until evening, shooting the breeze with Ted and Pinky, but Army came in with the sad news that Ozzie's body had been flown to Kunming and would be buried that afternoon. We checked into the transient officer's hostel, cleaned up, and borrowed a jeep to go to the graveside funeral services. The cemetery, off to one side of the field hidden by a grove of trees, consisted of long rows of aboveground concrete crypts that looked like small, attached Quonset huts. They were intended for temporary interment until the caskets containing the bodies could be shipped home. This was the first funeral I had ever been to, and I would attend only one other in China, although I lost many friends during my stay. Usually they were shot down in enemy territory and their bodies not recovered. In the rare instances that the bodies were recovered, they were sent to Kunming for burial.

The service, conducted by a Catholic chaplain, was simple and short, but the final volley of shots over the grave and the poignant strains of taps were very moving. Since that time I've attended many military funerals, and I'm always touched by the finality of the guns and taps, which are a fitting end to a military career, whether it be at nineteen or seventy-nine.

We went back to the hostel and that evening ate with the 26th pilots. Pinky Mace told us that two pilots from the 51st Group Headquarters would be with us on the trip. A Capt. Solon Kelley and, to our dismay, Lieutenant Colonel Amen, who had threatened to court-martial Moose and some of the other L-5 pilots for the buzz job at Landhi, would be leading the flight.

The food in Kunming was better than at Hengyang. The cuts of pork were recognizable and not so fat, the sugar wasn't fermented, and we had a real canned apple pie for dessert. The closer to the Hump, the better the food, seemed to be the rule.

The next morning Army, Jesse, and I reported to the flight line ready to roll. The colonel told us that he would lead the first flight of five and Kelley would lead the second flight of four. The three of us from the 75th would be with Kelley. I was on Kelley's wing, and Armstrong and Gray were the second element. Our destination was the airfield at Mohanbari, 500 miles away in Assam, one of the India bases of the Hump route. It was only a few miles from Chabua, where I had left India for China less than six months earlier.

We took off to the east and made a slow climbing turn to the northwest as we assembled the formation. Once out of sight of the field we shifted into combat formation because the Japanese sometimes attacked planes on this route. As we slowly climbed up to 20,000 feet, the foothills became more rugged and higher until we were over the Himalayas proper. Although I had crossed the Hump before, I had been in the back end of a transport and couldn't see too much. Now, in the cockpit of a P-40, I had a clear view of the terrain, and I could see why it was world renowned: high, rugged mountains, covered with snow for most of their height. There did not seem to be any valleys between them; another mountain started where one left off. They stretched as far as I could see, higher to the north and lower to the south, where they faded into hills in Burma. The highest peaks were 16,000 to 18,000 feet but seemed much higher to the northwest. It was an awesome sight, particularly as I'd never flown over any real mountains before. It was hard to believe that man had ever attempted to climb Mount Everest, which towered some 10,000 feet above us, out of sight in the northwest. That would require much more courage than flying combat.

Flying over this extremely rough country for an hour or so, it seemed that we would have as much chance of surviving a bailout if our chute didn't open as we would if it did open. When we were about halfway across, over the worst country, we found scattered to broken clouds below us. Right about then, our leader, Colonel Amen, called Kelley and said, "My clock has stopped, Kelley. You better take the lead." Kelley said Roger, and our flight slid into the lead. The mountains below us gradually changed into hills and then into the low tropical valley of the Brahmaputra River in Assam.

About one hour later we started to let down as the green belt of the Brahmaputra Valley came into sight. Kelley called the Mohanbari tower to find the direction of landing and put our flight into echelon. Once we had spotted the field, the colonel again took the lead, and we peeled off to land after a higher approach than we were used to, 300 feet instead of 30 feet. Evidently the colonel was still opposed to buzzing.

My landing felt different somehow, and while I was taxiing to the ramp I realized it was my first landing on a paved runway in six months. I missed the familiar sound and impact of the gravel hitting the flaps. The flight had taken three hours, and I was back in India's sunny clime.

We checked into the transient quarters, the familiar bamboo and thatch hutments with screened-in sides. Except for the materials, they were identical to our quarters in Sarasota. We hustled up to the mess hall for lunch and to our delight found that the main course was Spam with canned pineapple rings. We were the only transients; everyone else groaned at the sight of Spam since it was a staple of their diet. We were probably the only members of the U.S. armed forces who would kill for Spam, or for any stateside food, however mundane.

The colonel said we wouldn't be leaving until the next day, so we went to the officer's club, which was just a lounge adjoining the mess hall, and listened to records and read until time for supper. The menu was equally appealing: hot dogs with cheese, and ice cream for dessert. We thought we must be at the Plaza.

The next morning, after a good breakfast of pancakes with fake maple syrup, unfermented, we took off for Gaya. After a flight of three hours and thirty minutes over flat, generally featureless country, we arrived. Along the way the colonel asked Kelley to lead because of a compass problem, but he took the lead again for landing. The airfield was unimpressive, just a runway and a few buildings. We ate at a small canteen operated by the Red Cross—just sandwiches and tea, but made more enjoyable by being served by two attractive and pleasant American women.

Gaya was just an airstrip to me until a few years ago when my son, a professor of eastern religions, told me that Gaya was where, 500 years before Christ, Siddhartha Gautama attained the enlightenment that made him the Buddha. My son and I visited Gaya under such different circumstances: I, as a young fighter pilot with almost no knowledge of the history of India before the Raj, saw Gaya as an uninteresting refueling stop. Almost forty years later my son, a Fulbright scholar seeking to increase his already strong knowledge of Buddhism, saw Gaya as the birthplace of a worldwide religion.

As soon as the planes were refueled we took off and just under three hours later landed in Agra, the site of the Taj Mahal. I caught a glimpse of it as we approached to land, but we were in close formation and I couldn't look away for long. We asked the colonel if we could spend the next day in Agra so we could visit the Taj. At first he said no because we were due in Karachi the next day, but then he relented and said that we would leave for Karachi in the midafternoon, giving us time to see the Taj and still be able to arrive in Karachi before dark.

The colonel and Captain Kelley were staying on the base, but the rest of us, all first lieutenants, decided to go for broke and spend the night in a luxurious hotel. We scrounged a ride in a weapons carrier to the Hotel Agra, a beautiful old building and the best hotel in the city. We all looked pretty grungy in our wrinkled, sweat-stained khakis that we had flown in for several days. As we were checking in, we received looks that varied from quizzical to downright dirty from the Indian staff and from the well-dressed officers and ladies, both British and American, in the lobby. Obviously they did not realize they were in the presence of real combat pilots. No one said anything, however, and we made it to our rooms without incident.

The rooms were luxurious, far nicer than any place I'd ever been. They had spotless white walls and ceilings, with two enormous beds with white mosquito bars hanging from the high ceiling. All the chairs were white wicker, and there were two large, slowly rotating ceiling fans. It looked like a movie set, and I wouldn't have been surprised if Sidney Greenstreet and Peter Lorre had walked in. Jesse and I were in one room and Milks and Heelen of the 74th were in the next room, separated from ours by a gleaming bathroom. We flipped to see who got the first bath and Heelen won. About fifteen minutes later he called, and we found him soaking in a hot tub, smoking a big cigar, with a drink in his hand. He had adapted to his surroundings without any apparent difficulty. After everyone had bathed, we dressed in clean bush jackets, trousers, and boots and went to the main dining room, where we all ordered steaks and baked potatoes with pie à la mode for dessert. It was wonderful to feel completely clean and to eat at tables set with white tablecloths, napkins, and fine china. After dinner we sat around the lobby for a while, ogling the lovely ladies passing through and hoping Jesse would keep his lewd remarks to a whisper, then went back to our rooms for a most refreshing sleep.

The next morning, refreshed and eager, we ate early and then took a gharri, a horse-drawn carriage driven by a giant Sikh, to the Taj Mahal. When we arrived at the entrance to the grounds, we were besieged by Indians who wanted to be hired as guides as well as by the usual beggars. In addition to the standard cry of "Baksheesh, Sahib," they were shouting, "God bless the president of America," only they pronounced it Amer-EEK-a.

We selected a guide, rented the shoe covers that must be worn, and entered the grounds of one of the most magnificent structures in the world. Built in the mid-seventeenth century as a tomb for the favorite wife of the Indian ruler Shah Jahan, it houses the bodies of the shah and his wife. The perfectly proportioned white marble palace is surrounded by four white marble minarets and a large garden with reflecting pools. The inner walls have writings from the Koran in colored mosaic. I was sorry to see on the walls of the spiral staircases in the minarets that there were many names written in pen and pencil. Even more disappointing was that the names were all written in English.

Our guide was knowledgeable and told us a great deal about the early history of India. He suggested that we visit Agra Fort if we had time, so we asked him to guide us through it as well. Across the river from the Taj Mahal, it was a fascinating red stone fort that had been built much earlier. It was full of underground passages, complete with bats, dungeons, thick walls, wells, and barracks. When we finished the tour we hustled back to the hotel, checked out, and reported back to the flight line with about thirty minutes to spare. Kelley told us later that the colonel was prepared to blast us if we had been late. He would have been right to do so, as he had been kind enough to let us spend the day in Agra. It was an experience I was glad not to have missed.

We took off and flew an uneventful three hours and forty minutes to Karachi. I thought we would go directly to Landhi, but instead we landed at Karachi Air Base, where the P-40s would be inspected before being flown to Landhi. The giant dirigible hangar at KAB was visible from many miles away as we approached Karachi. After I peeled off to land, I noticed a long line of large aircraft parked along the flight line. They were much larger than the B-17s and B-24s I was familiar with. I was so engrossed in studying them that I nearly flew into the ground, but fortunately I recovered in time. The airplanes were B-29s of the 20th Air Force on their way to their new bases in Chengtu, China. I wanted to take a closer look after we landed, but they were closely guarded and only the crews were allowed near them. About six months later in China I was able to inspect one as closely as I liked.

We checked into the transient quarters, which were in the main terminal building, while Colonel Amen checked on our transportation to Panagarh, where we would pick up our new airplanes. He told us that we wouldn't be leaving until May 2, four days hence, so we would be free until the morning of May 2, when we were to meet him in the passenger area at KAB—four whole days on our own.

We caught the shuttle bus to Landhi and looked up a few of the permanent staff whom we knew. We stayed for supper and enjoyed the privilege of eating on the staff side of the mess hall for the first time. The food was the same but the difference in prestige was enormous. After dinner we attended the film, which was a good one—that is, Richard Arlen and Andy Devine weren't in it.

We spent the rest of the time in Karachi shopping, watching the latest movies in town, and eating the excellent food at the Karachi Officer's Club. I bought a good RCA Victor windup phonograph and some fifty records, all swing and jazz by the best big bands and combos. I had all the standards and several nonstandards, like Wingy Manone's "South with the Boarder," destined to become a big hit in the 75th.

Top left: Bring on the Zeros: Donald Lopez at three.

Top right: Lopez wearing a shearling suit for winter flying in open-cockpit PT-19s at the Embry-Riddle primary flying school in Union City, Tennessee.

Bottom right: Lt. Wiltz P. "Flash" Segura in his original zoot uniform in front of the barracks at Landhi Field, Karachi, India, 1943.

Lieutenant Lopez in front of a P-40M, Hengyang, China, December 1943.

Top: Lt. Lyndon R. "Deacon" Lewis in front of the Kawasaki Ki-48 Lily bomber he shot down in a head-on pass over Hengyang on December 10, 1943.

Bottom: Coolies breaking stones for gravel runways, Kunming, 1943.

Left: Lt. Jesse Gray with Lopez by tail of Gray's P-40, Kweilin, 1944.

Right: Maj. Elmer Richardson, 75th Fighter Squadron commander, with Maj. Witold Urbanowicz, second-ranking Polish ace.

Left: Capt. Jones Laughlin, flight surgeon, in front of his trusty ambulance.

Right: Three of the 75th's hardworking, well-dressed ground crew: Sergeants Carl Uhland, Jim June, and Charlie Waits.

Lt. Oswin "Moose" Elker behind the best mustache in China.

Earl Green and Moose Elker hamming it up after their return from enemy territory.

Hunk on a hill: Jesse Gray atop one of the distinctive mountains in the Kweilin area.

Top: Lt. Danny Daniels and Lope Lopez in front of the squadron headquarters sign at Yang Tong airfield in Kweilin.

Bottom: Lopez's P-40N on the fighter strip in Kweilin chewing on the wing tip of a Mustang, which ran into it on takeoff.

Top: Roommates and blood brothers: Lieutenants Green, Lopez, Gray, and Jones in front of the hostel at Kweilin, with their wings pinned to their chests, apparently to make up for the absence of hair.

Bottom: Comparing notes after a July 5, 1944, mission on which Lopez shot down an Oscar and Major Quigley shot down two (left to right): Lopez and Quigley, still wearing their escape kits, carried on every mission; Flight Surgeon Laughlin; Lieutenants Baldwin, Jones, Moehring, and Glass.

Seventy-fifth Squadron pilots in front of a P-40 at Chihkiang in September 1944 (left to right, standing): Lieutenants Segura, Alarie, Bellman, and Glass; Captain Kelley; Lieutenants Summey and Vayo; (on wing): Lieutenants Sanford, Gray, and Lopez and Captain Harper.

Dr. Francis P. "Butcher" Keefe, 75th Squadron flight surgeon and morale raiser, at Luliang late in 1944.

Top: Lt. Bob Bellman's Mustang burning on the field at Chihkiang, after a hung frag bomb exploded just after touchdown, killing Bellman instantly.

Bottom: Lopez with his new Mustang, *Lope's Hope III*, on the field at Chihkiang in October 1944. The first two *Lope's Hope*s were P-40s.

Lopez in the cockpit of his P-51 Mustang on November 11, 1944, after shooting down a Nakajima Ki-84 Frank on his hundredth mission.

Top: The B-25 from the Eleventh Bomb Squadron that overshot the runway at Chihkiang on January 19, 1945, with the loss of three lives. Dr. Keefe is in the foreground, and Lopez is with the group at the nose trying to rescue the flight engineer pinned in the wreckage.

Bottom: Mustangs of the 75th Fighter Squadron, with their new black tail markings, in formation over Chihkiang in early 1945.

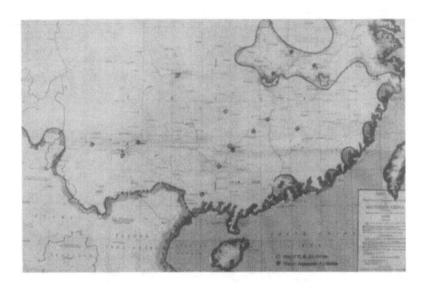

Japanese-held territory (shaded) in southern China as of April 1944, before the start of the Japanese offensive. By the end of the year, the Japanese had captured all the Allied airbases from Hengyang through Yungning (Nanning).

On May 2, after hanging around for several hours, we finally took off in a C-46 transport for Panagarh in south-central India, about 500 miles from Calcutta and almost 1,000 miles from Karachi. Some five hours later we landed on an airfield with hundreds of P-40s in varying stages of assembly parked on the ramp. The next morning we were assigned to specific aircraft and told to take them up and test them in the local area, since they had been flown only once since assembly. Mine was P-40N-20 number 43-23266. It had been flown for a total of three hours since it was manufactured in Buffalo. The colonel emphasized that we could do anything we liked except buzz, but buzzing was what we liked the most, so we all, individually, dropped to the deck as soon as we were out of sight of the field and buzzed hell out of the area. We had people jumping off trucks, oxcarts, and embankments and dropping flat on the roads. It was a thoroughly satisfactory morning—at least it was until we got back and the reports started coming in. Colonel Amen chewed us out royally, but it was well worth it.

Later that day we took off for the flight to Calcutta, landing at an airfield with the strange name "Dumdum." Since we were to leave on the fifth for Mohanbari, the lieutenants, becoming accustomed to the good life, once again opted to stay in a hotel. We checked into the Grand Hotel, which was well named, being even more grand than the Hotel Agra. Shortly after moving into our room we heard an in-line engine, popping and cracking, as they do when throttled back for landing. It sounded close, so Jesse and I rushed to the window, looked up, and saw nothing. We then looked down and were startled to see an RAF Spitfire below us with its wheels and flaps down. It landed a block or so away on one of the boulevards. We thought it was an emergency but learned later that the boulevard was used as a fighter strip for the Spitfires based there to defend Calcutta from bombing raids.

The next morning I went food shopping at the U.S. commissary, where I bought three barracks-bagfuls of canned food, including Spam, pineapples, apples, cherries, boned chicken and turkey, and some unfermented sugar. I felt like a kid turned loose in a candy store. Jesse loaded up as well, but he didn't have as much money to spend, since his pay had been reduced. We coordinated our buying, knowing all of our food would be shared with our roommates, Dick Jones and Earl Green. Some of the others loaded up on beer.

Calcutta was an extremely crowded city even in 1944. The English and the upper-class areas were beautiful, but the squalor in the slums was unbelievable. Most of the worst slum areas were off-limits to us, but the lower-class areas we drove and walked through were bad enough. Many people just lived on the streets, urinating and defecating on the sidewalks. All of the physically able were begging, and it was an ordeal to turn them away. One pass through there was a lifetime ration.

Later we were invited by an RAF officer, who had traded an RAF leather flying helmet to me for my AAF sunglasses that I never used, to visit a swimming club. We borrowed bathing suits and spent a wonderful day swimming and sunning in luxurious surroundings.

On the morning of the fifth we brought all of our belongings and purchases to Dumdum to load our airplanes for the return trip. The barracks bags were so heavy that I couldn't lift them into the baggage compartment through the small door on the left side of the fuselage. I emptied them on the ramp and climbed into the compartment, which went from behind the fuselage fuel tank all the way to the tail wheel. The oxygen tanks and the radio were in this compartment. I crawled back as far as I could and put one of the barracks bags up against the tail wheel. Jesse passed the cans to me, and I loaded all three bags, moving forward as the space filled up. After all the food was in I climbed out and loaded my records, the phonograph, and my B-4 bag with my clothes, as Colonel Amen watched in disbelief. I could barely close the door.

Not surprisingly, I was the last one loaded and the colonel was impatient to start. I jumped into the cockpit, strapped in, and checked my controls. The stick would barely move forward or back; the cable running back through the baggage compartment was obviously binding on something. While the others were starting their engines I jumped out, opened the compartment, took out the bag, the records and the phonograph, reached in, and found that a large can was pressing a turnbuckle on the elevator cable against one of the fuselage frames. I moved the can, threw in my gear, got back in the cockpit, and started up under Colonel Amen's glare. The stick moved freely, and I taxied out with a sigh of relief.

The sigh was premature. I came as close to buying the farm on takeoff as I ever have in all my flying, before and since. I never considered how far back the c.g. would move with all that weight in the aft fuselage; to me, c.g. stood for "commanding general," not "center of gravity." The first part of the run was normal, but as I gained speed I couldn't get the tail up. I was afraid to push forward too hard for fear of nosing up suddenly. The main gear left the runway first, and the nose came way up as the P-40 quivered on the edge of a stall. I pushed hard on the stick and cranked in forward trim to keep it from stalling. As the nose came down I pulled up the wheels and assumed a normal climb attitude. The airplane handled all right at normal flying speed, with some nose-down trim applied. Even though I would kill for Spam, I didn't want to be killed for it. I've often wondered what an accident investigator would have reported if I had crashed. He would have thought that a supermarket had hit the runway at 200 mph, and he wouldn't have been far off the mark.

After about three hours we reached Mohanbari and prepared to land. I wasn't anticipating any difficulties, since the airplane felt normal. Actually the c.g. had moved still farther aft, since I had burned all of the fuel in my belly tank and most of the wing tank. As I slowed down on the last part of my approach the tail felt heavier and heavier, even with full nose-down trim. As I stalled to land I was still using forward stick instead of full back stick, which is normal. The tail wheel hit first, with the main gear slamming down later. I was okay once on the ground, but I lost a lot of face on that landing. I heard later that someone who saw it thought I was a Chinese pilot.

Before we left for Kunming I reloaded my goods, moving my B-4 bag and the phonograph and records aft and the food as far forward as possible. I took it up for a test hop, and it handled fine, a little tail heavy but nothing I couldn't handle. I also decided to burn out the fuselage tank before the wing tanks to help keep the c.g. forward. The next day we took off and had an uneventful flight over the Hump back to Kunming.

At Kunming we learned that the Japanese had started a major drive south toward our bases from the Tungting Lake area. Their object was to drive us out of our eastern bases so that our fighters and bombers could not harass their transportation—the three Rs (road, railroad, and river) and their coastal shipping. We knew that the squadron would be flying a lot of missions and were anxious to get back as soon as possible.

The weather was bad the next day, but the following day we took off and headed for Kweilin. We made good time with a slight tailwind and with a little more power than usual. We landed on the fighter strip, refueled, said good-bye to our friends from the 74th, and took off for Hengyang.

Army, Jesse, and I made the flight to Hengyang in only one hour. We were like horses returning to the barn. We peeled off at zero feet, making our tightest patterns and smoothest landings in front of the assembled pilots. It was good to be home. Our holiday was over, and it was time to go back to war.

11

ENEMY ON THE MARCH

I rejoined the war on May 13, the day after I returned to Hengyang, attacking the shipping on the Yangtze. The river was alive with traffic, mostly sampans but with other larger boats as well. I was in one of the two low flights that strafed back and forth, crisscrossing the river as the boats desperately made for the shore, leaving many of them on fire and sinking. At times the sampans disappeared from view behind the geysers churned up by the thousands of rounds of .50-caliber slugs poured into the boats by the P-40s. We also came upon the first enemy trains I had seen. The Japanese did not usually operate trains in the daylight, but the clouds were low and evidently they weren't expecting our fighters to be in the air. We shot the engines full of holes, adding clouds of steam to the natural clouds, and set the cars on fire. Tracers ricocheting off the sides of the locomotives added to the display. All in all, it was a gratifying way to celebrate my return to combat.

Enemy activity had increased markedly with the breaking of the monsoon. The Japanese had started their long-heralded drive south from the Hankow area along the Siang River toward Kweilin and then down the railroad to Hanoi in French Indochina, now Vietnam.

Since the beginning of the war, the Japanese had been content to hold northeast China down to the Yangtze River, as well as the major coastal cities. Holding those areas kept many Japanese troops from the primary war theaters in the Pacific, and they were unwilling to tie up any more troops to capture the bases used by the small Fourteenth Air Force. By early 1944, however, the Fourteenth's B-24s and B-25s were sinking large numbers of Japanese ships. The vital work accomplished by the B-24s of the 308th Bomb Group is well expressed by this excerpt from the group's Presidential Unit Citation: "Operating from bases in China, the Group swept the East and South China Seas, the Straits of Formosa, the Gulf of Tonkin, through all kinds of weather, sinking and damaging nearly three-quarters of a million tons of vital Japanese shipping." Also, the B-25s and the fighters made it extremely costly to move matériel along the Yangtze or by land. The Japanese war machine depended heavily on this shipping to keep it supplied, so in late April they began a drive to capture the easternmost U.S. bases in China.

To support this drive, the Japanese had increased their air strength in China from an air division (Third Hikoshiden) of some 300 planes, about two-thirds fighters, to an air army (Fifth Kokugun) of more than 450 planes, also about two-thirds fighters.

Except for a few advisers, there were no American or other Allied troops in China. Still, we all believed that with the Fourteenth Air Force's control of the air and the large Chinese armies, we could stop the Japanese advance. It was not one of our better predictions.

The drive to the south started in late April, and by mid-May it was well under way. The Japanese air activity did not increase much in the beginning, but there were many more ground targets both for us and for the B-25s. Although we inflicted heavy damage and casualties, the Japanese ground forces moved inexorably toward their first major objective, the town of Changsha on the Siang River just south of Tungting Lake.

A few days after my return the operations officer told me that the P-40 I had flown back from India would be assigned to me. It was great to have my own airplane, especially a new one. Sgt. Ralph Key, an old hand from Texas, was assigned to be my crew chief, and he was a good one. Except for the failure of a new magneto on one mission, I never had an engine or airplane problem—a source of great comfort when flying a single-engine plane over enemy territory.

The first thing Sergeant Key did after completing the acceptance inspection was to install an electric starter. The P-40Ns had been delivered with hand-crank starters to save weight, but no one was willing to exchange the small amount of weight involved for the time and effort required to hand crank the inertia starters. The second thing, even more important in my mind, was to have the squadron "dentist," Sgt. Don Van Cleve, paint on the shark teeth and eyes, the distinctive markings made famous by the Flying Tigers. He also painted my name on the side of the cockpit and the squadron number 194 on the vertical fin, after painting out the serial number 323266. Purely by coincidence, the P-40 now on display in the National Air and Space Museum wears 75th Fighter Squadron markings, and the number on the tail is 194. Incidentally, Don Van Cleve is now the indefatigable president of the Fourteenth Air Force Association.

Sergeant Key asked if I had decided on a name for my P-40. I hadn't, but I was working on it. Naming one's plane was serious business. I'm sure we put at least as much thought into it as we put into naming a first child. Many pilots named their planes after their wives or girl-friends, but I had no special girl at that time. Dick Jones had named his Available, after the Al Capp character Available Jones. Jesse Gray named his Streak because of its speed, and Sack Tanner chose Bluebonnet Belle, after the Texas state flower. Earl Green had a list of some twenty names he was considering, but he never settled on one. I racked my brain, since this was one of the few decisions a lieutenant was permitted to make. Although I wasn't too happy with it, I had about decided on Pistol Packin' Mama, after a popular song, when Sack Folmar suggested "Lope's Hope"—an inspired name, I must say. It was just what I had been searching for: a short, distinctive name immediately associated with me. I told Sergeant Key, and he had it painted on the cowling, just above the exhaust stacks. It was an inde-scribable thrill for me to see my name on the airplane. I felt that I had really arrived as a fighter pilot.

A few months earlier, a Maj. Phil Loofbourrow had joined the squadron and begun leading flights. He was a graduate of West Point, the first I'd met. He was thin, quiet, and serious on the ground but an aggressive pilot and leader. Shortly after I returned to the squadron, Major Richardson finished his tour and left for the States, and Major Loofbourrow took over as squadron commander. He was a good one, always leading the toughest missions and sticking with a target until it was destroyed, regardless of the intensity of the ground fire. I flew as his wingman on a number of missions, and he was a smooth pilot, easy to fly with.

One morning we were standing alert when a flight of four P-40s came up from the south, dived toward the runway in tight formation, and peeled up for landing. They all made excellent tight patterns and good landings, which surprised us because they all had Chinese mark-ings. As they taxied to the flight line and parked, we went over to greet them. They were all American pilots from the Fifth Fighter Group of the Chinese American Composite Wing (CACW). This was a group of U.S.-trained and -equipped Chinese pilots led by Americans. Lt. Col. John Dunning, the deputy group commander, was leading this flight. He was a big, rugged man who was one of the most inspiring leaders I've ever met. His picture would make as good a definition of "leader" as any dictionary entry. More about him later. The group had just arrived in China and was to fly with us for a few weeks to learn the area and to gain combat experience.

As we stood around shooting the breeze with the newly arrived pilots, we heard a knocking sound from Colonel Dunning's fuselage. "Damn, I forgot Mac," the colonel exclaimed, and opened the baggage compartment door. Warrant Officer McCullough, looking somewhat the worse for wear, struggled out and then lifted out his tool box. He was the group maintenance officer and was there to maintain all four of his airplanes. It took plenty of courage to ride in the baggage compartment. It was completely dark, he couldn't communicate with the pilot, and he couldn't get out in the air or even on the ground without help. It was like riding in a coffin, and it could well become one if the P-40 had any problems. In addition to a liberal dose of guts, he was an outstanding maintenance officer and mechanic and one of the funniest people I've known.

I was pleased to be assigned as Colonel Dunning's wingman and flew with him on four or five missions. He was probably in his late twenties, more than six feet tall, and powerfully built. He was an experienced pilot who had been in the Army Air Corps well before the war, and he was spoiling for combat. On my first mission with him we went down to strafe a long line of trucks just south of the lake. I was following Colonel Dunning, and every time he fired I heard a strange noise in my headset. I first thought there was something wrong with his radio, causing it to screech when he pulled the trigger. After several passes I realized that every time he fired, he pressed the microphone button on the throttle and yelled, probably from sheer exuberance. Some months later, when he shot down his first airplane, he sang several verses of a ribald song ("Do Your Balls Hang Low?") over the radio.

The reason for our surprise at the fine patterns and landings made by Colonel Dunning's flight was the Chinese Air Force markings on the P-40s. We had been visited several times in the past by P-40s from the Chinese Air Force, as distinguished from the Chinese American Composite Wing. It was made up of older Chinese pilots who had been trained (after a fashion) before the war by a conglomeration of Russian, Italian, and other foreign instructors. It was like a circus when they landed at Hengyang. The older pilots always called the hostel when they learned that the Chinese Air Force was expected so that all the off-duty pilots could get down to the flight line to watch them land and enliven an otherwise dull day.

We were never disappointed by the show. Several nearly touched down with their wheels retracted and were driven off by red flares fired in front of them. There were always some ground loops, resulting in damaged wing tips at the least. I remember two taxi accidents, one wing to wing and one prop to tail. Once, two of them landed on opposite ends of the runway at the same time and somehow did not collide.

The main attraction, by far, was their traffic pattern, if you could dignify it with that term. There seemed to be no rhyme or reason to it, as if it had been choreographed by the Marx Brothers. Airplanes were flying at all altitudes and in all directions, with every combination of wheel and flap position imaginable. Sometimes they approached the runway in such close trail that two or three in a row would have to pull up and go around. Then there would be long periods when no planes landed. The problem was exacerbated when a second, not quite parallel runway was added at Hengyang. The runways came together at the south end of the field but then diverged 15 to 20 degrees toward the north. We used both runways for takeoff but landed only on the old runway. The Chinese, however, landed on both runways, and the fighters on final crisscrossed like the cars in those races on figure-eight tracks. We sometimes felt that it was dangerous to stand near the runway while this was going on, but we were too fascinated to leave.

Despite all of that miserable flying, there were never any serious accidents or injuries. I don't know which god they worshiped, but it was working overtime. On the other hand, the Chinese pilots in the CACW that we flew with later were very good, disciplined pilots who had been trained at Luke Field in Arizona.

The Japanese drive to the south continued, and our mission rate increased accordingly. We escorted B-25s on bombing missions near Tungting Lake, dive-bombed gunboats in the river south of the lake, and ran several fighter sweeps against Pailuchi airfield, where fighters had been reported on the ground—but they were gone when we arrived, undoubtedly warned by their radar, so we had to be content with shooting up the few buildings. We often scrambled to intercept incoming Japanese bombing raids, but they turned back well short of Hengyang and we never made contact.

On May 17, thirteen of our P-40s escorted B-25s to the Tungting Lake area. As usual, after the bombers headed back south, the fighters went down to strafe. They found a concentration of 5,000 Japanese cavalry and made a number of strafing passes, until Major Loofbourrow's electrical system was shot out and Maj. Bob Denny, from 23rd Group Headquarters, was shot down. He got over the first ridge of hills before he belly-landed in a rice paddy. Later, with the aid of the guerrillas, he made it back to our territory. The fighters arrived back at Hengyang low on fuel and trailed by about forty Oscars hoping to catch some sitting ducks in the landing pattern.

The eight P-40s on the ground scrambled and, oblivious to the five-to-one odds, dived into the enemy squirrel-cage formation with guns blazing. They shot down four Japanese and drove the rest off. None of the P-40s was lost, but all took some hits. Sack Tanner had to belly-land with the most completely riddled P-40 anyone had seen. The windshield, wings, and tail section were full of holes, but by some miracle Sack was not scratched. Bullets must have missed him by inches on both sides.

Late in May three flights of P-40s were on a strafing mission near Puchi Bridge. Two flights were down strafing, and the third was flying top cover. Ten or twelve Oscars dropped out of the clouds behind them and shot down Smedley, despite Anning's valiant attempt to drive the Oscar off Smedley's tail. The Oscar easily turned inside Anning, and Smedley was never seen again. Buckshot Smedley, by far the biggest pilot in the squadron, was also one of the most popular, and his loss was a blow. We kept hoping that he would be brought in by the guerrillas, but it was not to be. It would have been impossible to disguise the six-foot-one, 200-pound redhead as a Chinese peasant. I often wondered how someone so big was selected for fighters. We always enjoyed watching him land, because with the canopy open, he seemed to bulge out of the cockpit like a jolly red giant.

The Oscars made no attempt to attack the strafing P-40s, which by now were trying to climb up into the fight, but disappeared into the clouds. Lieutenant Balderson followed them into the clouds but couldn't locate them. He became lost in the process and, after some time, managed to locate and recognize the town of Changsha, which was still about ten miles south of the Japanese advance.

Baldy was almost out of fuel by this time and decided to make a belly landing on the deserted main street; the town had been evacuated by most of its population. He made a good landing but was a bit too fast and slammed into a concrete pillbox at the end of the street, smashing his head into the gunsight and suffering a depressed fracture.

The squadron was notified almost immediately by telephone that he was badly injured and in need of medical attention. Since there was no airfield at Changsha, our flight surgeon, Doc Laughlin, said that if we could get him up there he would bail out and try to save Balderson. Since all our airplanes were single seaters, that would have been impossible, but by good fortune a C-47 delivering fuel had landed about an hour earlier and was just about to take off. Major Loofbourrow explained the situation to the crew, and they volunteered to fly Doc up to Changsha.

Doc was fitted with a parachute and climbed in loaded down with his medical kit and other supplies. The cargo door was removed, and the Goony Bird took off escorted by eight P-40s. One of our pilots rode with Doc to brief him on the use of the chute and to show the C-47 pilot where to make the drop. According to our pilot, Doc showed no trepidation whatsoever and executed flawless form in bailing out immediately upon getting the signal. He landed right where he was supposed to and was rushed to the mission hospital, only to learn that Balderson had died just a few minutes earlier.

Doc got back to the squadron by jeep a few days later, with some intelligence officers who had been stationed in Changsha, and was the hero of the hour. We had always liked and respected this taciturn Texan, but his disregard for personal danger and his willingness to risk his life to save one of the pilots raised him still higher in our estimation.

He was awarded a medal for his bravery, and about three months later, possibly because of the bailout, he was promoted to major. Unfortunately, a fighter squadron was not authorized to have a major as flight surgeon, and Doc Laughlin was transferred to one of the squadrons in the 308th Bomb Group, the B-24 outfit. He was shattered by the transfer, because during his five months with the squadron he had been well indoctrinated in the standard fighter pilot drivel about the inability of bomber pilots to fly well and about the great danger of riding with them in their hulking creaky monsters. He regularly wrote to us about how much he disliked it at his new base at Chengkung, near Kunming. He said that even though the food was so much better because of the B-24s' frequent flights to India, he would forfeit the chow and the promotion to be back with the 75th.

About a month after he joined the 308th, one of the B-24s landed at our base and the pilot told us a strange tale about Doc. It seems that he had been flying in one of the B-24s to get his flying time in for the month. The B-24 was carrying fuel and other supplies across a strip of enemy territory to one of the eastern bases still in our hands. Doc, because of our frequent warnings about bomber pilots, wore his parachute and sat by the rear escape hatch whenever he flew. In the middle of the Japanese territory, one of the B-24's four engines coughed a little, probably because of a little water in the fuel. Doc Laughlin didn't hesitate a second; he opened the hatch and bailed out, only to watch the B-24 circle him in puzzlement as he descended in his chute. The B-24 went on with its mission, and Doc landed deep in Japanese territory, where he was picked up almost immediately by Chinese guerrillas. By the time the B-24 pilot told us the story, they had learned that Doc was okay and would be returning. When he got back four weeks later, he wrote and said that he enjoyed his stay with the guerrillas as much as anything he'd ever done.

The day after Baldy was killed, the weather was marginal in the morning and we weren't sure that we could get through to the target area. Major Loofbourrow told me to fly a weather reconnaissance up as far as Changsha. I took off and climbed up to about 8,000 feet on my way north through broken clouds. The clouds thinned out as I neared Changsha, and I could see that the squadron would have no trouble with the weather. As I started to turn for home, over Changsha I saw six or eight Oscars down low attacking the city. I searched the sky above for aircraft and, seeing none, started to dive on the Oscars, hoping to shoot down several before heading for home. At about 4,000 feet they still hadn't seen me, so I took one last look above; what had been empty sky was now full of Oscars. About twenty of them were diving on me, and some were already firing, although way out of range. I pushed the prop control to full rpm and rammed the throttle through the stop to the war emergency position and changed the direction of my dive slightly to make for some low clouds. My manifold pressure was up to about fifty-eight inches, and that scared me almost as much as the Oscars. The Allison engine did not thrive on such high power settings, and I was afraid it would come apart, so despite the Japanese on my tail I throttled back a little. I dived through the cloud layer and stayed on the deck for a few minutes, then zoomed back up through the clouds. The Oscars were just small dots in the distance heading north. They must have turned back when I reached the clouds, knowing they couldn't catch me, or perhaps Dave intervened.

I throttled back some more and continued on toward Hengyang, radioing that the weather was okay and that there were enemy fighters in the area. When I landed three flights of P-40s were being readied for a strafing mission in the Puchi Bridge area, where a lot of ground activity had been reported by Chinese intelligence. I briefed them on the weather and warned them about the Oscars that had come down on me out of the clouds.

When they reached the target area, they spotted a large truck convoy. Two flights went down to strafe and one stayed up as top cover, but at only 3,000 feet because of the clouds. Suddenly they were jumped by fifteen to twenty Oscars and Tojos. Earl Green, my roommate, was shot down in flames and bailed out, as did Moose Elker. Flash Segura shot one Oscar off Curt Scoville's tail and damaged another. Danny Daniels had dived away from the first attack, but looking back, he thought he saw two Japanese attacking a P-40, so he turned back to help. When he attacked he found that all three were Oscars. His airplane was clobbered, but he managed to break away and head for home.

At Hengyang we were told by the net that our P-40s were coming back followed by a gaggle of Zeros. I was in the alert flight, so we jumped into the cockpits to intercept the Japanese. As we were starting our engines, Danny's P-40 came into view from the north, trailing a heavy stream of smoke. He came right in without lowering his wheels—his hydraulic system was shot out—and bellied it in. The plane slid right past our flight, and Danny dived out onto the wing and rolled off as the P-40 slowed to a stop. We took off immediately and headed north, but the Japanese had turned back well short of Hengyang. We returned to land, anxious to see how Danny had fared.

We found that he was okay except for a cut on his head where it had banged the gunsight. He said that he was getting ready to bail out but decided he could make the field, not knowing that his hydraulics were gone. Later, the parachute rigger came into the alert shack to show us Danny's chute. He said, "It's lucky you didn't try to bail out, Lieutenant Daniels. Your chute was hit by an incendiary bullet that came up through the seat." Most of the silk was burned or charred, and had he jumped he would have been killed. Luck was with him.

Major Melloan of the 74th was not so lucky. Early in June he was hit by heavy ground fire while on a strafing mission, and his plane was severely damaged. He bailed out at low altitude and was killed. When his body was recovered, near his crashed plane, the search party found that his chute had been burned by an incendiary bullet and did not open properly.

In addition to the heavy daylight activity, with numerous combat missions and encounters with enemy fighters, the Japanese night bombers were active. Although we controlled the air in the daylight, we could do almost nothing to stop the night bombing. We did have the satisfaction of knowing that our B-25s and B-24s were doing the same thing to the Japanese at night. We were bombed fourteen times in May, usually by individual bombers that attacked at five- or ten-minute intervals over periods of several hours. Most of the damage was to the runway, which was easily repaired, but occasionally one of our irreplaceable aircraft was damaged or destroyed. There were also several false alarms when the bombers turned back before reaching Hengyang. Since we usually got the jing bao warning about thirty minutes before the first attack and the all-clear didn't sound until thirty minutes after the last attack, we weren't getting much sleep. The pilots and the ground crews, who often worked through the night anyway, were becoming exhausted. We went to bed as soon as we finished dinner in order to get as much sleep as possible before the first jing bao warning. For the same reason, we stayed in bed after the first warning and got up only when the three-ball alert sounded, then ran like hell to the slit trenches to get there before the bombs started falling.

We all threatened to stay in the sack instead of going to the slit trenches because the hostel had never been hit. The runway and the airplanes were the main targets. The incessant clangor of the three-ball gong usually persuaded us to head for the trenches, but one night Moose, Danny, and Bill Carlton decided to play the odds and stay in their beds. As luck would have it that night, for the first time, the hostel took a direct hit. A new snack bar had just been opened in the back of the hostel not far from their room. It was completely destroyed, and the windows were blown out in their room. They spent the rest of the raid under the beds, but fortunately they were not injured. From then on, they were leaders in the race for the slit trenches.

The bombing of the hostel coincided with the completion of the new hostel, several miles from the old one and the same distance farther from the town of Hengyang. It was a typical Chinese hostel, with long one-story buildings divided into about ten rooms with a washroom on one end. They were just washrooms; the latrines were outside. Curiously, all the buildings were painted bright yellow and stood out like beacons in the moonlight. Despite that, the new hostels were never bombed, at least by the Japanese. Perhaps they didn't realize that the buildings were part of the base.

Without radar it was next to impossible for our fighters to locate the bombers at night, although we tried on many occasions. The fighters just couldn't get close enough to the bombers to see them in the dark, even though we could sometimes make them out from the ground. Dick Jones and I came up with what we thought was a brilliant solution to this problem one evening while we were chatting with the base weathermen. They told us that a ceiling light and generator had just been delivered. A ceiling light is a fixed searchlight that projects a vertical beam that reflects against the cloud layer. Using triangulation instruments, the meteorologists can determine the height of the reflection above the ground and thus the ceiling. We decided to borrow the light and attach it to a swiveling gun mount and use it as a searchlight to mark the bombers for the fighters.

The generator was in a small brick building near the runway, so we had a gun pit dug next to it and set up the light. It seemed to work reasonably well, so Major Loofbourrow decided to send up a P-40 the next time we had a jing bao. The very next night, to our delight, the jing bao bell was sounded. Dick and I and the P-40 pilot headed for the airfield, and while the P-40 was preparing to take off we started the generator and tested the light. The plan was for the ground radio to tell our pilot when the Japanese Lily was starting its run so he could position the P-40 in the general area; then, as soon as Dick and I spotted the bomber, we would illuminate it with the searchlight and hold it in the beam for as long as possible, hoping that the P-40 could get close enough to shoot it down.

All went as planned up to a point. The Lily started its bombing run in a shallow dive, the P-40 sounded as though it was fairly close, and we spotted the Lily against the lighter sky. We turned on the light and got the bomber in the beam. That was the point up to which all went as planned. We hadn't planned on the Lily having a world-class gunner in the nose. As soon as the light beam hit the Lily, he hit the trigger and fired a long burst of machine gun fire that raked through our gun pit and against the wall of the brick building, showering us with brick fragments. We turned off the light with the speed of light and huddled in the bottom of the pit until he was almost out of earshot. His bombs had hit near the runway and slightly damaged a P-40. About an hour later the all-clear sounded and the P-40 landed. The pilot had gotten a brief glimpse of the Lily but lost it when it pulled up.

The next morning Dick and I went back to the searchlight. When we saw how close the bullets had come to us, we dismantled the entire rig and gave the light back to the weathermen. We approved of strafing only if we were the strafers, not the strafees.

A few nights later the squadron took another approach to shooting down the night bombers, but it fell apart even sooner, and with much more disastrous results, than the short-lived searchlight plan. The operations officer thought that the P-40s might spot the bombers if three of them were sent up to patrol at different levels and if ground lookouts radioed the Lilys' positions when they were spotted.

Sack Aylesworth, Joe Brown, and Flash Segura were to fly the P-40s and to take off in that order. (Aylesworth roomed with Tanner and Folmar, and for some reason all were called Sack, even though their names were Leonard, Vernon, and Jim respectively.) Since there were no runway lights, a jeep was parked at the far end of the runway with its lights on and the pilots took off toward it. The three pilots were briefed to take off at one-minute intervals to allow plenty of spacing.

Up at the slit trenches near the hostel the rest of the pilots were waiting for the fighters to scramble following the jing bao signal, hoping to have front-row seats for the shooting down of a few Lilys. We were baffled when we heard the P-40s start up and what sounded like three takeoff runs but never heard them in flight. The all-clear sounded a few minutes later, since the Japanese had turned back. We assumed that the mission had been cancelled, so we went to bed sorry to have missed the anticipated show.

The next morning we learned that even though they had turned back, the Japanese had scored a major victory. Aylesworth had taxied onto the runway, and in his methodical way (he was a tall, quiet farmer from upstate New York), he slowly advanced the throttle and started his takeoff roll. Joe Brown, a small, quick New York City slicker, was so eager to take off that he didn't wait a minute but blasted out onto the runway and rammed open the throttle. He had gone about 1,000 feet when he caught up with and cut the tail off Aylesworth's P-40. Aylesworth's plane veered off the runway to the left, hit a rock pile, and ripped the landing gear off before skidding to a stop. Joe Brown's landing gear collapsed, and he slid to a stop on his belly in the center of the runway. Here he made his smartest move of the night when he got out of the cockpit and ran as far away from the runway as he could. Segura did everything right. He waited the prescribed interval, taxied onto the runway, and started his takeoff. Just before lifting off, his gear straddled the fuselage of Brown's airplane. The prop ripped off and landed several hundred yards away, the gear collapsed, and the plane skidded to a stop on its belly some distance beyond Joe

Brown's plane. Flash said that the engine rpm, without the prop, reached about 50,000 before he could shut it off.

When we got to the flight line the next morning, the runway was covered with wrecked P-40s and assorted P-40 parts, much more damage than the Japanese usually inflicted with their bombs. It looked as though the Chinese Air Force had made a night visit. Major Loofbourow didn't seem particularly upset by the incident, taking into account the difficulty of night takeoffs with no lighting. I'm sure that much of his attitude was due to his relief that no one had been killed or even injured.

A few days later we got the welcome news that both Moose and Earl Green were alive and in the hands of the guerrillas. So many of our pilots survived after being shot down that we didn't give up hope for a long time, unless we learned that they had been killed.

The Chinese had developed a most efficient system for rescuing downed pilots. If one was able to get to a peasant, the peasant would get him to one of the organized guerrillas, many of them former troops of the local warlords, or to another peasant who knew how to contact the guerrillas. If the pilot was down close to the Japanese, the guerrillas were skilled at hiding him until the search was over. Then they dressed him as a Chinese peasant and took him back to friendly territory. They were risking their lives by helping us, because the Japanese would have executed them out of hand if they were caught, but that did not deter them. It was reassuring to know that we had a good chance of making it home if we had to bail out or belly in.

Bill Carlton and Flash Segura were especially relieved to hear that Moose was okay. Several weeks before he was shot down, Moose had received a Dear John letter from his girlfriend stating that she had married a Marine warrant officer named Godwin. As was the custom, Moose had circulated the letter among the officers. He didn't seem particularly upset; in fact, he said that he was going to name his aircraft the Mrs. G. Bill and Flash, however, weren't going to take this insult to their buddy lying down. They wrote a long, mournful letter to Mrs. G., telling her that Moose was so upset by her letter that after brooding for several days, he had volunteered for a suicide mission on which he had been shot down and was now missing in action. About the time she would have received the letter, Moose was actually shot down and was missing. If the word that Moose was okay hadn't come in when it did, a missing-in-action telegram would have been sent to Moose's parents, and Mrs. G. might have felt much needless guilt.

Several times late in May, because of the increasing number of bombing raids, we flew the P-40s down to Lingling for the night to ensure that they wouldn't be damaged. As the Japanese moved south, we lost more and more of our warning net and were afraid that the fighters might get caught on the ground by a raid just at dusk. We were always glad to go to Lingling, just thirty minutes south, because the food was good in the hostel there, including the chef's specialty, chocolate pie. Chocolate pie is a treat anytime, but you can't imagine how good it was to us, who hadn't tasted a decent dessert in many months. We never learned where the chef got the ingredients.

It was beginning to look as though we would have to leave Hengyang permanently if the Japanese couldn't be stopped. It was frustrating to destroy so many troops and transport from the air and still not be able to stop them. We had little respect for the Chinese troops, especially their leaders. Quite often they drifted away before the Japanese advance without even the pretense of fighting. Chiang Kai Shek was apparently husbanding his strength, both in troops and equipment, to use against the communist forces in north China when the current unpleasantness with the Japanese had ended.

I've often wondered why the guerrillas were so effective while the regular troops were so ineffective, since the Chinese were, in general, hardworking and intelligent and had a deep hatred of the Japanese. The difference was, I believe, the leadership. The regular troops were, in most cases, poorly led, poorly trained, and poorly fed. The guerrillas, on the other hand, were led by some of their own, lived off the land, and knew their area intimately. They did not engage in much actual combat against the Japanese but hurt them as much as possible by helping downed airmen to escape and by acts of sabotage.

Although the constant strafing missions may sound repetitious and even boring, I can assure you they were not. Each mission was a little different, and there was always the threat of enemy aircraft to keep a pilot alert. As Wing Commander Geoffrey Page, a World War II RAF ace and a good friend, said, "How could a young man be bored when he has a fast airplane to fly, a uniform to wear, and something to shoot at?"

12

FIRE AND
FALL BACK

June continued just as May had ended—with missions and more missions. On June 2 I flew three dive-bombing and strafing missions of two and a half hours each against Japanese troops and equipment in the town of Tsungyang. There seemed to be more and better targets on each successive mission, and we were causing extensive damage.

The next afternoon there was a bizarre incident reminiscent of the Chinese Air Force visits. The 76th Fighter Squadron, equipped with P-51s, had a detachment operating in our area from Lingling, about thirty minutes south of us. They had been having trouble with the wing bomb racks on their Mustangs. Often they could not get one of the bombs to release in the air, only to have it drop off on landing when the wheels contacted the runway. Without our knowledge, their CO had told them that if they couldn't shake off the bomb in flight, they should make a low approach to Hengyang and bounce their wheels on the runway in the hope of causing the bomb to fall off. We were baffled when a Mustang dropped out of a homebound flight over Hengyang and began letting down. He approached the runway from the north, opposite to our usual landing direction, let down to within a few feet of the runway, and then pushed the stick forward to bounce his wheels. His actions were letter perfect, except for one minor detail. He had forgotten to lower his wheels. The prop ripped off and went flying off to the side of the runway, and the engine sounded as though it were coming apart. The Mustang came skidding down the middle of the runway, following the bouncing 500-pound demolition bomb that had been dislodged by the impact. As we saw the bomb approaching, we all broke for the ditch in back of the alert shack. One of our smaller sergeants couldn't get through the windows or doors of the alert shack because of the press of bodies with the same idea. He solved the problem by running through the wall. The interlaced bamboo walls were extremely tough, and I'm sure they would have stopped a jeep. Such is the propulsive power of panic that he didn't even remember going through. The bomb did not explode because the arming propeller on the nose bent on impact with the ground and could not spin off and arm the fuse. It was some time before the 76th pilot lived down that colossal goof, performed in front of an entire rival squadron.

In another week of continued multiple missions, we lost several more pilots, one of whom, Lieutenant Noonan, spun in on final approach. He tried too tight a turn at low airspeed and snapped into a spin too low to recover. Also, our planes were in need of more maintenance than could be accomplished in the short intervals between missions. The ground crews worked at night to keep up but were handicapped by the poor lighting and by their own weariness, since they worked all day as well.

Our group commander, Tex Hill, after conferring with Major Loofbourrow, wisely decided to send the 75th back to Kweilin for a short rest and to move the 74th up to Hengyang. On June 7, we flew all the flyable P-40s down to Kweilin except one that was left for Major Loofbourrow, who remained at Hengyang to brief the 74th CO and to make sure all our squadron personnel and equipment had proper transport to Kweilin.

Segura and about fifteen other pilots were flown to Kweilin in a C-47. We landed in the P-40s about an hour before the C-47 arrived and were telling all the 74th pilots who were leaving for Hengyang the next morning how rough it was up there. On the flight down in the Goony Bird (C-47) Flash found several large first-aid kits. He broke into them and used all the bandages, tape, mercurochrome, and splints to make our 75th pilots into reasonable facsimiles of the soldiers in the Revolutionary War painting "The Spirit of '76." Well-bandaged head wounds, liberally sprinkled with mercurochrome, were his specialty, but he was no slouch on splinted arms and legs. The 74th pilots went out with us to meet the C-47 when it taxied in, and they were convinced that things were indeed rough at Hengyang when Flash and his moaning band of walking wounded got off the plane. In fact, some of us who knew better were almost convinced. Things could never get too serious with Flash around.

That evening we all gathered around the 74th's shortwave radio to listen to the reports of the Allied invasion of Normandy. We stayed up most of the night until the reports indicated that beachheads had been established. It was the beginning of the end of the war in Europe now that the Allies had a foothold in France. On the day before June 6, D-Day, the Allied forces in Italy had retaken Rome from the Germans. In Burma, General Stilwell's force was just about to capture Myitkyina, and in the Pacific our forces were advancing on Biak. The Russians had stopped the Germans on the Rumanian front. Only in China, where we had no ground troops other than the Chinese, were the Allies in trouble. The Fourteenth Air Force's gallant but futile attempt to stop the Japanese advance proved the statement made by Air Marshal John Slessor, RAF: Air power "cannot by itself defeat a highly organized and disciplined army, even when that army is virtually without air support of its own."

The next morning the 74th took off for Hengyang, and we assumed their base defense duties. We didn't do any flying, and the ground crews used the time to good advantage to get the aircraft back into shape. A few replacement aircraft were flown in from Kunming, and they too were readied for combat. I can't say too much about the skill and devotion of the ground crews. There were no hangars or shelters, so all the work had to be done in the open. Despite the heavy workloads and the primitive working conditions, we had virtually no in-flight maintenance problems with the aircraft or the armament. Spare parts were in short supply, but the crews were passed masters of the art of cannibalizing, using parts from damaged or out-of-commission planes to keep others flying. I don't recall ever having one of my machine guns jam in a P-40, and I had engine problems only twice, both due to magneto failures.

At Kweilin we were based on the fighter strip, not the main runway, at Yang Tong Airfield. The 74th usually operated from this strip. It was so narrow that the wings overlapped when two P-40s took off in formation. When our aircraft were parked along the runway during the daylight hours, their noses extended over the runway edge.

A few days after we arrived I was in the alert shack reading when I heard a flight of P-51s from the 26th Squadron, which had flown in the night before, start up and taxi into takeoff position. After completing their runups and mag checks, they started their takeoff runs. A few seconds later one chopped the throttle and aborted the takeoff. I assumed he had some kind of an engine problem, but someone outside yelled, "Hey, Lope, that Mustang just ran into your airplane." I rushed outside with everyone else to see the damage to my P-40. It looked undamaged from a distance, but it had a P-51 wing tip embedded in the front of the fuselage right in the middle of the shark mouth. It looked as though the P-40 had spitefully bitten off the wing tip of its slicker, faster compatriot. A closer examination revealed that the P-51 wing tip had hit the P-40 prop and the front of the lower engine cowling, ripping off the tip and leaving it caught in the teeth area.

Surprisingly, the only damage turned out to be to the lower section of the cowling, known as the bathtub to the mechanics, that covered the oil and coolant radiators and the bottom of the engine. It also served the all-important role of tooth bearer. My crew chief, Sergeant Key, removed the damaged bathtub and replaced it with a spare that had not yet had the teeth painted on. He carefully inspected the P-40 for other damage but could find none. The prop had rotated when it was hit, so the engine was not overstressed. I took it up for a short test hop and everything checked out. My morale suffered for a while, since our painter did not have his equipment with him. I became a toothless tiger and had to gum the Japanese for several weeks.

The 74th, under Maj. Barry Melloan, took over where the 75th had left off, flying several missions a day against the advancing Japanese. Although the 74th inflicted heavy losses, destroying hundreds of boats, trucks, and horses, and thousands of troops, the Japanese continued to advance.

The enemy ground fire was intense. On June 15 Major Melloan's plane was hit; unlike Danny Daniels in May, Melloan was forced to bail out, only to be killed because his parachute had been burned by an incendiary round. The same day, Major Cruickshank, the second in command of the 74th, was hit and bailed out successfully, landing in a tree. He was seen to get out of his chute and start walking south. He made it back to Hengyang, with the help of the guerrillas, and took command of the 74th.

The next night Hengyang was heavily bombed with almost no warning because of the loss of much of the warning net. The morning of June 17, Tex Hill, the group commander on the scene, decided it was imprudent to continue to operate from Hengyang. He ordered the 74th back to Kweilin and moved the 75th up to Lingling. I flew my toothless airplane, along with the rest of the squadron, on a river sweep in the Chuchow area, just south of Changsha, which was now surrounded by Japanese troops. We landed at Lingling after that mission, and I flew two more strafing and bombing missions that day against the troops surrounding Changsha. Despite our support over the next few days, the Chinese troops surrendered and the Japanese took over Changsha. There seemed to be as many Chinese troops as Japanese, but the Japanese were better equipped and better led. Most of the Chinese troops were uneducated peasants with little idea of why they were fighting. To the north of Changsha the Chinese troops had melted away before the Japanese. A few hundred Japanese often took positions defended by thousands of Chinese. In Changsha itself the Chinese Fourth Army gave up the city without a fight. Most of the Chinese leaders seemed interested only in saving themselves and their belongings. Chiang Kai Shek didn't trust his generals in Hunan Province, through which the Japanese were advancing, and they in turn distrusted him, so no one was willing to commit the forces necessary to stop or at least slow down the Japanese.

There was some good war news from China despite our losses. The B-29s that I had seen in Karachi had bombed the Japanese mainland from their bases at Chengtu. It was the first time the Japanese mainland had been bombed since Jimmy Doolittle's Tokyo raid on April 18, 1942.

The evacuation of Hengyang was so sudden that the runway and buildings were left intact. On the morning of June 22, when I reported to the flight line, I noticed that the crew chiefs were removing the belly tanks from twelve of our P-40s, mine included, and replacing them with 1,000-pound demolition bombs. Major Loofbourrow told us we were to bomb the runways and buildings at Hengyang. I was gratified to learn that my target was our old hostel building. Since there would be no ground fire to worry about, we were to make our runs in turn so that a second pilot could be assigned to a target if the first one missed.

On the takeoff I made a stupid mistake. I forgot that I was carrying a bomb instead of a belly tank, and as soon as I had my wheels up, following normal procedure, I switched my fuel selector to the belly-tank position. About a second later the engine sputtered and quit, and I nearly sprained my wrist switching back to the main tank. The engine started up instantly, but I was still embarrassed by my goof. I felt much better about it later when the pilots on the ground said that as far as they could tell, every pilot on the mission had made the same error. We had all flown with belly tanks for so long that the switchover was a conditioned reflex.

Over Hengyang we started our bombing runs. The first flights laid their bombs along the runway, the delayed-action fuses allowing the bombs to penetrate deeply before exploding and thus make much larger craters. When my turn came I rolled into my dive, aiming at the center of the hostel some thirty feet from my old room. I strafed the building on the way down and released the bomb as I pulled my gunsight pipper through the aiming point. I pulled up in a wingover so I could see the target. I thought at first that the bomb was a dud, but then the delayed-action fuse exploded the bomb and our hostel was blown to bits. As best I could tell I had hit it dead center. I had finally marked "paid" to my account with the rats. I'm sure there were few survivors, unless rats desert sinking hostels as well as ships and had moved out when we did.

The next day the weather was marginal, with heavy broken clouds to the north, but it looked as if we could get through, so eight of us took off to strafe targets of opportunity in the area around Changsha. We hoped that the Japanese would not be expecting us because of the weather and might be caught in the open. I was the element leader in the second flight, and when the flight leader turned back because of engine trouble, I became the flight leader. We made it to the target area through holes in the clouds and found that the Japanese were indeed moving openly. We were able to strafe and frag-bomb several large cavalry groups. In addition to killing many of the troops and horses, we caused many of the horses to panic and run off in all directions. The Japanese used cavalry and pack horses extensively in China because of the roadless, rough terrain.

Our flights had been briefed to separate on the way home to inspect two different areas for signs of troop activity. My area had no visible activity, so I turned for home only to find a solid wall of clouds between us and Lingling. We climbed to about 15,000 feet and searched to the east and the west without finding a hole. Since we had no flight instruments, I decided to try to get through by flying down the river right on the deck under the clouds, which were at about 100 feet. I put the flight in trail and slowed down so that we could negotiate the turns in the river. I unfastened my parachute harness and opened the canopy to make it easier to get out if I hit the water. We were about halfway back and feeling more confident about making it when a P-40 appeared heading straight toward us, also on the deck. He saw us at the same time and zoomed up into the clouds, where he must have done a combination wingover and hammerhead stall, because he came out of the clouds behind us flying in our direction. The clouds got a bit lower ahead, forcing us almost to the surface of the river, and I wondered if we could get through. Since we had no alternative, we continued on.

The ceiling lifted gradually as we neared Lingling, and we were able to climb up and fly a normal formation. I saw that it was a 74th Squadron P-40 that had joined us.

After we landed I found that the pilot was my good friend Dick Mullineaux. He said that he had become separated from his flight and had tried to make it down the river but had been forced back when the clouds got too low. He decided to fly north of the clouds and try to make it over them. When he saw us he was so glad not to be alone that he would have followed us underwater if necessary.

June 26 was as action-filled as anyone could hope for. In the morning I took part in an eight-plane offensive reconnaissance mission in the area just south of Changsha, where a large movement had been reported by Chinese intelligence. The weather was marginal, which gave us a better chance of finding the troops on the move. They usually stayed under cover during daylight in good weather. Sure enough, we surprised a force of more than 1,000 infantry soldiers leading hundreds of supply-laden horses. They were in the worst possible location, for them, in a deep railroad cut several miles long, with steep, almost vertical sides. We were carrying the ideal bomb load for this situation: parafrags. The first flight dropped its frags at the front end of the column, and the second flight dropped theirs in the rear, temporarily stopping either forward or rearward movement. The clouds were so low that we didn't need top cover, so all eight planes strafed at once. The troops were so tightly packed in the narrow cut that it was difficult to miss them. We flew up and down that cut, strafing until the two flights had expended all of their 10,000 rounds of ammunition, leaving a mountain of dead and dying men and horses. The flight leader had radioed that we had located the troops, and two flights from another squadron were diverted to the railroad cut. They arrived soon afterward and continued the slaughter. Probably because of our deep enmity toward the Japanese, no one ever expressed anything but satisfaction on a mission like this, except that many pilots regretted having to kill the horses. Killing the men bothered no one.

Later in the day P-40s from the 74th, 75th, and 118th (the 118th Tactical Reconnaissance Squadron had joined the 23rd Group in May) and P-51s from the 76th flew a joint strafing mission against targets in the area just south of Hengyang. The weather had improved, and the P-51s were flying top cover. Toward the end of the mission, when the P-51s came down to dive-bomb, a 74th P-40 pulled up from a strafing run and cut the tail off a P-51. Both planes crashed and both pilots were killed.

It was a bad month for 74th Squadron COs. A few minutes after the midair collision, Major Cruickshank, who had just walked back from being shot down on June 15, was shot down again, both times by ground fire, and had to bail out. He landed hard and injured his back and neck. Despite the pain, he made for the hills but was accosted by two men in peasant clothes who tried to lead him in the opposite direction. He resisted, and when they used force, he killed one with the machete from his parachute escape kit. He wisely didn't use his .45 because of the noise. The other man ran away, and Major Cruickshank found a good hiding place after seeing Japanese soldiers searching for him. He finally made contact with some wounded Chinese soldiers who helped him to the south. After several days he found a truck carrying evacuees to the south and caught a ride to Lingling, arriving on June 30. The doctors found that he had suffered some kidney damage in the bailout, and he was sent back to the States. Usually pilots were sent home after being shot down behind the lines once, but the action was so fierce during this period that the rule was ignored.

Late that afternoon, we had a three-ball alert without benefit of a warning from the net. The Chinese were evacuating the area in the enemy's path, and the net was falling apart. One of our fighters on the way home had spotted a large flight of Oscars heading for Lingling and had radioed the warning. Our P-40s and the 76th's P-51s scrambled and clawed for as much altitude as possible. There was a thin cloud layer at about 10,000 feet, and when we reached that height Tex Hill told all Charleston planes to stay below the clouds and all Pontiacs to go above. (We had recently been given new squadron call signs: Detroit for the 74th, Charleston for the 75th, and Pontiac for the 76th.) I was flying as element leader in Red flight, led by Bill Carlton. As the P-51s pulled up into the clouds I saw about twenty Oscars come down through the clouds several miles away on our right rear quarter. I called, "Charleston Red leader, Zeros at five o'clock level." Bill said, "Where?" and I repeated my call. He said, "I don't see them. You take the lead."

I immediately broke hard right, jettisoned my belly tank, and headed for the Oscars. As we approached, the Oscars broke up and went in all directions. I lined up one, but just as I got within range he flipped into a tight turn, and I couldn't get enough lead to fire. I rolled over and saw an Oscar below me. I dived after him, and he went into a tight right turn. I wouldn't have been able to hit him, but he suddenly reversed his turn, and I nailed him before he could turn in the opposite direction. I must have killed the pilot, because he went into a gradually steepening dive without any evasive action. Just to be sure, I followed him in the dive and fired a long burst into the fuselage. I pulled out, and he went straight into the ground close to the field. As I climbed back up, keeping my eyes open for Japanese, I saw that the P-51s had come down and the Oscars had left. After circling for about fifteen minutes to make sure they were gone, we were cleared to land.

It was satisfying to shoot down an enemy fighter, especially right over my home field. Air-to-air combat is what every fighter pilot is trained for, and even though ground attack is dangerous and important tactically, it doesn't come close to air combat for exhilaration and satisfaction. The one-to-one, dueling aspect of air fighting is, to use a current expression, where it's at.

On landing I found that Lt. Army Armstrong had not returned and that a P-40 had been seen to dive straight into the ground, probably shot down by an Oscar. Although a search was conducted, he was never found. A group of our ground crew gave me hell because they had been standing by a slit trench near the field cheering as I shot down the Oscar. When I fired the extra long burst at the diving plane, they all had to leap back into the trench, as my bullets were spattering into the ground dangerously close. One said, "If I have to be shot, I prefer to be shot by the enemy."

That evening we learned that the Japanese had taken the base at Hengyang and were about to surround the city. Since we could no longer count on any warning, Tex Hill decided to move all the aircraft out of Lingling and to use it only as a staging base for missions. The 75th flew back to Kweilin, where we were to be based for several months. The 74th was back on the fighter strip, so we were based at the south end of the main base at Yang Tong. The Eleventh Bomb Squadron, the B-25 outfit that we had often escorted, was on the north end.

Yang Tong took some getting used to. We were surprised when the flight leader signaled us into left-echelon formation as we neared the field and flabbergasted as we stayed in that formation and then peeled off to the right for landing. None of us had ever landed from a fighter break in anything but a left-hand pattern. It felt extremely awkward and unnatural. Once we were in the pattern, however, the reason became clear. The beautiful mountains, among which the base was laid out, were too close to the left side of the runway to allow a normal pattern. After a few landings it felt as natural as a left-hand pattern.

On June 29 we lost one of our most popular pilots, Lieutenant Vurgaropoulos, or Vurgie, as he was called. His Greek heritage had made him a bit of a philosopher, and he liked nothing better than to sit around and discuss any subject at length. His favorite subject was air power, and he was a strong disciple of Alexander De Seversky's writings. Most of us were in general agreement but usually argued against De Seversky in order to watch Vurgie fume and fuss. He was short, about five feet four, with heavy eyebrows and a fierce mustache. Despite his lack of height, he walked kind of hunched over, which made him look even shorter. He also flew with the seat in the lowest possible position and was almost invisible in the cockpit. The first time I flew as his wingman, I kept pulling up above him so that I could see down into his cockpit and reassure myself that the airplane was occupied.

His habit of sitting so low, which he said made him less vulnerable to enemy fire, was probably a contributing factor in his death, along with target fixation. He was up in the north strafing Japanese cavalry when he flew right into the target on a strafing run. When a pilot has a good target he is often tempted to keep shooting just a little longer, sometimes until it is too late to pull out. I think that, plus the difficulty of judging height from such a low position in the cockpit, was the cause of his death.

We lost two more P-40s that day, but fortunately one of the pilots, the indestructible Flash Segura, made it back safely. He was leading a strafing mission in the Hengyang area. One of the pilots in his flight dived down to drop his parafrags on some river boats. Just after he released his bombs, his right wing was blown off and he crashed into the river and exploded. One of the bomb parachutes must have opened prematurely and caught on the bomb rack, arming the bomb and causing it to slam against the wing, where it exploded.

Segura was leading the planes back to Kweilin after the mission. Since he was out of the target area and quite tired from two tough missions that day, he was relaxing in the seat. Suddenly the engine exploded. Smoke and flames were pouring out the exhaust stack area. Flash unbuckled his seat belt and dived over the side of the cockpit, since the fuel tanks could explode at any moment. As he dived out, he was hit on the calf by the horizontal stabilizer, flipping him end over end. He managed to stop tumbling and pull his ripcord, but he had loosened his leg straps, allowing the chest buckle to come up and hit him in the jaw, knocking him out. He recovered almost immediately and was relieved to find himself floating to earth under a beautiful white canopy. He landed safely, gathered up his parachute, and limped along until he found some Chinese soldiers who had been attracted by the explosion of his P-40 hitting the ground. They led him to the trusty rail line, where they flagged down a train on which he returned to Kweilin, bruised and tired but otherwise all right. We had not been too worried, since he had been seen to bail out safely by the others in his flight.

As far as he knew Flash had not been hit by enemy fire. Another of our airplanes had exploded in much the same manner a few days earlier. Fortunately, it too was over our lines, and the pilot, Lt. Joe Focht, had bailed out successfully. The squadron engineering officer had been trying to get more hours out of our engines between overhauls. The extra vibration or gasket deterioration had caused the intake manifold to rupture, spraying the fuel-air mixture on the hot engine. Both of the P-40s had about the same number of engine hours when they exploded. After one more such incident, a week or so later, we went back to the old, shorter engine overhaul period.

The next day I flew on a long offensive sweep deep into Japanese territory. It was led by Tex Hill, and I'll never forget the informality of the briefing for the mission. We had about sixteen planes on this mission, from both the 75th and 74th. Tex stood up in front of the assembled pilots and said, "Y'all follow me." It was quite a contrast to the formal briefings for the 1,000-plane raids by the Eighth Air Force in Europe that we had seen in the movies. It revealed as much as anything the difference in the magnitude of effort in the two theaters. We found large troop and supply concentrations and destroyed many of both, but we ran into strong headwinds on the return trip and after four hours and twenty minutes had to land at Lingling to refuel before returning to Kweilin. Thus ended our successes in the air and on the ground: always frustrating because of our loss of territory.

13

A HOT AND HEAVY JULY

July 1944 was a hot month, in terms of both weather and action. All our efforts were dedicated to stopping the advance of the Japanese troops. The 75th flew hundreds of sorties (a sortie is one plane on one mission—eight planes on one combat mission equals eight sorties); I flew twenty-seven missions, all but one were offensive missions.

Maj. Don Quigley took over the squadron, as Major Loofbourrow was promoted to deputy group commander. Although we hated to see Major Loofbourrow leave, the squadron and I couldn't have been more pleased with the choice of Major Quigley as his replacement. Quig had been with the squadron for more than a month and was highly regarded as a pilot and as a person. He had been with the 80th Fighter Group in India and Burma before coming to China and had a great deal of experience in the P-40. He was about five foot eight, dapper, with a trim mustache, and looked the way we thought a fighter pilot should, something like David Niven in *The Dawn Patrol*.

I had flown as element leader in his flight many times, and he led the squadron as he did his flight, by example. He managed the difficult task of being one of the pilots without any loss of dignity or failure to realize who was in command.

On one of the first missions in that hot July I fully realized what a devastating weapon the parafrag was. We caught a group of Japanese boats, resembling landing craft, crossing a corner of Tungting Lake. There were about twenty boats, all loaded with troops. We had three flights of four, and my flight stayed up as top cover while the others attacked the boats with parafrags and guns. I was watching the low flight while the three others in my flight watched for enemy planes. When the lead plane's parafrags exploded in the middle of the boats, the lake within a radius of about 100 yards turned to froth instantaneously. It looked just the same for the others in the low flights. Each plane carried six parafrags, and the havoc wrought by the shrapnel fragments of bomb casing hurtling outward at several thousand feet per second was enormous, both to the men and the boats. Several boats were sinking, and all appeared dead in the water after the first pass.

The low flights strafed until almost out of ammunition, then we exchanged roles, and my flight came down to bomb and strafe. The devastation looked much worse from up close. About half the boats were sinking or had sunk. The water was full of bodies and swimming soldiers, and the boats and the water were tinged red from the blood. When my flight finished with them there were few, if any, soldiers left alive. Despite the carnage, my only feeling was satisfaction at having eliminated so many of the enemy, whom we regarded as little more than animals because of the atrocities they had committed so callously in China, Burma, and Bataan.

Another frightening aspect of parafrags, if one is needed, is the interval of horror between the opening of the parachute and the moment when they hit and explode. The helpless terror the troops feel watching the inexorable approach of death must transfix them with fear. Of course, the sight of the shark-mouthed P-40s diving at them with guns blazing probably didn't do much for the reenlistment rate either. Although there is nothing sporting about war, I always felt that machine guns aimed at specific targets were a bit more sporting than frag bombs and other "To whom it may concern" shrapnel devices.

July 4, 1944, was the second anniversary of the formation of the 23rd Fighter Group from the disbanded AVG. Although the American Volunteer Group was in combat for only six months, its record was amazing: 299 Japanese aircraft destroyed in the air, with the loss of only 8 P-40s in combat. Even more important than the numbers was the defeat of the up-to-then invincible Japanese. We were proud to wear the mantle of the Flying Tigers and continued to use the tactics developed by General Chennault for them with great success. We used the strengths of the P-40, diving speed and rugged construction, to overcome the maneuverability of the Zeros and Oscars. We always kept up our speed and never tried to out-turn a Japanese fighter. If one evaded us with a tight turn we just kept diving, then climbed up and attacked again.

On the anniversary we were scheduled to escort twelve B-25s to the Liling area, where they were to bomb a supply dump of fuel and ammunition. Our twelve pilots sat in their cockpits watching the B-25s take off toward us from their area on the north end of the runway. As they climbed to the south to form up, we started our engines and took off toward the north.

My engine had checked out fine before takeoff and ran normally until we were in formation above the bombers and were turning on course. Suddenly it began to backfire and vibrate as though the pistons were changing cylinders. I throttled back instantly, thinking of the P-40 engines that had exploded in flight in the last few weeks, and signaled my flight that I was returning to land. The engine sounded and felt almost as rough at low power, and I fervently hoped that it wouldn't blow up before I could land.

Despite my concern, another emotion dominated my thoughts, the macho monster, fear of being thought afraid—one of man's strongest and, in this case, most ridiculous fears. To make sure that no one thought I was returning to avoid having to fly the mission, I circled the field once with the engine smoking and backfiring so that everyone on the ground knew that my engine trouble was not imagined. Fortunately the engine kept running and I was able to land safely with both body and ego intact. I told the pilots and crew chiefs who had come out to see me land, or crash, that I wanted them to hear the backfiring to celebrate the Fourth of July. Upon inspection, Sergeant Key found that a magneto had shorted out and upset the timing. After seeing how crestfallen he was over the first maintenance problem we had ever had, I was sorry that I had circled, because it embarrassed him and made him sweat me out for a few extra minutes.

My fear and the actions based on it were completely irrational, since I had flown more than fifty missions without ever aborting (turning back before reaching enemy territory); this mission was not as danger-ous as many I had flown. I think I was driven, in part at least, by the pilots' feelings about the few men who did regularly abort on the tough missions. One of the newer pilots aborted every third or fourth mis-sion and always on ones that might be a bit more dangerous. He could find things wrong with an airplane in flight that the crew chiefs would have been lucky to uncover during a 100-hour inspection, which took several days and required partial disassembly of the airplane. He never turned back, however, before we reached enemy territory, because that way it was credited as a mission, not as an abort.

Once when he was in my flight, he pulled up next to me, just about when I was expecting him to, and signaled that he was turning back. Although we normally maintained radio silence until we reached the target area, I asked, "What's the problem now?" He replied, "There is a loose wire behind the instrument panel," and peeled out of the formation. I looked at my panel and figured he must have x-ray eyes, because no one could see behind the panel from the pilot's seat. Surprisingly, he always acted as though he flew his missions the same as everyone else and seemed completely insensitive to the squadron's feeling about him. Pilots would tolerate any fault but lack of courage or apparent lack of courage.

In the late seventies the 75th held a squadron reunion in Nashville that was attended by many of our pilots. Someone asked if the pilot who had aborted so regularly was coming. There were loud cries of agreement when I said, "He started here but turned back at the Mississippi."

A new pilot in one of the other squadrons gave every appearance of being a real eager hotshot all through training, but on his first mission he saw some light flak, peeled out of the formation, and fled for home. He overshot the base in his panic, got lost, and had to bail out. He got back safely and was immediately transferred to the Fourteenth Air Force's only C-47 squadron as a copilot. There are hazards in all types of flying, and less than a month later the Goony Bird in which he was flying flew into a mountain in bad weather, killing all aboard.

This fear of combat presented itself in many forms. Later that year a major was attached to the 75th to gain some combat experience prior to taking over a squadron. He had a great deal of flying experience, having been an instructor and squadron commander at an advanced training base in Georgia for most of the war. We soon found that he was extremely single-minded. His only goal was to survive the war unscathed.

His motto was "Safety through Hypochondria." He knew more medical symptoms than the flight surgeon and used them all to keep from flying. After about a month of this, the CO got fed up and forced him, on threat of court-martial, to get into an airplane and take off on a mission. The major was also an expert on airplane hypochondria and landed almost immediately with a rough engine, whose roughness could be detected only by more sensitive ears than we possessed. After the mission the CO told him to pack and be on the first plane back to group headquarters, where he finished out the war. He achieved his goal and survived the war intact. But then, so did I and many others who had the same goal but who did not demand a guarantee. A lot of time and money would have been saved if the weenies could have been weeded out during the selection process, but usually the problems did not appear until the enemy did.

On July 5 I came close to not making that goal because of a few seconds of inattention to the job at hand. We were to escort B-25s to a target in the Changsha area. The twelve B-25s took off, followed by twelve P-40s. Quig was leading the mission, and I was leading the second flight. The third flight was from the 33rd Fighter Group, stationed in the Chengtu area guarding B-29s. They had flown to Kweilin with eight P-40s the week before to help stop the Japanese drive.

The bombers were flying at 10,000 feet, and we were a couple of thousand feet above them. As we came abreast of Hengyang, I spotted fifteen to twenty dots in the distance at about ten o'clock level to Quig's flight. From the way they flew in a gaggle, not a fixed formation, I was sure they were Japanese. I called them out to Quig, and we dropped our tanks and turned toward them, staying between them and the bombers. We opened up to full power to pick up as much speed as possible during the coming fight. The Oscars broke up as we approached, flying in all directions. I saw several below me and dived toward them. I fired at one at long range and got a few strikes on the fuselage before he broke into such a tight turn that I made no attempt to follow.

I spotted another Oscar in a turn a little below me and fired at him from a tight descending turn to the right. In order to hold enough lead I pulled through so far that he went out of sight under my nose. After firing a short burst I relaxed the turn slightly until he appeared. I corrected my alignment, pulled through until he disappeared once again, and fired a longer burst. When I eased off my turn again he came into view, still in the same turn, but blazing from the engine and wing roots. It was a beautiful sight, one of the best that a fighter pilot can experience, blazing evidence of victory in one-to-one combat, but I didn't stop to admire my handiwork. Instead, I continued my dive until I was sure my air was clear and then climbed back up into the fight.

I made passes at two other Oscars but got no hits, since they broke sharply and zoomed up out of range. My last pass was made from a dive, so I kept diving to keep my speed up. When I turned to climb back into the fight, there was no fight. There were no airplanes in sight, no P-40s, no Oscars, no B-25s. It was hazy, so I continued to circle and climb without seeing any planes. Looking down I saw a parachute descending toward the town of Hengyang. Since I had never seen or heard of a Japanese pilot bailing out, I was sure it was one of our pilots. He was at 6,000 or 7,000 feet, so I dived down to get in close and try to identify him. I did not get near enough to recognize him but saw he was a tall American with a leather jacket and khaki pants. He waved as I went by, his final contact with an American. I planned to watch until he landed so I could report his position, but a Japanese pilot had other plans.

A few seconds later there was a terrific impact and earsplitting noise. It felt as though a giant had dropped a tractor trailer on my plane. An enemy had dived on me while I was watching the parachute, when I should have been watching my tail. He hit me with explosive rounds in the rudder and left aileron, shredding both badly. Another round or two had exploded on the armor plate just behind my head and blown holes in the canopy and, it felt like, in my head.

I instinctively slammed the stick into the front right corner of the cockpit and went into a twisting dive. Pulling out at about 1,000 feet and looking back, I was relieved to see nothing. To this day I haven't seen the Oscar that clobbered me. He either didn't try to follow me down or couldn't keep up in the dive.

At that moment I declared the fight officially over and headed for home, keeping my eyes peeled. I called on the radio but couldn't raise any of the other planes. I climbed slowly to 5,000 feet on the return trip, flying at a low cruise setting, since my left aileron was in bad shape. One of the hinges was badly damaged, and it was trailing long streamers of fabric, but it seemed to operate normally.

About fifty miles north of Kweilin I called the ground station with my individual call sign, Charleston Three Two, to report my position. When I reached the field I slowed down even more, made a straight-in approach, and landed. The others had landed about fifteen minutes earlier, and when I taxied in all the pilots were in a group talking about the fight with the participants. Sergeant Key, smiling broadly, jumped on the wing and began patting me on the back and helping me off with my chute, greatly relieved that I hadn't been shot down. He did a classic double take when he noticed the damage to the plane. He was proud of its condition and its outstanding in-commission (ready for flight) record and faced a lot of extra work to repair it. I don't know how he did it, but I was flying it again two days later.

As I got out of the plane, all the pilots crowded around to inspect the damage and to get my report on the fight. Tex Hill walked up, clapped me on the shoulder, and said, "Be careful you don't get the Purple Heart, son."

In the debriefing I learned that Quig had shot down two Oscars and that our resident Indian, Chief Sanford, a full-blooded Winnebago, had been shot in the toe and was in the hospital. That Japanese pilot must have been a good shot to hit him in the toe, the little toe at that. It was not a serious wound, and Chief was okay, except that he limped for a few weeks. He was flying again in a few days. It would have been the perfect wound for some of the less eager pilots, who could have stayed grounded for months.

Lieutenant Haynes of the 33rd had not returned. He was a tall pilot who had been wearing a leather jacket and khaki pants, so I reported that he had bailed out and must have landed in or very close to Hengyang, which was completely surrounded by Japanese troops. He was never heard from again. If he landed in Hengyang, he may have fought with the tough Chinese Tenth Army that held off the Japanese for more than six weeks before they were overwhelmed. They put up what was by far the most determined resistance of any of the Chinese troops.

Earl Green, my roommate, who had been shot down late in May, returned to the squadron. We had known for some time that he was safe, but he was so deep in Japanese territory that the guerrillas kept him in place for more than a month before they started him on the long trek back. To our surprise and delight, he appeared one night, unshaven and dressed in black Chinese clothes. Because we knew he would be back, we had kept his clothes, food, and mail for him.

Earl had a harrowing tale to tell. A large group of Oscars had dived out of the clouds behind them, and in an instant, he and his element leader, Danny Daniels, had both been hit. Danny had been wounded, and although his own plane was hit, Earl drove off the Oscars that were attacking Danny, only to be hit and set afire by another Oscar. He bailed out without being burned just as his plane burst into flames. His chute opened several thousand feet above the ground, and just as he was breathing a sigh of relief, a lone Oscar made a strafing pass at him. The attack missed, but almost before Earl could catch his breath, the Oscar was coming back on another pass. Fortunately, Earl was skinny, and he said it seemed as though the rounds from the nose guns were straddling him: "I started to swing the chute wildly, then climbed up the shroud lines and looked out through the little hole on top." The Oscar made three more passes at Earl but never touched him.

Not to be denied, when Earl reached the ground, the Japanese strafed the chute, but he was at the far end of the shroud lines under a bush and received only a small cut on his foot from a shell fragment. It was, nevertheless a wound inflicted by the enemy, and Green brought back a certificate from a Chinese doctor attesting to his wound to justify the award of a Purple Heart. Our feelings toward the Japanese were not improved by this incident. I hadn't heard of any pilots being strafed in their chutes in Europe, but the Japanese had done it many times in the Pacific. Since the Japanese rarely bailed out, it was difficult to reciprocate.

A few days earlier another of our pilots, Jack Blanco, had also walked back with the aid of the guerrillas. He had been down only a few days, since he had been close to the lines when he bailed out. Blanco was thin, almost scrawny, so Moose took a picture of him in his shorts in the same pose as a picture of the Michigan All-American running back, Tom Harmon, that had appeared in *Life* magazine. The year before, Harmon had bailed out of a B-25 over the jungles of Brazil and walked through the rain forest for several days until he reached a river and was rescued. His photo in *Life* showed him standing by one of his rescuers in his shorts. The caption read, "My football legs saved me." Moose put it on the bulletin board, and next to it he pinned the photo of Jack with the caption, "My bird legs saved me."

Jesse Gray, two other pilots, and I had a day off the flying schedule on July 8, so we got the cook to make some sandwiches with the Spam we had brought back from India. We packed them in a musette bag along with some canteens of boiled water and went on a picnic. We took a jeep into Kweilin, then hired a sampan to take us south on the beautiful Li River.

Once we were a few miles south of Kweilin, it seemed as though we had entered another world. The river flowed in gentle curves through the small valley between the sharply etched mountains, which seemed to change color when viewed from different angles. It was easy to see why this area was famed throughout China for its beauty. We saw a few peasants but no airplanes, no soldiers, and no military vehicles. It was a scene of the utmost tranquillity and a most relaxing interlude for us. We picnicked on a sandbar, skinny-dipped in the river, despite the rules against swimming in the river, and returned late in the afternoon enjoying a completely different view of the mountains as the sun was setting. It was a short but effective R&R.

The next day Jesse and I climbed to the top of the mountain behind our hostel. We spent an hour or so on the peak, enjoying the panorama of the airfields and the mountains. The mountains were steep, but the numerous jagged rocks provided good purchase for the climb.

The following morning it was back to war. We flew two long missions a day for several days. The Japanese were still moving south in force, and Hengyang was surrounded but still in the hands of the Chinese. On July 17 during an offensive reconnaissance north of Hengyang, Quig was leading the first flight, and I was leading the second. Quig had started down with his flight to strafe in the area about twenty miles south of Changsha. The Japanese were reported to be using the small airfield in the bend of the river that we called Dog Dog two-four.

He had almost reached the deck when I saw two aircraft about ten miles to the north at roughly my altitude. They looked like Japanese but were circling and not getting any closer to us. I started climbing toward them and told Quig to get back up since there were Zeros in the vicinity. He led his flight back up to the enemy's altitude, while I leveled off several thousand feet above them.

I kept searching the sky for more Zeros, since I had never seen the Japanese fly with fewer than ten aircraft in a formation. They were behaving so strangely—keeping their distance while allowing both our flights to get above them—that I felt certain they were decoys of some sort. Quig evidently thought so too, because he told me to act as top cover while he went after them. I climbed a bit higher as we jettisoned our parafrags but held onto our tanks until we were sure we would be in a fight. Quig's flight had jettisoned its bombs before starting back up from the deck. After releasing the frags I hoped that we didn't have to dive anywhere in that area before the slow, drifting bombs reached the ground.

The two Japanese must have been the rawest of rookies. Not until Quig turned toward them did the Oscars seem to notice the P-40s. They turned in our direction, and as they got closer I could see that they were still carrying their drop tanks. They began firing at Quig's flight from far out of range, almost a mile away. Neither of them took the usual violent evasive action as the P-40s closed with them. Instead they made gentle diving turns away from the attack. Quig got behind the first one and set him ablaze with his first burst. The Oscar nosed over and dived straight to the ground.

Another P-40 fired at the second Oscar from behind, and it belched a tremendous cloud of oily black smoke that poured out for a few seconds, then it nosed into a 20- to 30-degree dive. About ten seconds later a second P-40 came up behind the Oscar and fired a burst into it. The pilot instantly bailed out. He was the first and only Japanese any of us had ever seen use his parachute. Since the Oscars had little or no armor plate, the pilots were usually killed or too badly injured to bail out. Also, they wouldn't have lasted long with the Chinese if they did bail out.

The chute opened immediately, and he began drifting toward the airfield at Dog Dog two-four. The P-40 that had hit him first dived toward the parachute with his guns blazing and shot the pilot to ribbons, leaving the body drifting toward the airfield. After searching the sky carefully, Quig took his flight down and made a pass at the airfield, but there were no signs of aircraft or activity. We completed our strafing mission and returned to Kweilin.

During the debriefing I found that Jesse had been flying the P-40 that made the first pass at the Oscar and that Joe Focht made the second pass. Jesse was the one who had strafed the pilot in the parachute, mainly because he was the closest. Everyone was eager to get even for Green's being strafed in his chute.

Naturally both Jesse and Joe claimed the second Oscar—there was no doubt that Quigley had gotten the first one. Jesse, showing much of his dad's temper, threatened to beat up Joe and anyone else who said that he shouldn't be credited with the victory. He also refused to share it with Joe when that was suggested. To quote Jesse, "By damn, I shot him down, and I'm getting the victory."

I told what I had seen and that it seemed to me that Jesse had inflicted so much damage that the enemy was starting to bail out when Joe fired his burst into the Oscar. I'm not sure that my statement was regarded as totally unbiased, because Jesse and I had been roommates since we'd been in the squadron. In fairness to Joe, when he attacked the Oscar it was no longer smoking and was fair game.

Joe offered to withdraw his claim, but Major Quigley said that since there was no interest in sharing the victory, he would decide by the toss of a coin. He flipped the coin and Joe won. Jesse stomped out in a rage and left for the hostel. An hour or so later, when we all went to the hostel (in this case more appropriately spelled "hostile"), Jesse had removed all of Joe's belongings from the large room that ten of us were occupying and had thrown them on the ground outside. Still raging, he told Joe never to set foot in that room again. Joe, who was much smaller than Jesse, wisely did not argue and moved into another room.

Quig made it up to Jesse the best way he could. He knew that Jesse's promotion had been held up because of his problems with the censors ("By damn, no one can tell me what to write to my mother"). Quig wrote a letter to 23rd Group Headquarters, to be added to Jesse's file, stating that Jesse and Joe had both claimed the same airplane in a fight and that Jesse, with outstanding good sportsmanship, had relinquished the claim so that Joe could have the victory. Despite being the lie of the century—Goebbels would have been embarrassed by it—it worked, and Jesse's period of punishment was reduced.

We wondered if the Japanese pilots' obvious lack of ability indicated that the enemy was running short of experienced army pilots in China. We had seen no previous evidence of it, but we knew that hundreds of Japanese Navy pilots had been lost in the Battle of Midway in June 1942. Just a month before, on June 20, 1944, in the Battle of the Philippine Sea, about 275 Japanese Navy pilots had been shot down by U.S. Navy pilots. Our Navy pilots called it the Great Marianas Turkey Shoot. We thought it possible that experienced Japanese pilots from China had been withdrawn to help out in the Pacific Theater. In later combats, however, the Japanese seemed to fight as well as ever, so it was unlikely that many had been withdrawn.

It was hot and humid in Kweilin, and it was difficult to stay cool except when flying at altitude. We moved our beds outside to try to catch a bit of breeze, but it didn't help much because we had to sleep under a mosquito bar that blocked most of the breeze. We were all exhausted from so much flying, and the lack of sleep added to the problem. The frequent night bombings and bombing alerts further reduced the chance to sleep. Many of us, me included, developed heat rash, or prickly heat, on our chests. It was most uncomfortable, especially under the parachute harness chest strap when flying at low altitude. We took to flying the return legs of missions with the canopies open, shirts or flying suits open to the waist, and parachute chest strap unbuckled to let some cool air blow on us. It helped a bit, but the rash didn't go away until the powder that the doc had requisitioned finally arrived.

A few days after the Case of the Inept Oscars (we thought in these terms from reading so many Perry Mason stories), eight of our P-40s were flying a mission in the area north of Hengyang. Just before we reached the target area, I spotted twelve fighters roughly paralleling our course about five miles to the west and several thousand feet higher. The formation did not look Japanese, but the fighters seemed to have radial engines. Rather perplexed, we thought they might be Oscars flying in a U.S.-type formation to fool us. As we were wondering, they dived toward us. We jettisoned our tanks and bombs and turned into them.

At about half a mile from us they pulled up, and we saw that they were Chinese Air Force P-40s. They had painted the front of the engine cowling and the spinner white, causing the nose to appear much shorter. We continued our mission, really irritated over the unnecessary jettisoning of the bombs and belly tanks that had been flown over the Hump to Kweilin at such great cost. When we landed, Major Quigley heatedly told our intelligence officer to get word to the Chinese Air Force not to make passes at us for any reason.

A few days later, despite the warning, they did the same thing to another of our missions. This time, because he knew of our experience, the leader didn't jettison anything but turned toward the apparent attackers just in case. This time Quig sent a message to the Chinese, through our group headquarters, that if they made any simulated attacks on us in the future, we would shoot them all down. That did the trick, and we never saw them again.

We had never seen any evidence that they were engaged in combat. There were no intelligence reports indicating that they were strafing or supporting their ground troops in any way. Also, although our planes were constantly in the combat area, we had never seen them except for the two simulated attacks. Their primary value, as far as we could determine, was the comedy relief they had provided when they landed at Hengyang.

We were finding it much more difficult to locate the Japanese troops, since they had dispersed throughout the countryside and were traveling in the early dawn and late evening, when we could reach them only by flying at night either going or coming. Night landings were out of the question at Kweilin because of the proximity of the mountains to the runway and the complete lack of runway lighting.

Quig decided that we could make night takeoffs, however, without too much danger and that if we could hit the target area at first light we would catch the Japanese by surprise and blast them. The next morning eight of our most experienced pilots went to the flight line at three to prepare for a three-thirty takeoff. I flew as an element leader in Quig's lead flight.

Four jeeps were parked along the left side of the runway with their lights shining across the runway. The leader of each two-man element used them to line up the takeoff while the wingmen flew formation on the leaders. We flew with our running lights on and climbed straight ahead until above the mountains, then made one circle to form up and headed north. We climbed to about 12,000 feet and flew well to the west of the river and railroad running from Hengyang to Kweilin.

It was quite beautiful, with the gently bobbing running lights and the soft blue-red glow of the exhaust stacks, and it became more beautiful as the sky lightened and the P-40s emerged from the darkness, first as silhouettes, then becoming whole airplanes bathed by the faint light of dawn. As soon as we could see well, we turned off our lights. It was the first time most of us had ever flown formation at night, and it was a strangely tranquil experience.

At the south shore of Tungting Lake we turned east, throttled back, and began letting down toward the river. Quig had decided to do without top cover, and all eight of us roared down to strafe. We hit the river just as it became light enough for us to pick out targets on the ground. The surprise was total; the Japanese were all along the river, eating, removing camouflage nets and loading trucks, forming up to move out on foot or on horseback.

We essed back and forth along the river and road, dropping our parafrags and strafing—trying to spread the destruction over as wide an area as possible in order to keep the Japanese in the open for a while as they regrouped. Eight more P-40s, from the 74th, had taken off right at dawn, and we hoped they would arrive before the troops could get back under cover. Later they told us the Japanese were still milling around in the open and they were able to inflict severe damage.

The next morning we tried the same thing, only this time we came from the east, out of the sun, and once again caught the Japanese with their pants down, literally, since many were bathing in the river. Group intelligence thought we had a built-in surprise and could continue this tactic indefinitely, but on the fourth try two of our planes were shot down and many were hit by the heavy ground fire. One of the pilots made it back because he was able to get several miles from the river before bailing out, but the other went straight into the ground. After that, we occasionally ran night missions but never on two nights in a row. None was ever as successful as the first two, however.

Since the Japanese were moving in small groups through the more remote countryside and were holing up by day, we needed another method of locating them. It appeared in the person of Lt. Malcolm Rosholt. He was a former journalist who had been in China for many years and was fluent in the language. He was now an intelligence officer attached to the headquarters of the commander of the Chinese Army in that area, Marshal Hseuh Yo, the Little Tiger of Changsha.

Rosholt, a tall, slim, scholarly looking and acting man, was based at Chensien, a small village with a tiny airstrip about forty-five minutes northeast of Kweilin. He was in close contact by means of radios and runners with the Chinese guerrillas in the area, from whom he received reports on the location of Japanese troops. When he learned of worthwhile targets, he would radio Kweilin, and the 75th would send two P-40s to land at Chensien and be briefed by him. He would often give the lead pilot a large-scale map of a small area, showing individual houses and groves of trees marked in red. Two flights of P-40s would leave Kweilin about thirty minutes after the first two aircraft and fly to Chensien. The first two would then take off and lead the way to the targets. The leader would attack the first target himself by bombing and strafing it, and then he would lead his wingman and the other pilots to the remainder of the targets, marking each one by firing a burst into it—just another example of the 75th's personalized service.

The first few times we did this, Sack Folmar led the flight of two and I was his wingman. After that we alternated, each flying as leader with different wingmen. In retrospect, landing at Chensien was a hairy operation, since the field was so short, about 2,000 feet, and we were landing with a full load of fuel and bombs. To add to the difficulty, there was a ten- to fifteen-foot dike at the approach end of the runway. At the time, however, we didn't give it a second thought, thanks no doubt to the misplaced confidence of youth.

One of my most memorable and absolutely most frightening experiences took place on a Chensien mission. I took off for Chensien in the early afternoon with Lt. Paul Moehring as my wingman. We landed and joined Lieutenant Rosholt for our briefing. He said that a group of several thousand Japanese cavalrymen was reported to be heading south in the Chaling area, which is east of Hengyang. The precise position was unknown, and we were to reconnoiter the roads at low altitude in the hope of finding them. For some reason I was carrying parafrags and Paul had demolition bombs.

We took off and flew at about 5,000 feet to the search area, then let down to a few hundred feet and flew in gentle S-turns in loose formation so that we could both search. After about twenty minutes of fruitless searching, we came upon an open area bordered by a large stand of trees at the base of a small mountain. There was a compound with several houses on the edge of the open area.

It all looked so serene, but as I passed over the trees I saw a flash of something white. I couldn't make out what it was, so I made a wide circle, climbed a bit, then nosed down and fired a short burst at it. The woods suddenly came alive, with soldiers and horses pouring out onto the field in wild disarray. What my eagle eyes had spotted was the back end of a white horse.

I whipped around and made a pass at the troops, dropping my frags and strafing. Most of the troops scurried into the compound for cover, so I told Paul to climb up and dive-bomb it. He scored a direct hit, and then we strafed until we were out of ammunition. We left the area and began climbing for home. As soon as I was able to contact Kweilin, I radioed the code word that meant I had located the Japanese.

When I landed, the ground crews swarmed over my plane checking for damage, refueling, and rearming. The 75th planes were out on a mission, and the intelligence officer told me to take off as soon as possible and lead the 74th to the target. Capt. Ted Adams would meet me with twelve P-40s over the fighter strip, and we would hit the troops before dark, after which the 74th would land at Lingling to stage for a morning mission. I said it might be too dark for me to land back at Kweilin as instructed, but he said we would chance it. I said I hoped that *we* don't buy the farm.

I joined the 74th over the field, then headed north. Since I knew where the targets were, I stayed well to the west of their location and came around the back of the mountain to hit them out of the setting sun. It couldn't have worked out better. The troops were forming up to march, apparently thinking we wouldn't attack so late in the day. We swooped in, sowing our parafrags, and then came back around to strafe the mass of dying, wounded, and totally disorganized men and horses. After about six passes, I saw that my coolant and oil temperature gauges were right on the peg. My heart nearly stopped—coolant and oil overheating meant that the plane had been hit and was losing coolant. From the time of the hit, I had about two minutes until the engine would overheat and seize completely. I was horrified at the thought of bailing out in the midst of all those troops we were strafing. To add to my fear, my airplane's spinner was a different color from the others, making me easily recognizable, and I was sure to be high on their hate parade. I had not only found and strafed them earlier but had also returned with all my friends to finish them off.

I opened my coolant shutters wide as I turned east and started climbing to minimum bailout altitude and to put as much distance as possible between me and the Japanese. I called Ted and told him I was going to bail out, and he followed me to report on my position. I stuffed my special map in my shirt and opened my canopy so I could get out as soon as the engine stopped. To my surprise and great joy, the coolant and oil temperatures began to drop. I flew east for a few more minutes and both needles went back into the normal range. I called Ted, with difficulty because my mouth was so dry that I couldn't have spit for a million dollars, and told him it was a false alarm but I was returning to Kweilin, since I had all the war I needed for one day. Ted went back and made a few more passes, then headed for Lingling, while I flew back to Kweilin as fast as possible and landed with just enough light remaining to make out the mountains and the runway.

When I parked, all the pilots who had landed from their mission about an hour earlier were there sweating me out because of the approaching darkness. I told Sergeant Key what had happened, but he couldn't figure it out until he had inspected the plane with a flashlight. I had been hit by ground fire several times and one of the slugs had hit the latch on the coolant shutter handle, allowing it to close all the way. The fully closed shutters and the high power setting I was using caused the overheating. It really wasn't a close call, but it was as close as I wanted to get.

In that hot month of July, about the midpoint of my combat tour in China, I completed twenty-seven missions and flew eighty-two combat hours. That amounted to slightly more than one fourth of the total missions and hours I amassed during my entire tour.

Volume 5 of *The Army Air Forces in World War II* includes this summary of the efforts of the Fourteenth Air Force task force defending against the Japanese advance:

> From May 26 through August 1 its planes had flown 5,287 sorties, over 4,000 of them by fighter aircraft. A total of 1,164 tons of bombs had been dropped, and more than a million rounds of ammunition had been expended, chiefly in strafing attacks. Out of an overall strength of approximately 150 aircraft, 43 had been lost but only three of that number were credited to enemy pilots. It was estimated that the task force had cost the enemy 595 trucks, 14 bridges, some 13,000 casualties, 114 aircraft, and more than 1,000 small boats.

It concludes that if the prospect of stopping the Japanese was hopeless, it was no fault of the air task force.

14

TOUGH
LOSSES

August was for me the best of times and the worst of times, to borrow a phrase. I scored another victory and was recommended for the Silver Star, but I lost two good friends and my trusty P-40 *Lope's Hope*.

We flew fewer missions in August than we had in July because there were many days of heavy clouds that made it impossible to reach the target area. This bad weather helped the Japanese immeasurably, as they were able to advance along the roads and river with impunity. They were even able to use the railroads, with steam engines and with small gasoline-powered vehicles on grooved wheels.

To deny them the use of the railroad, we bombed the tracks regularly, trying to destroy as much of them as possible. At first we were not too successful, since the bombs, dropped at low altitude in level flight, skipped along the roadbed and, as often as not, exploded harmlessly in the air. Our efficiency improved markedly, however, with the arrival of a new development, the spike bomb. It was a standard demolition bomb with a long steel spike screwed into the nose fuse cavity. When dropped from a slight dive, the spike would stick into the ties of the roadbed and hold the bomb in place until it exploded.

Despite the improvement, our destructive capability was limited by our inability to carry more than two bombs per aircraft. The B-25s, however, were very effective. Using both spike bombs and the 75-millimeter cannon, one B-25 could destroy several miles of track on a single mission.

Often, when the weather was too bad for the squadron to fly, Quig and I would fly two-man missions with me as his wingman. We knew the country like the backs of our hands, and we would fly up the valleys and the river looking for targets. Usually the ceiling was a little high in the area north of Lingling, so we could get up to about 500 feet. This made it easier to spot targets and much easier to strafe. A pilot has to be able to nose down slightly in order to shoot accurately at ground targets.

Quig and I always found many good targets on these missions. The Japanese weren't expecting our fighters to be up, and we were on them before they knew it. The most common targets were small groups of men and horses on the roads or boats on the river, but occasionally we located trucks. We seldom were hit or even fired on because of the surprise, but now and then they were ready for us. They had most likely been warned by radio from upriver.

On one such mission Quig was diving on some boats when I saw two soldiers in a gunpit cut into the side of a hill firing at him with what looked like 20-millimeters. The gunners were concentrating on Quig's P-40 and didn't see me following him. I dived on them from behind and cut them to pieces. As I pulled up I saw them sprawled on the bottom of the pit along with the guns.

I really enjoyed those missions. Low flying is exhilarating in any circumstances, and I felt that we were accomplishing a lot for the cause. Also, I took a certain amount of pride in almost always being chosen by Quig to fly with him. With the ego of a fighter pilot, I thought he couldn't have made a better choice.

Since the squadron was based at Kweilin, it was a much longer flight to the Tungting Lake area than it had been from Hengyang—more than 300 miles longer, in fact. Often when we went up to the lake, we had to land at Lingling on the way back to refuel. From there we would either go back to Kweilin or, more often, fly another mission to the lake area on the way back. We kept a small detachment at Lingling to supervise the refueling and rearming, although we pilots helped as much as possible.

On one mission, just as we were pulling up from strafing a supply dump far to the northeast of Hengyang, my wingman, Mouse Carter, called and said that he had been hit in one of his tanks and was losing fuel; he didn't think he could make it back to Kweilin. I told him to land at Lingling, but he was new to the squadron and wasn't sure he could find it. I called Sack Tanner, who was leading the mission, and told him I would lead Mouse to Lingling and then fly on to Kweilin.

We pulled out of the flight and took up a course for Lingling. As we approached Lingling, Mouse and I dived down to the deck to make a fighter landing approach to the north. Since I wasn't going to land and wanted to head south anyway, instead of peeling up to the left I pulled straight up into an Immelman while Mouse made a normal peelup and landed.

About an hour after I landed at Kweilin, our operations office was notified that Mouse was on his way back. Since everybody watched all landings, we went out to the side of the runway to wait. Instead of landing from the north as we usually did, he approached from the south and, in front of our alert shack, pulled straight up into an Immelman. He hadn't rolled out on top before the operations officer's phone was ringing. It was the wing commander, General Vincent. It seemed that he too watched landings whenever possible, and he wanted to know who in the hell was doing aerobatics over the field. He didn't want anyone screwing around with his precious aircraft. I told Major Quigley what had led Mouse to do the Immelman and then later told Mouse that there are things you can do at a forward base that you can't do near wing headquarters.

On August 4, Quig led an eight-plane mission to strafe north of Hengyang, with me leading the second flight. We spotted a small group of boats carrying gasoline on the river just north of Hengyang, and I took my flight down to bomb and strafe them. We dropped our parafrags, stopping the boats, and then strafed them until they all were blazing. We continued along the river toward Hengyang and a few miles farther on found more boats unloading gasoline cans. My flight made several passes, setting the rest of the boats and a large cache of gasoline on the shore ablaze. The targets were so numerous that I kept strafing until I was out of ammunition. I called to Quig that we were coming up since our guns were dry.

He was just starting down with his flight when I spotted a bunch of Japanese circling over Hengyang. We headed toward them and saw that there were twelve Oscars covering six or eight Aichi D3A Val dive-bombers that were attacking Hengyang. Vals were the wheels-down-and-welded dive-bombers used by the Japanese at Pearl Harbor. It was the first time I had seen them, but I wouldn't soon forget them.

As we closed on them Quig instructed everyone who was out of ammunition to go home and told his flight that he was going down after the Vals. I signaled my element leader to take the flight home. They peeled off to the south, and I went after the Oscars. I figured that Quig's flight could use some help in keeping the Oscars off them and that the Japanese couldn't tell that I was out of ammunition.

I made a diving head-on pass through the Oscars, and they scattered like birds in all directions. When an enemy fighter is diving on you, the last thing you do is try to see if he is firing at you. Break first, think later, is the rule. I stayed in a steep dive until well past them and then zoomed back up and turned into them for another pass. I glanced down for a second just in time to see a Val dive straight into the river, then I went through the Japanese again. Several turned after me this time, but I was going too fast. I looked down again and saw another Val crash in flames. Quig's flight was certainly doing its job. After several more passes, the rest of the Vals fled to the north and the Oscars followed. I continued my dive to the south and joined up on the tail end of Quig's flight.

As we landed and taxied in, we were met by the rest of the pilots, who knew we had been in a fight. During the debriefing Quig said that he had shot down two Vals: one had gone into the river and the other had crashed in flames. I told the intelligence officer that I had seen both of them crash and could confirm them.

Quig asked me if I had been out of ammunition. When I answered yes, he said, "I thought I told everyone without ammunition to head for home."

I replied, "I heard you, but I thought I could keep the Oscars off your back while you went after the Vals."

"You must have done a hell of a job," he said, "because none of them came down on us."

Later that day he said that he had recommended me for the Silver Star. His recommendation was approved, and I was awarded the medal about six months later.

The next day eight P-40s from the 75th and eight from the Sixteenth Fighter Squadron flew what was a major mission for us, sixteen airplanes. We rarely had more than eight fighters to send on a single mission. Intelligence had reported a major concentration of supplies and equipment in the area north of Changsha ready to be moved south. All of the aircraft were carrying demolition bombs. The 75th was to provide top cover for the Sixteenth on the initial attack, and then the squadrons would switch roles.

Sack Folmar was leading the mission, and I was leading the second flight. About halfway to the target my wingman, the aborter, turned back with some problem. Both squadrons flew at about 12,000 feet, but as we approached the target area the Sixteenth dropped down to

8,000 feet. The supply dump was right where it had been reported, on the east bank of the river above Changsha.

Just as the second flight of the Sixteenth rolled into its dive-bombing run, amid fairly heavy flak, I spotted a group of dots coming toward us from the north. I called them out to Sack, and we turned toward them, climbing as we went. We held onto our belly tanks and bombs until we were sure we would make contact. As we approached them, I saw there were about twenty Oscars and Tojos. They were definitely attacking, so we jettisoned our tanks and bombs. The Japanese were diving on the Sixteenth planes climbing up from their dive-bombing runs. We bounced the Japanese from the front quarter, and they broke in all directions. The Oscars broke to the sides and up, but the Tojos, which could dive much better than the Oscars, continued downward after our low fighters. I fired at one Tojo from out of range to chase him off the tail of a P-40. I didn't see any hits, but he pulled off his intended victim. I saw another Tojo below me attacking a P-40. Instead of the normal mottled green camouflage, this Tojo was painted all black except for the large red balls on the wings and fuselage. I fired at him and saw a few strikes on the aft fuselage. To my surprise, instead of turning, he went into a steep dive toward the river. I got directly behind him in an almost vertical dive and fired a long burst into him. I could see the flashes of my strikes dancing all over his fuselage and wing roots. Suddenly I realized how low I was and made a high-g pullout to keep from hitting the water. I blacked out for a few seconds, and when my vision cleared there was no sign of the Tojo, but there was a series of enlarging concentric circles on the river that looked like something had made a big splash.

As I climbed back up, I saw that the remaining enemy planes were all climbing away to the north. There were three oil fires burning on the ground near the river. We strafed the supply dump until low on ammunition, then headed back for Kweilin. As we regrouped, I saw that all the 75th planes were with us but that the Sixteenth was short a man.

After we landed, I claimed the Tojo as a probable, since I was sure he had gone into the river. I hoped that my gun-camera film would show him too low to pull out. When I described my attack and its location, Sack said that he had seen the Tojo go into the river and thought there was no way that I could avoid the same fate. The Tojo was then changed to a confirmed victory. Sack and one of the Sixteenth pilots had also shot down Tojos, and one of the Sixteenth had crashed in flames.

A few days later, on August 8, Flash Segura was flying my P-40 on a strafing mission in the Hengyang area. I was off the schedule that day, and Flash's airplane was being inspected. Hengyang was still surrounded by the Japanese but was holding out. Our fighters were constantly attacking the surrounding troops to try and relieve the pressure, but the Japanese continued to pour in replacements. They had committed fifteen divisions plus five brigades to this drive, called Ichigo, determined to capture our main bases.

Flash was leading the mission and took his flight down to strafe, leaving the second flight up for top cover. Ground fire was heavy, and Flash felt several hits, but none seemed to have caused any substantial damage. After a few more passes he started to climb back up and switch places with the top cover flight.

During the climb he noticed that the oil pressure was dropping and the oil temperature was rising. He knew that the engine would seize in just a few minutes without oil, so he leveled out and headed south to get out of Japanese territory. The oil pressure continued to drop, and all the temperature gauges were on the pegs. The engine was starting to run really rough, so he decided to bail out before it caught fire. He shut off the engine, pulled the nose up to lose speed, and dived over the side. This time, unlike his previous bailout, he went under the horizontal stabilizer without hitting it. His chute, or more correctly, my chute, opened normally, and he drifted down to a safe landing in an area between the Japanese and Chinese forces. He was some distance from both lines, and since it was midafternoon he prudently decided to wait until dark before trying to join the Chinese. He gathered the chute and settled in a small hollow to wait. After an hour or so he became hungry. He had flown several missions that day and had eaten only a small sandwich between missions. He unzipped the so-called jungle-kit backpack of the parachute, which contained a machete, fishing gear, compass, and a large bar of extremely hard, unmeltable chocolate. Everything was there but the chocolate. He was, to put it mildly, chagrined to find that it was gone; I had already eaten it. He suffered through the rest of the afternoon, and when it became dark he reached the Chinese lines and got back to Kweilin late the next day by jeep.

As soon as he saw me he started to give me hell for having eaten the emergency ration in my jungle kit. I didn't answer but went to the parachute rack, got out his parachute, and unzipped the back—no chocolate. I unzipped the backs of several more chutes—no chocolate. Everyone had eaten their chocolate. Starvation or even hunger was not generally a problem when we were shot down, and none of us had thought twice about eating the chocolate. Besides, why all the fuss about chocolate, when I had graciously refrained from saying, "Where in the hell is my P-40?"

Sweets were in short supply in China. Except for occasional candy and fruitcake from home, our main supply was the four Tootsie Rolls we were given each month along with a few cans of beer, a few cartons of cigarettes, and two cans of a chocolate drink called Toddy. Since I didn't drink or smoke, I always traded my beer for Toddy and my cigarettes for Tootsie Rolls. Toddy had some sort of preservative that coated your mouth with wax, but it was worth it to have a chocolate drink.

We also received a ration of two ounces of whiskey per mission. I saved mine until I had a full fifth and gave it to hardworking Sergeant Key. One month my gift backfired; Sergeant Key got drunk, took his rifle, and went looking for the first sergeant, who was most unpopular with everyone in the squadron, officers and enlisted men alike. Luckily Sergeant Key was unable to find him, but Key was threatened with court-martial and loss of rank before the CO wisely decided to forget the whole thing. From then on I gave my whiskey to the sergeant in more manageable doses.

I was assigned another P-40 a few days after the loss of *Lope's Hope*. It had been transferred in from another squadron and was an earlier model than my first plane. I never got around to having the name painted on the nose because we were all too busy.

I got off to a bad start in it. On my first mission I was down strafing when I felt some hits from ground fire. As I glanced at my instruments, I saw the needle on the airspeed indicator drop to zero, and the altimeter started rotating aimlessly. Since I could see that the pitot tube on the left wing was intact, I was sure that the line from the tube to the instruments had been cut. I flew the next ten or so missions without an airspeed indicator or altimeter, but I had flown the P-40 so much by now that I didn't need instruments. I could land right on the end of the runway every time without difficulty.

Twice during the next week we were part of coordinated attacks on what had become a major Japanese airfield, Pailuchi, at Yochow on the northeast corner of Tungting Lake. The missions were planned by Lt. Col. John Dunning, and he and Colonel Rouse, the group commander, led the Fifth Fighter Group, CACW, on both of them. Colonel Dunning was a master tactician as well as a master pilot, and he snookered the Japanese at their own game, in effect hoisting them on their own radar.

We knew, both from intelligence and from experience, that the Japanese had radar in the Yochow-Hankow area and that their fighters would be scrambled to intercept incoming bombing raids. On the first of these missions, sixteen P-40s from the 75th and 74th escorted fifteen B-24s from the 308th Bomb Group to a target to the northeast of Yochow. The B-24s flew at about 15,000 feet, with our fighters about 2,000 feet above them.

Just as the bombers were releasing their bombs, I spotted a large gaggle of fighters approaching from the west. I called them out to the leader, and we turned toward them to stay between the attackers and the B-24s, which were turning for home and descending slightly to pick up speed. The thirty or more Oscars and Tojos made a half-hearted dive toward the bombers but turned back as we headed toward them.

The Japanese were not very aggressive for some reason, and they turned and climbed away to the west. We had been briefed not to go after the fighters if it meant leaving the bombers, so with some reluctance we rejoined the bomber formation. After we got back to Kweilin and landed, we learned the reason for those instructions.

The Fifth Fighter Group had taken off with sixteen P-40s from Chihkiang, about 150 miles west of Hengyang. The planes had flown down close to the hills until they reached Tungting Lake, then they dropped to just above the water to stay under the radar and avoid detection. With precise timing and navigation, the group hit the Japanese just as they were landing from intercepting the B-24s. Most of their aircraft were on the ground, but a few were still in the pattern circling to land.

There was mass confusion and panic among the Japanese as the sixteen P-40s suddenly dived into their midst, strafing and parafragging. At least two Oscars collided on the runway trying to take off. Six or eight Japanese were shot down, most with their wheels down for landing, and every airplane on the runway and ramp was destroyed or severely damaged. Colonel Rouse then led his planes away as suddenly as they had appeared, without the loss of a single P-40.

Less than a week later Colonel Dunning ran a modified version of the first mission. I wasn't in the escort flight this time, but the script for the B-24s and the escorting fighters was the same as on the first mission. The major variation was that the Japanese never got off the ground to make even a token interception. The Fifth Fighter Group P-40s, led by Dunning, hit them as they were taxiing out for takeoff. This time only one or two got airborne, and they were shot down immediately. The rest were destroyed on the ground as many of the Japanese got out of their planes and ran for cover.

Again the P-40s escaped unscathed, except for the loss of one that hit the water and blew up on the flight across the lake on the way in. The Japanese had had enough and, radar or no radar, evacuated Pailuchi Airdrome, using it only as a forward staging base from then on.

Despite those successful missions and our control of the air, things began to deteriorate around the middle of August. Because of losses and battle damage, we had only twelve to fifteen serviceable planes left instead of the twenty-five authorized. The strain of flying so many missions took a greater toll on the airplanes than on the pilots.

Moose Elker led a mission of eight P-40s to strafe in the area north of Changsha. As we passed Dog Dog two-four on the way north, we spotted several Japanese airplanes parked along the runway. We finished our strafing mission, and as we approached Dog Dog two-four on the way back, Moose took the lead flight down to strafe the airplanes while the second flight stayed up for top cover. I was watching Moose's flight as they swept across the airfield and saw both sides of the runway light up with automatic weapons fire, with tracers all around the flight. One of the P-40s suddenly began trailing white smoke, and I yelled, "Someone in the low flight is trailing coolant. Better get the hell out of there." Moose looked at the other three P-40s and saw that none of them was smoking. He said, "Oh shit, not again," and turned west. We followed him from a distance so as not to give his position away to the Japanese. He was soon well away from the river, and I was relieved to see him bail out and his chute open. As Moose said later, "I landed on my ass in a guerrilla's front yard."

After we landed, the other pilots in Moose's flight said that the airplanes were dummies used just to draw us down into the ground fire. It worked well; all four of the aircraft were hit, but only Moose was hit in a vital spot. I could appreciate how ducks must feel when they approach decoys in front of a duck blind.

Although we were sure that Moose was okay and would walk back, we were downhearted because we knew he would have to leave the squadron. It was standard practice to send pilots home or at least keep them from flying combat in China if they were shot down in Japanese territory. If the Japanese learned the pilot's name from his parachute or from the plane and he were shot down a second time and captured, the pilot might be tortured into revealing information about the guerrillas who had rescued him the first time.

Moose had argued, when they tried to send him home after he walked back the first time, that since his airplane had exploded and burned and he had brought his chute back, there was no way the Japanese could have his name. Group headquarters accepted his reasoning, and he was allowed to keep flying, but we knew that it would not work a second time.

Moose was one of the most popular pilots in the squadron. Besides being a first-class combat pilot who always pressed home his attacks regardless of the opposition, he had a great sense of humor and helped to keep morale at a high level. His latest trick was to see who could lean at the greatest angle, both forward and to the side, at attention, without falling. Strangers visiting the squadron would have thought that they, or we, were completely insane. Everyone was practicing leaning, alone or in groups. Moose was the undisputed champion; he could lean at impossible angles with no apparent strain.

A day or so later I almost made a major purchase of agricultural real estate, or, in the vernacular, bought the farm. That dreaded disease, target fixation, that killed Vurgaropoulos and others just missed getting my favorite pilot, me. I was making a pass at a compound with some horses and soldiers in the open area. As I got closer, I saw more men hidden under the front overhang. I steepened my dive to bring my guns to bear and kept firing too long. I thought I would fly through the building as I hauled back on the stick with all my strength, pulling at least 6 g. My wingman said that I pulled the heaviest streamers he had ever seen off my wing tips and that I had cleared the roof by inches. The leader of the high flight said that he too was impressed by the size and duration of the streamers seen against the ground. About a week later he was leading a mission in the same area, and when he landed, he said, "Lope, I flew over that compound you nearly hit, and the streamers were still there." Streamers, of course, never last more than a few seconds.

The day after my close call, we suffered a real loss. Sack Folmar had been strafing some troops up near Changsha under heavy ground fire when suddenly his plane burst into flames and dived into the ground. He was killed on his 121st mission. The normal tour was 100 missions, but Sack had volunteered to stay on. He was a fine pilot and leader and a good friend who never missed a mission, despite constant bouts with dysentery. He was a wonder at finding Japanese on the ground. Tex Hill said that Sack worked the country like a champion bird dog. Although we took the deaths of our pilots as a matter of course, Sack was such a mainstay and good friend that it was hard to think of his not being there.

Later in the war Dick Jones and I were stationed at Eglin Field, Florida, about forty miles from Sack's hometown of Pensacola. Dick and I called his parents, and the following weekend we borrowed a car and spent the afternoon with them and other members of his family. The shock of his loss had eased, and they wanted to know all we could tell them. They were gratified to learn how highly he was regarded, as a pilot and a man, by his squadron mates. Admittedly, it was a small compensation for a life, but I'm sure our reminiscing helped ease the pain. Giving your life for your country was more easily accepted in World War II than in later wars, because the entire country supported the war and believed that the Nazis and Japanese had to be defeated at all costs.

The day after Sack's death, the intelligence officer gave me a small canvas bag with a long red streamer attached. I said, "What's in this, a rock?" He said there was a rock and a message for the surrounded Chinese troops in Hengyang. They had lost radio contact a few days before, and I was to drop the message in the city on the way back from the mission. On the return flight I peeled out of the formation and dived to about fifty feet above the main street of Hengyang. I opened the canopy just like in the movies and threw the bag over the side as I approached the building used as the headquarters, but unlike in the movies, I didn't salute. I didn't see any signs of life in the city, so I'm not sure anyone received the message. If the commander of the Chinese was in the headquarters, it was a good news, bad news situation for him. The good news was that he would receive a message from his commander; the bad news was that it was tied to a rock approaching at 250 mph. Two days later we learned that after more than six weeks of a heroic defense by the Chinese Tenth Army, the Japanese had taken the city. If the other Chinese troops had fought as well, we might have stopped the Japanese.

A few days after that, Quig was shot down. His flight was down strafing some troops along the river north of Hengyang. It was a large concentration of troops, and he led the flight on several strafing runs. I was in the top cover, and as he was making his third pass I saw his P-40 burst into flames, continue on for a few seconds, and then plow into the ground. I yelled, "Was that Quig?" His element leader replied, "Yeah, but he bailed out." The low flight pulled up from the target. They didn't continue to strafe because they might hit Quig or at least infuriate the Japanese even more. We returned to base in low spirits. We hated the thought of losing Quig, both as a friend and as a commanding officer. I was certain that the enemy would kill him if he survived the minimum-altitude bailout; we all thought he was dead, although he was officially reported as missing. After the war we learned that he had indeed survived the bailout, been taken prisoner, and spent the rest of the war in a prison camp.

When we landed and reported the loss to Tex Hill, he said that losing Folmar and Quigley in the same week was like losing two right arms. Tex could always get the most meaning into the fewest words.

During a stretch of bad weather, we caught up with the news of the rest of the war, some from intelligence digests but most from the shortwave radio. The Allies were sweeping through France and had liberated Paris on August 25, while the heavy bombers of the Eighth Air Force by day and RAF Bomber Command by night pounded Germany with thousand-plane raids. The long-range P-51s were now able to escort the American bombers to and from the target, greatly reducing the threat of the German fighters. In the Pacific, Tinian and Saipan in the Marianas Islands had been captured and were being readied for use as B-29 bases. The B-29s were bombing Japan from their China bases, but the missions were few and far between because of the long distance to be covered and the necessity of flying all their fuel over the Hump. The Soviets were driving the Germans back toward Germany along the entire Eastern Front. They had retaken much of Rumania and were threatening Hungary.

We were without a CO for about a week. Then Segura, Gray, Jones, and I, along with a couple of the other senior flight leaders, were called up to Tex Hill's office to meet our new CO, Major Home.

He was small, dressed in a clean, well-pressed uniform (a rarity in China), with a number of ribbons (more of a rarity in China) and shiny paratrooper boots. He had already served a combat tour, early in the war, flying P-40s in the Pacific. We were impressed with his appearance and apparent eagerness for combat and thought he might be a pretty good replacement for Quig. How wrong we were.

15

THE BREAKING
OF A MUSTANG

September and October were the most discouraging months I spent in China. The Japanese advance toward Kweilin from the north and toward Liuchow, about 100 miles south of Kweilin, from Canton continued. Despite our strong efforts in the air, we were forced to evacuate our main bases. The Japanese were well on their way to achieving one of the goals of their drive, a land transportation link from Peking to Indochina. Meanwhile, the squadron's morale plummeted under the miserable leadership of the new CO.

By early September, battle damage and losses had left the squadron with only four serviceable airplanes, so the group commander took us off operations for a short rest. One of the fighter groups in the Chengtu area was switching from P-40s to P-47s, and we were to get fifteen of the P-40s. Segura, Gray, Jones, three other pilots, and I were sent to Chengtu to ferry them back. We went by C-47 to Kunming, and the next day we flew to Chengtu in a C-87, landing at the main base.

Chengtu was in Szechuan Province, about four hours, as the P-40 flies, northwest of Kweilin. The country was relatively flat in that area, but the Himalayas rose sharply from the plains about eighty miles to the west. The flat land and the distance from the Japanese bases were factors in the selection of Chengtu for the B-29s of the newly formed 20th Bomber Command. The B-29s were to carry out a plan for the sustained bombing of Japan, code-named Matterhorn. At the time of the decision to implement Matterhorn, China was the only Allied territory from which the B-29s could reach Japan. When Chengtu was selected, 300,000 Chinese were put to work to build the airfields, using primitive hand tools and ample doses of sweat labor to construct the gravel and mud runways. Dozens of airfields with long runways were required for the bombers and the fighters that were to protect the bases. The B-29 runways required tremendous effort because of their length, 8,000 to 10,000 feet, and the extra depth needed to support the heavy bombers. Working night and day, the Chinese completed the runways in a few months.

The B-29s made their first raid on Japan on June 14, but they were unable to carry out the sustained effort expected of them. The missions required more fuel than could be ferried over the Hump. In the months that followed, the B-29s made sporadic raids on Japan, Manchuria, and other targets from China, but it was not until they moved to the newly captured islands in the Marianas in late 1944 that they became really effective.

Since the complex of bases in the Chengtu area was spread out, we were flown by C-47 to the field where the P-40s were based and met the pilots who were to fly the other eight P-40s. Heavy rain and low ceilings kept us from leaving for two days, but on the third day the weather was marginal and we decided to have a go. Segura was leading, and he thought we could make it at least as far as Chungking, about an hour to the southeast, where we could land and reassess the weather.

We had to dodge around some low clouds but made it to Peishiyi, the airfield at Chungking, without difficulty. Chungking was the wartime capital of China and Chiang Kai Shek's military headquarters as well. Peishiyi was the headquarters for the Chinese Army and for the Chinese American Composite Wing, commanded by Brigadier General Morse.

We moved into the transient hostel, which was far better than our hostel in Kweilin, more like our first hostel in Hengyang without the rats. The rooms were smaller, and there was a large recreation room with Ping-Pong tables and, best of all, hundreds of paperbacks that we had not read. Most of them were the special Armed Forces Edition paperbacks, including classics and assorted novels. There were far more than we ever got in the squadron.

That night we were delighted to find that the food was excellent. It was stateside food, not Chinese, and we, the group from the 75th, ate an embarrassing amount. Breakfast was just as good, featuring pancakes with nonfermented syrup. We told Flash to be sure the weather was perfect before we left, since we wouldn't mind staying a few extra days. As usual, Flash was way ahead of us. He had already told the base operations officer that Kweilin was socked in and there was no chance that we could leave that day.

After two and a half days of lounging around the rec room, reading, and waiting for the next meal while Flash regularly checked the weather and convinced the ops officer, as only Flash could, that it would be suicide for us to try to leave, General Morse called Flash to his office and told him that the 23rd Group was desperately in need of our aircraft and he should leave that afternoon. Although the weather was worse than it had been the past two days, we at least had to take off, since we had been given a direct order. I suspect that Morse was eager to see us leave because we were putting a tremendous dent in their rations.

Everyone managed to down a huge lunch and reluctantly made preparations to leave. I had loaded my bag with as many books as I could stuff in, but remembering my problems with the load of canned goods, I carefully tied down my bags as far forward as possible in the baggage compartment. We took off and followed Flash in a serpentine path as he dodged the worst of the weather and led us over the field at Chihkiang, where we could have landed if the weather had been too bad to proceed. I saw the field through a hole in the clouds but gave it only a cursory glance, not realizing that it would soon be our base for the rest of my stay in China. The weather looked a little better to the southeast, and we made it into Kweilin without incident.

When we taxied in to the flight line, I saw that there was a shiny new P-51C parked on the 75th line. I found that it was assigned to us and that we would be replacing our P-40s with P-51s within the next two months. I made up my mind to get checked out in the Mustang as soon as possible.

The next day I wasn't scheduled to fly, but I went to the flight line anyway and sat in the P-51 cockpit for a while to familiarize myself with the controls, which were close enough to those in a P-40 that I had no difficulty figuring them out. After about an hour, I went back into the alert shack to ask the CO if I could fly it. He wasn't there, and in fact there was no one there who outranked me, even though I was just a first lieutenant, so I gave myself permission.

I climbed in, started the engine, and taxied to the south end of the runway, where all the pilots and crew chiefs were out in front of the alert shack to watch. After checking the mags, I lined up with the runway and opened the throttle. The Mustang had a semilockable tail wheel, so it was much easier to keep straight on takeoff than a P-40, which always tried to escape from the straight and narrow. Also, it accelerated much faster than a P-40, but the takeoff run was about the same because it lifted off at a higher speed. The landing-gear retraction was simple because there was just a single handle to move from down to up, instead of the up, down, neutral, and operating trigger of the P-40. Another simplification was the automatic coolant shutter controls. Surprisingly, the cockpit was smaller and the pilot's visibility was not as good as from a P-40.

I climbed up to 10,000 feet in what seemed like half the time a P-40 took and flew around for about ten minutes to get the feel of the Mustang. It handled well, so I went through a series of stalls in the clean configuration and with the wheels and flaps down. It had a sharper stall than the 40 but recovered normally. I decided to try a few maneuvers over the field, both to try out the airplane and to show off a bit for the gallery below.

All this time I had been running on the internal wing tanks, as was standard in a P-40. The small fuselage tank in the 40 was always saved until last because it would feed by gravity if the fuel pump failed. The Mustang's fuselage tank was part of what made it a great airplane. Its large capacity gave the Mustang its outstanding long-range capabilities. Besides being large, it was farther back in the fuselage, causing the Mustang's center of gravity to be too far aft for safety in other than gentle maneuvers. The pilot's manual—which, unfortunately, I had never seen, since there was not one with the plane—prohibited aerobatics with much fuel in the fuselage tank. Standard procedure in a Mustang called for using the fuselage tank first after emptying the drop tanks.

With perfect assurance, reflecting the élan of the fighter pilot, I dived down and pulled through in what was to be a large loop. As I pulled the loop a little tighter on top, the airplane did a sloppy half snap roll into a right-side-up attitude. In other words, it made an Immelman out of the loop. I didn't give it too much thought, being concerned mainly about how good it must have looked to those on the ground. Providentially, I climbed up a few thousand feet and dived down to start an Immelman. Just before I started to roll out on top, the airplane seemed to tighten up the loop by itself, then stalled violently and went completely out of control.

I was totally disoriented for a moment and was being tossed like a rag doll around the cockpit. Every few seconds I was suspended by my safety belt as I got a closer look at the mountains and airfield through the top of the canopy, where, as any fool knows, the sky should have been. I moved the controls in the approved recovery from an inverted spin and a normal spin without any results. The rapid approach to the earth continued. I was beginning to think about bailing out, when I chopped the throttle and, to my great relief, the gyrations stopped and I went into a straight dive toward the ground. Dives I knew how to get out of, and I made a long gentle pullout to avoid the possibility of a secondary stall. After flying around for another ten minutes, I came in and made a gentle peeloff, flew a wide pattern, and landed. The Mustang was easy to land and much easier to hold straight after landing than the 40. I didn't know what had caused the problem, but I knew enough to avoid anything requiring pulling back hard on the stick.

After I parked, the other pilots all crowded around and someone yelled, "What in the hell was that, Lope?" I explained, "That was a new maneuver I just invented called the Tootsie Roll." It must have made quite an impression. In 1978 I attended a reunion of the 75th, and when I walked in to register, Earl Green, whom I hadn't seen since 1945, saw me and yelled, "Done any Tootsie Rolls lately, Lope?"

Major Home had made a few changes while we were gone. He appointed a new operations officer, whose main qualification for the job, as far as I could tell, was that he was just as short as Home. He was liked well enough as a person, and there was no question whatsoever about his courage, but he was not a very good pilot, certainly not one that we would want to follow into combat. Home also was making a lot of stupid statements about our excessive losses while strafing and bombing that he intended to eliminate. We all agreed with the thought but not his suggested remedy, to stop strafing and bombing. He even threatened to have the bomb racks removed from the P-40s. Since we rarely flew escort missions, if we didn't bomb and strafe we would be of little use to the war effort. We doubted that the Japanese would be deterred if we flew great formation above them. When I say "we," I mean Segura, Gray, Jones, and a few of the other senior flight leaders. We were all irritated that Segura hadn't been made operations officer because, in addition to his skills as a pilot, he was a natural leader both in the air and on the ground. The squadron would have followed him anywhere.

Home also decided that the 75th wasn't ready to go back into action, although we now had enough planes. We spent the next few days test flying the transferred P-40s after our maintenance crews had checked over them. We spent a lot of time bitching about Home and his attitudes, completely the opposite from our previous COs. We in the 75th believed, and the record bore out our belief, that we were the best fighter squadron in China. We had been blessed with a series of outstanding, hard-fighting commanders, and we bitterly resented the idea of having some weenie CO trying to move us from the top of the heap.

We knew that the Japanese were still advancing, but we were shocked two days later, on September 11, when we were told at breakfast that Lingling had fallen a few days earlier and we would be moving from Kweilin to Chihkiang later in the day. It was the start of the evacuation of Kweilin. Because of my experience in the P-51, one fifty-minute flight in which I had nearly augured in, I flew it to our new base, a little more than an hour to the west of Kweilin. The complex of bases at Kweilin were completely evacuated, and the runways and facilities were destroyed within ten days of our departure. A few weeks later it was captured by the Japanese. It was deeply discouraging to have to retreat when we had regularly defeated the Japanese in the air. Without good ground troops, there was little we could do, considering how few planes and how little fuel were available to us. My mother even wrote and said, "Why are you in the only theater where we're losing?" All I could say was "I'm doing my best, Mom."

When I arrived at Chihkiang I found that four more Mustangs had been delivered there for the 75th. We moved into the hostel, and some of the other pilots checked out in the new airplanes. I didn't know it then, but I had flown my last mission in a P-40. The P-51 I'd first flown was assigned to me, and as soon as possible I had "Lope's Hope III" painted on the nose. Not only did I give up the P-40, but my great crew chief, Sgt. Ralph Key, also received his orders to go back to the States. I hated to see him go because he was a good friend as well as a top mechanic, but he had been overseas for two and a half years and was long overdue for rotation. A C-47 that flew some of our ground crews from Kweilin was leaving for Kunming, and he was able to catch a ride almost immediately. I barely had time to say good-bye before he left. It was hard to get used to having someone else help me on and off with my harness before and after missions, and it was some time before I felt as confident about the condition of my airplane as I had when he was crewing it. Cpl. Jack Harrier, who replaced him, did a first-class job, but I didn't have too many missions left to complete my tour, so we never built up the same rapport.

The ground crews deserve a tremendous share of the credit for the fine performance of our squadron. They got up before dawn every day to ready the airplanes for the morning missions. They performed their arduous tasks late into the night in all kinds of weather to keep their charges in top shape. They refueled the fighters from 55-gallon drums with hand pumps and strained the fuel through chamois to filter out the water, rust, and other sediment, and they did it in the broiling sun in the short periods between missions. At the same time, the armorers clambered on and under the hot wings, manhandling the heavy bombs and ammunition belts and changing gun barrels when necessary. Every night the guns were carefully cleaned and lubricated, and the airplanes were inspected for damage, while plugs (twenty-four per engine) were changed if necessary, new magnetos were installed, and carburetors were adjusted. This monotonous work was done day in and day out without the relief of days off, which the pilots got regularly, and without the exhilaration of flying exceedingly unmonotonous missions.

The ground crews, especially the crew chiefs, fought the enemy vicariously through their pilots. They thrilled with every victory and successful mission, suffered when the airplane was damaged or the pilot was wounded, were devastated when their pilot was lost and overjoyed when he turned up safe. They received few promotions and fewer medals, but their dedication was unequaled.

This excerpt from the Fourteenth Air Force history describes the operations and operating conditions in China during that period:

> Forays against cavalry and bombing of supply dumps were alternated with sweeps up the Siang River and across Tungting Lake to catch the supply fleets. Mechanics worked all night in the steamy heat to repair damage from missions, replace worn parts, and have a full complement of planes ready for a dawn takeoff. As fast as planes returned from combat, armorers hung new loads of demolition and frag bombs under the wings and reloaded the guns. On many a mission pilots barely had time to dash to the alert shack, report on the mission, and be briefed on the next target before they were back in their cockpits on a new mission. As a result of the dissolving of the radio net, there was little weather information available, and they flew their own weather recons at dawn every day.

After a few days at Chihkiang, where our squadron was under the tactical command of Colonel Dunning, we were shown the two small grassfields, code named Texas and California, used to disperse some of the aircraft during full-moon periods, when bombing by the Japanese was likely. The P-51s were not camouflaged, and it was decided that they would always be dispersed, since the silver finish would show up brightly in the moonlight. On September 12, I flew my P-51 to Texas and spent the night, returning early in the morning. The other 51s were being inspected and were not in commission.

Two days later, when Major Home told me to lead the five Mustangs to Texas for the night, I had no idea that the overnight would become an overnightmare. Texas was not much more than 2,000 feet long and shaped like an acute isosceles triangle. Since there was barely room for a P-51 to turn around at the small end of the field, I briefed the pilots to land at least 45 seconds apart so that the preceding airplane could clear the end of the field before the next one arrived.

We took off at dusk, flew to Texas in loose formation, and peeled off to space ourselves for landing. I landed and turned at the end to taxi back down the left side of the field. When I was well clear of the end, Skip Stanfield rolled past me and started to turn to taxi. I turned to face the field, shut off my engine, and was climbing out of the cockpit just as the number three Mustang, flown by Dick Jones, was passing in front of me on his landing roll. Out of the corner of my eye I saw the fourth Mustang coming up behind Dick's plane at high speed. Pappy Parham had not only landed too close behind Dick, but he had also landed long and hot and probably couldn't have stopped at the end of the field. The problem of stopping was solved when he ran into the back of Dick's Mustang. His prop cut into the tank behind the cockpit, and it exploded with a fearful fireball. Dick's plane was turned 90 degrees by the impact and was now pointing toward my plane, while Pappy's Mustang went up on its nose, balanced for a second or two, and fell back onto its belly as the gear collapsed.

I rushed toward Dick's plane to help him get out, but he had released his straps and was running along the wing by the time I got there. He had a burn on his cheek but was otherwise uninjured. A few seconds later, Pappy came running around from behind his plane carrying his chute. He was not injured at all. I ran back to my plane to move it because Dick's plane was aiming directly at mine, and I knew the guns would be going off soon from the fire. I obviously was a bit flustered, because I first tried to push the four-ton airplane by myself, with no success whatsoever. Then I jumped into the cockpit to start the engine and taxi it out of danger, but forgetting that the engine had just been shut down, I primed it too much and flooded the carburetor. The prop was turning over and flames were pouring out of the stacks, but it didn't start for what seemed an eternity, probably a full ten seconds. Once it started, I taxied it several hundred yards away and walked back to where Dick and Pappy were crouched behind a stone roller, watching the fire.

I yelled to Skip to see if he was all right; he said he couldn't get his airplane past the fire, so he had parked it as far away as possible and was lying in a ditch, also watching the fire. A few minutes later the last airplane landed safely, parked down near mine, and the pilot, Lieutenant Beard, came to join us behind the roller. He had been recently transferred to the squadron, so we weren't too well acquainted.

Since everyone was safe, we settled back to enjoy the fireworks, which were spectacular, to say the least. More than 500 gallons of gasoline, 2,000 rounds of ammunition, two oxygen tanks, two containers of colored flares, and various magnesium parts make quite a show. The whole countryside was lighted and Chinese spectators were coming from everywhere to watch. We were laughing and joking about having our own Fourth of July, how it was the best we had ever seen, and that we should pass the helmet among the Chinese to collect for the entertainment.

Suddenly, to our utter amazement, Beard started cursing us. He said he'd never seen such a bunch of heartless bastards. How could we laugh and joke while Stanfield was burning to death in that inferno. He had joined us after I had checked with Skip and thought that Skip's plane was in the crash. To further discomfit him, we said that Skip would have wanted us to enjoy his cremation, especially since it was such a flamboyant way to go, and that Skip always did things with a touch of class. We went on with this charade for a while, becoming more and more heartless, until he stomped away in a rage. He didn't appreciate our sick humor, even after the rest of us, Skip included, joined him in the hostel about an hour later. Thus ended the infamous Texas barbecue. I'm not sure that the women of the world could have survived the loss of Skip. He was an extremely handsome and youthful-looking blond known to the squadron as the Golden One.

The next morning the hostel manager took Dick Jones and me by jeep to a small clinic about five miles away run by a Navy doctor. I had no idea what he was doing there, and he didn't volunteer any information. The doctor was probably tied in with some intelligence team. He treated Dick's burn, which he confirmed was superficial, and we drove back to Texas. The manager said that he would drive Dick and Pappy back to Chihkiang that afternoon.

Somewhat apprehensive, Skip, Beard, and I flew back to Chihkiang and landed. When Major Home came out to the airplane I told him that 40 percent of the squadron's Mustangs had been destroyed. He didn't seem too concerned, once he knew that both pilots were okay. He said that three more Mustangs were en route from Kunming. We were holding this conversation on the wing of my Mustang when suddenly I heard a radial engine, looked up, and saw an Oscar diving straight toward the runway. I yelled, "Zero," and jumped off the wing to head for the ditch, as did Skip and Beard. I was surprised that no one else ran, and we were relieved and embarrassed to learn that it was a captured Oscar that had been flown in that morning and had just taken off before we arrived. It was lucky for the Chinese Oscar pilot that we hadn't crossed paths in flight, because he would surely have been the first Chinese pilot shot down in an Oscar.

The next day, September 16, I flew my first mission in a P-51. Dick Jones, Jesse Gray, Joe Brown, and I flew top cover in Mustangs for two flights of CACW P-40s that were to strafe in the Hengyang area. Colonel Dunning had informed Home in no uncertain terms that we would indeed continue to strafe and bomb. One of the wing-tank fuel caps was loose on Dick's plane and he was streaming fuel, so he switched to that tank to burn it out first and continued with the mission. We reached the target area, and the P-40s were just starting down, when ten or twelve Oscars and Tojos dived out of the clouds and jumped us. One of them latched on to Dick, who racked it into a tight turn to get away. Since his fuselage tank was still full, he snapped into a Tootsie Roll, and as he went spinning down, we heard the Japanese pilot say, "That's what I call *ee*-vasive action."

I pulled up above the Japanese, rolled over, and dived on them. As I lined up on a Tojo, he went into a tight turn. I was able to get enough lead to fire, but when I pulled the trigger, all four guns jammed after a few rounds. I was really frosted, because I had gotten some hits on his fuselage with the few rounds that I fired. I'm certain I would have nailed him had the guns fired properly. Jesse and I dived on two that were down low, but they pulled away into the clouds, as did the others.

Dick had recovered, and the four of us regrouped over the P-40s and completed the mission. When we got back, I found that Jesse's and Joe's guns had also jammed when they fired them in a high-g turn. This was to become a serious problem for us in the P-51Bs and Cs. The Mustang wing was so thin that the four .50-caliber machine guns, instead of the six we carried in the P-40, had to be tilted to the side to fit. It affected the belt feed mechanism, which stopped feeding ammunition at 2 to 3 g. There was no problem with strafing, which was normally done at 1 g, but it made air combat almost impossible. The feed was modified a few months later, which helped, but the problem was never fully solved until the P-51Ds, with thicker wings and six guns mounted upright, replaced the Bs and Cs.

The gun problem was all the more irritating because the Mustang was so much faster than the Oscars and Tojos that we didn't have to dive to evade their attacks. We could easily outrun them in level flight. Although the Mustang was no more maneuverable than the P-40, it (except for the guns) was more than a match for the Japanese.

The next six weeks were miserable as both the weather and the squadron's morale deteriorated. I flew only two missions in that period, one escort mission that did not encounter any opposition and one strafing mission. It was the first time I had strafed in the P-51, and I did not like it as well in this role as the P-40. I preferred the six guns to the four of the Mustang, visibility was better from the P-40 cockpit, and the P-40 seemed to handle better for strafing. Possibly that was because I had more than 400 hours in the P-40 and fewer than 15 in the Mustang.

Our respect for the CO diminished daily. He never led or even flew on a squadron mission the whole time he was there, and he saw that the squadron flew as few missions as possible. Many times when the weather was marginal he called off flying, although we had flown any number of missions in worse weather in the past. He said that our tight formation flying, which we did only when close to the base before landing, wasn't up to snuff, so he made us fly locally to practice, wasting precious fuel and time. It was especially irritating, because we could fly formation as well as anyone. He never took the trouble to evaluate our combat formation, since that might have entailed flying a mission.

Colonel Dunning was becoming more and more fed up with Home; they were as unlike as two men could be. Dunning was a firebreather who led every tough mission, while Home was all talk and no action. Dunning finally told him to stop wasting fuel with all this practice flying and try burning some in combat. As a result of this demand, Home started flying private two-man missions with the operations officer as his wingman. They would take off in two Mustangs, disappear to the east, and return in about three hours. We didn't know what they did, but we knew what they didn't do: they didn't go near the ground, because they used a lot of oxygen, and they didn't fire their guns, because the tape over the muzzles was unbroken. The ground crews were as demoralized as the pilots; what little pleasure they got was through the pilots' exploits, and we were doing nothing.

The only thing worse than Home's leadership was his flying ability. He consistently made the worst landings I had ever seen. The ops officer wasn't too good, but Home was deadly. Each landing was a barely controlled crash. He would stall too high and drop it in from ten feet or more, then the next time he would fly it into the ground and all but embed the wheels in the runway. We all took pride in our flying ability and good landings. It was embarrassing enough when any 75th pilot made a terrible landing, but doubly so when the CO made one every time in front of our pilots and the CACW pilots in the next alert shack.

Home finally ripped it completely when he and his wingman came back from one of their mystery missions and were interrogated by Colonel Dunning instead of by the intelligence officer. When Home told him they had seen several Japanese fighters taxiing on the field at Dog Dog two-four, Dunning yelled, "You little bastard, why in the hell didn't you go down after them?" Home made some lame excuse, and Dunning stomped away after telling Home to stay the hell out of his sight. After that, Home sent Segura or me to the nightly operations briefing by Colonel Dunning. Dunning would end his briefing by telling the 75th representative to "pass the information on to the little son of a bitch," or some similarly complimentary epithet. Things had to be really bad for a professional soldier like Colonel Dunning to refer to a squadron commander in that way to the commander's subordinates; the colonel could tolerate anything but cowardice, especially in a CO.

For three straight weeks in October I didn't fly at all. That was primarily because of the weather but also because Home's operations officer kept most of the senior flight leaders on the ground while sending some of the others on half-assed missions. Segura, Jones, Gray, and I were really fed up. With little else to do, we had a lot of time to bitch. Home must have gotten wind of our bitching (it would have been hard not to), so one night he called a meeting of all the officers in his room.

When we were all assembled, he harangued us for a while about all he had done for the squadron and how he demanded loyalty from all his officers at all times. He paused dramatically and said, "Segura, stand up. Have you been telling all the new pilots that I was a yellow, no good son of a bitch?" Segura, standing at attention, said quite seriously, "No, sir, I don't know how they found out." It took us all, Home included, about ten seconds to register the comment. Home turned bright red, while we all fought to suppress our laughter, with little success, except for those in the front row. Home immediately dismissed us and said, "Segura, come see me in the morning." If possible, Segura's reputation for wit and courage was even higher than it had been. Early the next day, in the alert shack, he ordered Segura to take one of our P-51s that had lost its canopy in flight and fly it to Texas and not to return without his permission. Segura, glad to get a chance to fly, climbed into his Mustang convertible, took off under the low clouds, and disappeared to the northeast. We checked by phone and learned that he had landed safely, although I'm sure Home didn't care.

The next day the weather was clear, and around noon a sparkling P-51 with 23rd Group markings landed. It was Colonel Loofbourrow, now the group commander, who had gotten out of a sickbed to fly to Chihkiang and relieve Home as CO. He said he was sorry for not doing it sooner, but he had been ill and was unaware of what was happening to his squadron. Home left that afternoon by C-46 for Wing Headquarters at Luliang, where, we heard, he became wing mess officer. It was probably just wishful thinking, but he surely had tried to make a mess of the 75th.

We sent the happy word to Texas for Segura to return, because he was to be in charge until we got a new CO. Segura finally showed up two days later and was overjoyed to find that Home was gone. Flash had not wasted his time at Texas. He said that he had found a Chinese painter who had camouflaged his plane so well that he couldn't find it for two days. He had decorated the plane with the name of his fiancée, later his wife, Joy Rita, in flowing script. Instead of the standard small Japanese flags denoting victories, he had painted a sky and cloud scene with large Japanese flags billowing on flagpoles, one for each of his victories. Those billowing flags symbolized the way we all felt with Home gone, free as the breeze.

Shortly thereafter Flash received orders to return to the States. What a loss to the squadron—his wit, leadership, and constant good humor had been a major boost to morale, especially during the difficult days of the Home regime. Flash had a successful Air Force career, retiring as a brigadier general with the same reputation he enjoyed in the squadron. He is without a doubt one of the funniest and finest men I've known. He went on to become a successful businessman. Just recently he told me he had bought a Rolls Royce and was going to have a shark's mouth painted on the front. Knowing Flash, he may not have been kidding.

About ten years later, when I was a student at the Air Force Institute of Technology, Capt. Bill Skliar was in the seat next to me for most of our classes. In the course of becoming better acquainted, we were discussing various COs under whom we had served. After talking about some of the good ones, I said that the worst one I'd ever served under or even heard of was Home, although I didn't mention his name. After I had described his actions, Bill allowed that he sure sounded bad, but he had served under a worse one. He then described the actions of the CO of the squadron he had just left to attend the school. I said he had a strong case but still thought mine was the worst. Finally we got around to the names of our respective candidates and found that they both were good old Home. He was still setting new standards for nonleadership.

The next week, on the first of November, we received word that sixteen Mustangs were available for us to pick up at Kunming immediately, and the ops officer told me that I was to lead our remaining fifteen P-40s to Luliang that afternoon. Luliang, where 23rd Group Headquarters and the rear echelon of our squadron were based, was only a short distance from Kunming.

There was an overcast at about 6,000 feet, and we would have to fly no lower than 10,000 feet to clear the mountains en route. The weather was good at Luliang and the overcast didn't look too thick, so I decided to give it a go. We had no operating flight instruments and couldn't climb through an overcast of any thickness without the strong probability of spinning out. I briefed the pilots that we would try to zoom through the overcast in elements of two in trail. My wingman and I would go first and would let the others know by radio how thick it was.

We took off, made a wide circle, and came across the field in show formation, since this was a memorable occasion, the last flight by the 75th in P-40s, and climbed on course to the southwest. We leveled out just below the overcast and picked up as much speed as we could, then I zoomed up at a fairly steep angle and popped out on top 1,500 feet higher. I started a slow circle and called to the others to follow. It was a bit like watching a dolphin show at Sea World, seeing the P-40s pop up through the overcast in pairs. The old reliables seemed to be enjoying it. We assembled and proceeded to climb on course toward Luliang, about two and a half hours away.

Navigation was always a bit dicey in China because the maps were not too accurate, there were few prominent landmarks, and we had little or no weather forecasting, especially of the winds. I corrected enough to the north to be sure that I wouldn't pass to the south of Luliang if I missed it. There was a small lake at Luliang and two large lakes near Kunming. If the weather was as reported, I was sure that I would be able to spot the lakes by looking to the south. We were about fifteen minutes out, according to my time and distance calculations, and I had just spotted the large lakes at Kunming, when Dick Jones called and said that he had seen some bright flashes on the ground at about ten o'clock from us. I turned toward them, and as we got closer, I could see that the flashes were the sun reflecting off silver B-24s on the ground at Luliang, the China version of a navigational aid. We landed and taxied to the designated area, where we were met by Capt. Myron Levy, our adjutant, who said we would be spending a few days in Luliang since the P-51s were still being inspected.

During the next few days I ferried a couple of P-40s to Kunming and checked on the progress of the P-51s. On my second trip I met our new CO, the fifth I'd served under, who was also checking on the Mustangs. He was Maj. Clyde B. Slocumb, of Doerun, Georgia. He had already flown a tour in China with the Sixteenth Fighter Squadron when it had been attached to the 23rd Group. He had a pleasant and relaxed manner, and I liked him at once. He turned out to be as good as Home had been bad. I stayed in Kunming with Slocumb, and the next day the rest of the pilots came over in a Goony Bird. Each was assigned a Mustang and told to test hop it that day. It was the first flight in a P-51 for some of the pilots, so we gave them careful cockpit checks. That afternoon Slocumb said he had decided how he wanted to mark our new airplanes. The shark teeth didn't look good on a P-51, so he decided to paint the entire tail section a dull black.

No sooner said than done. He went away and came back shortly with a spray gun, a compressor, masking tape, and several gallons of paint. He never said where he had gotten them and we didn't ask, but by that evening we had painted all the airplanes. The next day we took off for Chihkiang with Slocumb leading and with me leading the second flight. About halfway there he had some problems with his radio and instruments. He rocked his wings till I came up alongside, then signaled for me to take the lead, so I led the rest of the way in. When we were in sight of the field I waved to him to lead the squadron over the field before landing. Our shiny silver Mustangs with dull black tails made a beautiful sight that did much to restore our pride and morale. We were now within four of our authorized strength of twenty-five fighters, and they were all P-51s.

Later that day, Major Slocumb gathered all the pilots in the alert shack and introduced himself. He said he knew we'd been having problems, but we were going to rejoin the war. Everyone was as impressed with him as I was. He asked the ops officer and me to stay and go over the records and capabilities of the pilots. He saw that I had 99 missions and that one more would complete my tour. He said he would need some experienced leaders for a few months and asked if I would continue past 100 missions. I said I would be glad to.

The next day we got word that Group wanted one or two P-51s to fly to Hankow at night to strafe the searchlights that were locating our night bombers. Segura had flown one such mission just before he left. I said that I would go, but Slocumb decided that he and the ops officer would go the following night and that I would go the next time we sent bombers to Hankow. They took off singly at about 10:30 p.m. on November 10, and Slocumb returned alone after midnight. They had not flown to Hankow together, since they had separate targets, and he had seen nothing of the other Mustang. A few weeks later we learned that the ops officer had gotten lost on the return trip and had bailed out safely far to the west of us when his fuel ran out. I was honored and pleased when Slocumb appointed me operations officer and second in command of the squadron.

The next morning one of the reconnaissance flights reported Japanese aircraft on our former airfields at Hengyang, Lingling, and Kweilin. As soon as we could brief, I led a mission of sixteen Mustangs to attack all three bases. I would lead all the planes to Lingling, where we would attack any Japanese aircraft we found, then I would proceed south to Kweilin with eight while Captain Kelley, a recent arrival with combat experience in Europe, led the second eight north to Hengyang. About halfway to Lingling my wingman pulled in close and pointed to his canopy, which looked as though it was about to rip off. I waved him back to Chihkiang, but he shrugged to indicate he wasn't sure how to get there. I signaled to him to steer 284 degrees, and he peeled out of the formation. He proclaimed me a master navigator after that because he held that heading slavishly and crossed the landing end of the runway. I never told him it was just a rough guess aimed only at bringing him within sight of the field.

I took the first two flights down over Lingling at high speed, but as there was no sign of activity, I started climbing toward the south while Kelley took his flights toward Hengyang. As we were approaching Kweilin, I heard a lot of commotion on the radio, shouts of "Zeros" and "Break," and someone said, "Get up here, Lope!" I turned north, rammed the throttle to almost full power (I had to leave a small margin for the rest of the formation), and started a gentle climb so I would be above the Zeros when I got there. Even at our high speed it took some thirty minutes to reach the Hengyang area. The radios had long been silent, although I tried to call Kelley several times when I was sure I wouldn't block out calls from others in his flight. I made several circles in the haze, searching for other aircraft without spotting any. I was just starting down to take a look at the airfield when I saw a group of about fifteen enemy aircraft flying in our direction, but several thousand feet below. We dived toward them—I don't think they had seen us yet—and made a quartering head-on pass at the leader, which I identified as a Nakajima Ki-84 Frank. I saw many strikes on his engine, and smoke began to pour out. I broke off and pulled into a tight right turn to fire at one of the Japanese in the rear, but all of my damned guns jammed as I fired. That was the second chance at a victory I'd lost because of those useless guns. The Japanese broke down into the haze layer and we lost them. We searched for a while with no luck, and then went down and took a look at the airfield, but there were no airplanes there either, so we climbed to the west and returned to Chihkiang.

Kelley had landed with the remains of his two flights about thirty minutes before. His flight had been surprised by a mixed flight of Oscars, Tojos, and one or two Franks. Three Mustangs had been shot down immediately (Gadberry, Miller, and Taylor), and a fourth, Riley, had been badly damaged but had gotten well back into our territory before bailing out. We thought the first three were dead, but Gadberry returned a few months later and Taylor was taken prisoner. That was the worst loss we had suffered in the air in one fight since I'd been in China. Kelley and the survivors of the first attack had claimed four Japanese destroyed and two probables, while I claimed the one I had left smoking as a probable and Rosenbaum, the element leader in my flight, claimed an Oscar probable. Two weeks later Chinese intelligence reported that nine Japanese fighters had been found on the ground, so all our probables were confirmed.

As soon as we had refueled and rearmed, we went back to the Hengyang area with twelve airplanes to see if we could find any Japanese. Slocumb went along, but he told me to lead since I knew the territory better. He had no problems with ego. We found nothing, but on the way back some broken clouds had formed just over the mountains. I stayed well above them since I was sure there would be big enough holes over the field to dive down through. Someone called and said, "Lope, better get under those clouds." I didn't answer but held my altitude, even though I thought it must have been Slocumb who had called. Since I was leading the mission, I would use my best judgment, but I wasn't sure how Slocumb would react. The same call was repeated twice more, but I stayed at my altitude, expecting to be chewed out when we landed. There were only scattered clouds over the base, and we landed with no problem. I approached Slocumb with some trepidation and explained that I didn't think it would have been smart to be screwing around in the mountains under the clouds. He didn't know what I was talking about, and when I told him, he asked the assembled pilots who had called. One of the junior birdmen flight officers, who had joined the squadron a few weeks earlier, said that he had called because he was afraid we would have to make an instrument letdown when we got back. Slocumb chewed him up one side and down the other for giving advice at all, for not identifying himself, and for giving such bad advice. That mission, my hundred and first, was the last combat mission I ever flew in China. Fittingly perhaps, it and my hundredth were flown on November 11, 1944, Armistice Day.

16

CLIPPED
WINGS

I had expected to fly missions for several more months, but as soon as the report of my mission number 101 reached Group, they sent a message that I was not to fly another mission. One hundred was the limit, and Group was now strictly enforcing the rule because several pilots had been killed after passing 100, and there was no shortage of replacement pilots. Slocumb asked me to stay on for a while and help run the squadron. I said that I would stay as long as he needed me and that I could lead the flight that always remained on base alert when missions were out and so release another flight leader for missions. I had mixed feelings about this arrangement: pride in being asked to stay and disappointment in being barred from flying combat.

The situation in China was still grim. The city of Kweilin had been captured on November 10, Liuchow had fallen on the next day, and on November 22 the Japanese took the last Allied airfield along the corridor that ran from Hankow to Hanoi. We still had several bases to the east of the corridor, but the Japanese troops were moving toward them.

There was great fear that the Japanese would advance from Indochina and try to take Kunming, the vital China terminus of the Hump. Lt. Gen. Albert Wedemeyer, who had replaced General Stilwell as the theater commander, moved Chinese troops from Burma to China to oppose the drive, which fortunately never materialized.

We did have some good news. When Stilwell's forces captured Myitkyina in early August, Hump aircraft were able to fly much farther to the south and thus at a much lower altitude. In effect they were flying around rather than over the Hump. Within a few months the tonnage carried over the Hump had doubled and the Fourteenth Air Force supply of fuel and ammunition increased markedly.

In the rest of the world the Allies were advancing on all fronts. In the Pacific, MacArthur's troops had landed in the Philippines, while the U.S. Navy had virtually destroyed the remainder of the Japanese Navy in the Battle of Leyte Gulf. In Europe, the Germans were being driven back into Germany itself from France, Italy, and the Soviet Union. German cities were being hit by 1,000-plane raids as the Luftwaffe's day and night fighters were seriously handicapped by lack of fuel and the enormous loss of experienced pilots.

About this time, in September 1944, a new flight surgeon was assigned to replace Doc Laughlin. He was Dr. Francis P. Keefe, a surgeon from Olean, New York. He was in his thirties, already a fellow of the American College of Surgeons, married with several children. Since he was a surgeon, he was immediately nicknamed Butcher, or Butch. His medical skills and experience were highly regarded by his peers. The other two doctors at Chihkiang always deferred to him in any medical situation, although one of them outranked him. (Dr. Keefe died in April 1990, and I was honored to write a tribute to him in the 75th Fighter Squadron newsletter.)

He became much more to the squadron than just its flight surgeon. He knew that a fighter-squadron flight surgeon didn't have many calls for his services beyond the routine minor problems. Fighter pilots were only rarely wounded and even less rarely did they crash in the vicinity of the base. They either came back unwounded or didn't come back at all. He therefore dedicated himself to raising and maintaining the morale of the pilots, a task he was well suited for because of his fine sense of humor. I think he could have made it big in vaudeville had he been so inclined.

Despite the difference in our ages and experience, we became good friends. He had been practicing medicine for a number of years, and I, although not wet behind the ears, still had some dampness in that area. Our friendship began shortly after he arrived and I was appointed operations officer. He informed me that it was the primary duty of the operations officer to see that the flight surgeon got his four hours of flying each month in order to qualify for his flying pay. That had been so far down on my list of priorities that I had never given it a thought. I realized that it was extremely difficult for a nonpilot to get flying time in a single-seat fighter squadron, but I said that I would do my best.

The CACW had an old airplane that had been in the Chinese Air Force at one time. It was a North American NA-56, an export version of the BT-14, a two-seat trainer with fixed landing gear. I asked Warrant Officer McCullough if I could borrow it to fly with the doc, and he, with some reluctance, agreed. I soon understood his reluctance. Few of the instruments worked, the propeller control was so worn that the rpm fluctuated wildly, the elevator trim tab was hooked up backward, and McCullough warned me not to touch the right brake because it would lock.

With misgivings, but unwilling to lose face, I got Butch strapped in the rear seat and I climbed into the front. He was much more confident than I was as we started up and gingerly, erratically taxied to takeoff position, making all left turns, some of 270 degrees. If anyone had been watching my path from above, he would have thought that the plane, or the pilot, had been fueled with rice wine. I took off and climbed up to 3,000 feet, just below the base of the overcast, and started circling the field with gentle turns. After thirty minutes I asked Butch if he wanted to fly, and he eagerly took the controls. Except for a tendency to climb into the overcast from time to time, he did extremely well and stayed at the controls until I took over for landing. I returned that antiquated contraption safely to the CACW, but it shook and rattled so much in the air that I never risked another flight in it.

Flying time was still a problem, so I asked Capt. Monte Lyon (who commanded a detachment of three B-25s from the First Bomb Group, CACW, operating from Chihkiang) if Doc could fly with him on his test flights. He said that both Doc and I could fly with him, since he didn't use a copilot on most test flights. The flights were usually just short functional tests before the airplanes were loaded for their night bombing mission. They stayed over the Japanese airfields for most of the night, dropping occasional bombs more for harassment than destruction. The B-25 was extremely noisy in the cockpit, but I found that it handled well when Monte let me take the controls. On one flight, he let me make the takeoff. The doc was standing behind me, and as we started to roll, he leaned forward and began loudly reciting the Lord's Prayer in a wonderful display of confidence (not in me but in God).

On one of our B-25 flights, after we were airborne, Monte and I decided to let the doc log a mission, so I suggested that we strafe the town of Paoching. It was a mostly undefended village, with a small garrison right on the edge of Japanese-held territory about 100 miles east of Chihkiang. Monte said, "When I hear the name 'Paoching,' especially when it is followed by 'undefended,' it makes my blood boil. Let's go strafe it!" I flew the airplane toward Paoching while Monte took Doc into the nose and showed him how to operate the machine gun. Doc fired a practice burst, then Monte came back to the cockpit. Unfortunately, or maybe fortunately, the weather was too bad for us to reach Paoching, so it remained unstrafed and left Doc a saver rather than a taker of lives.

Doc's flying problems were solved a few weeks later when our engineering staff finished modifying our last P-40 into a two-seater by removing the fuselage tank and installing a second canopy. From then on the doc got most of his flying with me in the P-40, although we still flew in the B-25s now and then. In the P-40 we flew to Texas, which Doc had heard so much about but had not seen, and once we flew to the top of a mountain to the west so Doc could inspect a shrine that we could see outlined against the sky from Chihkiang. I was beginning to feel like a tour guide, except that Doc delivered the spiel.

The squadron was flying missions regularly, but without me, in the Yochow to Kweilin area, attacking Japanese transport of every type. It was hard to get used to not flying on the missions, but my operations duties took a lot of time, which helped. I did fly on a few interception missions when enemy aircraft were reported coming our way, but none ever reached the field, so I logged the missions as test flights to stay out of trouble.

When I became operations officer I moved into the hostel room with the CO and the intelligence officer, our unofficial headquarters. We had desks in the alert shack as well. The intelligence officer had joined the squadron at the same time as Slocumb. He was a big, florid, high-school football coach from Dallas named H. B. Harrison, who was well liked and respected. Since he proclaimed several times that his niece thought he was "the man who laid the chunk," whatever that meant, he was known as Chunk Harrison. He had a seemingly inexhaustible supply of "last" bottles of stateside liquor, which he and Slocumb consumed at regular intervals. The fact that I did not drink made me a most welcome roommate for them.

As ops officer I was able to review all of the intelligence summaries, and I was impressed by the effort that the units under the overall command of Gen. Casey Vincent (23rd Fighter Group, Fifth Fighter Group CACW, Eleventh and 491st Bomb squadrons, and Third and Fourth Bomb squadrons CACW) had made to stop the Japanese advance. In little more than two months, they had flown 5,287 sorties and dropped 1,164 tons of bombs. With only about 150 aircraft, they had wreaked havoc on the enemy's transportation lines but had lost only 3 airplanes to enemy aircraft.

There was a shortage of space in the hostel, so two new pilots, Ernest Harper and Sam Dance, moved in with us. Both were captains with a lot of flying experience but no combat. Sam and I quickly became good friends. He was tall and thin and had been raised on a plantation in Monticello, Georgia, so I called him Massa Sam, and before long everyone else did too. He had been married shortly before he came to China to a lovely WASP (Women's Airforce Service Pilot) who was stationed in Texas. When he was assigned an airplane, I helped him paste a *Cosmopolitan* magazine cover that looked like his wife on the side of the fuselage. We covered it with clear paint, and to my surprise, it never ripped off. We made an agreement that he would teach me all he knew about women, which he said was all that was worth knowing, if I would teach him about combat flying.

Apparently he was a better teacher than I was. About a month later he went on a dive-bombing mission over Hengyang led by Slocumb. When they returned Sam wasn't with them. I climbed up on Slocumb's wing and asked, "Where's Massa Sam?"

"I'm afraid there's no more Massa Sam, boy," Slocumb said. "He went straight into the ground on his dive-bombing run. He must have been killed by flak."

It was a real blow, to me and to the squadron. He was a fine pilot and would have taken over as operations officer in a few months.

Shortly thereafter we had another tragedy, much more immediate because we all saw it. Our armament officer had devised a method of carrying more bombs on the P-51s, which had plenty of lifting power but only two bomb racks. He mounted a 500-pound demolition bomb on each rack, then attached two sets of stabilized fragmentation bombs to each demolition bomb by short cables slung over the center bomb. Each set of stabilized frags had six small frag bombs mounted on a long, finned rod. With this arrangement a P-51 could drop two 500-pounders plus twenty-four frag bombs on a single run. One of my former roommates, Bob Bellman, known as the Joker because his smile was identical to that of the Batman cartoon character, was on a dive-bombing mission to Kweilin armed with this bomb load. One of his bomb racks did not release on his run, but he was not aware of it until another member of the flight called him. He spent most of the return flight trying unsuccessfully to jettison the bombs.

When the mission returned I noticed that one Mustang kept circling at some distance from the field while the others landed. I asked the flight leader what was wrong, and he told me that Bellman still had his bombs on one wing. He could have landed safely if it had been only the demolition bomb, because they were quite safe in the unarmed condition, but frags were another story. They were touchy and might explode even though not armed. Bombs can be released so they will not explode if the cockpit arming switch is left in the safe position. I sent up a Mustang to inspect the bomb from as close to Bellman as possible, then I climbed into the cockpit of a parked airplane, raised Bellman on the radio, and told him to try releasing the bombs while pushing over instead of while level or pulling positive g. I thought that the negative g might release the jam. He tried that several times, but the chase pilot saw no change. He tried porpoising the airplane to both positive and negative g with the electrical bomb release button held down and also with the manual release handle pulled. He tried releasing at 6 g and at high and low speed. He tried it at landing speed with gear and flaps down. All to no avail. The bombs remained firmly in place.

I was finally out of ideas, and none of the pilots, armorers, or crew chiefs had any suggestions to offer. By then Major Slocumb had joined us at the flight line, and he agreed that it was not worth the risk to try landing with the bombs on. The decision was made, and although he had fuel for at least another hour of flight, I told Bellman to go to the east of the field, head the airplane east, and bail out. He replied that he didn't want to lose the airplane and wanted to risk the landing. I said, "The hell with the airplane, bail out." Again he said that he would rather land. Slocumb got on the radio and said, "Bob, this is Major Slocumb. Forget about the damn airplane. Bail out. Don't try to land. It's not worth the risk." But Bellman was adamant; he would not bail out and was determined to land. He was a tough, high-spirited young man who knew how precious airplanes were in China and thought that the bombs were firmly lodged in the rack. Finally I told him that he could land in about fifteen minutes but to keep trying to shake the bomb in the meantime.

I told the chase pilot to land and had our pilots taxi our planes to the far end of the runway. I asked the CACW, in the next alert shack, to move its planes as well. Major Slocumb sent all personnel to the slit trenches behind the shacks while he and I and the doc got behind a large stone roller. A hush seemed to come over the field as Slocumb fired a green flare and Bellman came down to land. He flew a gentle pattern and made a smooth touchdown. He had rolled about 200 yards, and we thought he had made it, when suddenly all hell broke loose. The bombs dropped onto the runway and the frags exploded, setting the plane on fire and killing Bellman instantly. The Mustang, with a dead hand on the controls, rolled slowly down the runway, with flame and smoke pouring out of the fuselage, and then eased off to the right of the runway, coming to a stop in the soft dirt with the engine idling. We made a desperate but futile attempt to put out the fire with our small hand extinguishers, but it was burning too fiercely. We couldn't get near the cockpit but could see Bellman slumped in the seat, apparently dead. Doc Keefe later established that he had been killed instantly by the bomb shrapnel. The aft fuselage burned in two, causing the airplane's nose to rise sharply. It was an eerie sight, the nose pointing heavenward with the prop still turning over and poor Bob still strapped in his grotesque funeral pyre. The engine finally quit running, but the fire burned for hours. It was not until late that night that they could remove the body.

I was thankful not to be involved in that gruesome task. Bellman's death hit me harder than previous ones, because I had the nagging feeling that I should have some way persuaded him to bail out. Also, I think that not being permitted to share in the danger by flying combat added to my sense of guilt.

Although we had never had any trouble before with that bomb load, Slocumb prohibited its further use. He got no argument from the pilots.

Our mission activity was slowing because of the weather, but since the Mustangs had operable flight instruments, we were not as handicapped in bad weather as we had been in the P-40s. We now had a radio beacon at Chihkiang, but we didn't have the proper receivers for it in the P-51s. On several occasions when our fighters were due back and a solid overcast had moved in, we were able to get a C-47 or C-46 to home on the beacon and circle above the overcast. Our fighters used them as markers for starting their letdowns to the field. That was done only when the ceiling was well above the tops of the mountains in the area.

In late November we had two large surprise visitors a week or so apart. One afternoon we got a message that a B-29 would be making an emergency landing at Chihkiang in about thirty minutes. I doubted that a B-29 could land on our short runway (not much more than 3,000 feet long), especially since a sharp drop-off, almost a cliff, at the approach end made pilots tend to come in too high, especially bomber pilots. Not this bomber pilot. The B-29 broke out of the clouds right on schedule with one engine feathered, made a low pass to look over the runway, and then started a long straight approach. He was a master; the wheels cleared the end of the runway by about 2 feet, and he touched down gently in the first 200 feet and rolled to a stop without excessive braking, then taxied clear of the runway and parked. He did such a good job that I was tempted to break the fighter pilot's code and praise him.

We swarmed around the airplane, *The Deacon's Disciples*, piloted by Maj. Deacon Miller. Few of our pilots and none of our enlisted men had seen a B-29 before. He said that while they were bombing Formosa some flak had shot out one engine and caused them to lose so much fuel that they couldn't make it back to Chengtu. We spent the evening chatting with him and the crew about the B-29 operations. The next morning two C-46s arrived from Chengtu with repair crews and fuel, and the Deacon and his disciples took off for Chengtu that evening. The 20th Bomber Command was nervous about leaving one of its valuable B-29s on the ground so close to Japanese territory. It was an interesting interlude for us.

About two weeks later a second B-29 dropped in. This one had one engine feathered and one windmilling and was nearly out of fuel. It came straight in without looking over the field, and when the pilot landed (a bit longer than the Deacon's but still a good landing), he thought the runway was even shorter than it was, so he pulled the emergency brakes, locked both wheels, and sank almost wheel-deep in the gravel runway. This left us with two very short runways instead of one moderately short one, since the B-29 was embedded almost exactly halfway down the runway. We cleared our narrow taxi strip of parked aircraft so we could use it as a runway to provide fighter protection. The C-46s came in as before and landed on the taxiway with no trouble, but it was several days before the Chinese coolies could dig a ramp and allow the B-29 to taxi out. It then had to wait another day until the runway was repaired before it could take off. I'm sure the crew was as glad to leave as we were to see them go.

A few days later Slocumb had to go to Luliang for a week to handle some squadron business, leaving me in charge. While he was gone we were visited on separate occasions by the wing commander, Gen. Casey Vincent, and by our new group commander, Col. Ed Rector. Vincent was the prototype for the *Terry and the Pirates* character, Vince Casey. Rector, one of the original Flying Tigers, was right up there with Skip Stanfield in the handsome department. Both were aces.

The first we knew of General Vincent's visit was when his beautiful silver, stripped-down B-25, *The Silver Slipper*, appeared overhead and landed. We knew the airplane well, since it had been based at Kweilin when we were. He taxied it in front of our alert shack and shut down the engines. The Chunk and I met him as he climbed out of the hatch. He returned our salutes perfunctorily and asked where Major Slocumb was. I told him he had gone to Luliang that morning for a few days. When he learned that I had been left in charge, he looked surprised and, glancing at my first-lieutenant bar, said, "Jesus, you really have a lot of rank around here." Despite being a hardened veteran, I still wasn't shaving regularly and looked very young. I showed him around and answered a few questions about the condition of the squadron, after which he said to give his best wishes to Slocumb, whom he had flown with on Slocumb's first tour, and took off.

A few days later Colonel Rector landed in the first P-51D we had seen. It was beautiful, with its bubble canopy and *six* guns. Even without the 23rd Group insignia on the fuselage, I recognized Ed Rector, since I had seen his picture many times in *God Is My Copilot* and other books about the AVG. He was on his first inspection tour of all the squadrons in the group. I got all the pilots together to introduce him, and after chatting awhile, he said he wanted to inspect our auxiliary field, called California, for possible use as a base for another squadron. I offered to lead him over it in another Mustang, since it was a bit hard to spot unless you knew the area. But he didn't want to risk landing his new Mustang where the ground might be too soft from all the rain we'd been having, and he definitely wanted to land and inspect the surface and the surrounding area for hostels and other facilities. I then offered to guide him from the back seat of our two-seat P-40, but he insisted that I fly it, since I knew the area.

After lunch we climbed into the P-40 and took off for California. After a flight of about twenty minutes I spotted the field and circled for a while so Colonel Rector could get a view of the layout. I flew down the grass runway a few feet above it, and it appeared dry. To add to my confidence, a number of Chinese officials and soldiers were giving us a thumbs up and laying a panel to show the direction of landing. I peeled up, landed, and taxied to the area indicated by the Chinese and cut the engine.

We climbed out, and the Chinese delegation, the leader of whom spoke good English, gave a comprehensive tour of California that lasted about an hour and a half. After much bowing and handshaking, they left and we returned to the P-40. To our dismay, the main wheels had sunk several inches into the soft earth. The two-seater was light in the tail anyway, and I was afraid it would nose up if I attempted to taxi it out of the mud. Colonel Rector agreed, and after some discussion he decided that he and the Chinese would hold down the tail by leaning on the horizontal stabilizer while I tried to taxi the plane forward by blasting the engine. I volunteered to sit on the tail, but he said since he spoke some Chinese he would do it. I climbed in, started the engine, and on his signal blasted the throttle until the wheels started to roll, then throttled back and taxied onto firmer ground. He signaled for me to cut the engine, and when I climbed out I saw that the home-made back canopy had been ripped off by the slipstream, fortunately without decapitating any of the Chinese or, heaven forbid, Colonel Rector. Somewhat embarrassed, I retrieved it and stored the remains in the baggage compartment. When I started to climb into the back seat so the colonel wouldn't have to ride in the open air, he waved me into the front seat. We climbed in and took off for Chihkiang, fervently hoping that nothing else would go wrong. As we flew back, I was more worried about what Sergeant Hogan, who had laboriously fashioned the back canopy, would say than how Colonel Rector was enjoying the air.

After landing I found out just how he had enjoyed the air. "The wind wasn't a problem," he said, "but the end of that two-foot hair ribbon tied to the top of your helmet flipped me in the face all the way back." I had gotten the idea for the ribbon from some World War I movies. I thought it looked great when I landed with the canopy open. He took it all in good humor, and even Sergeant Hogan took the news about the canopy philosophically, possibly because I told him in front of the colonel.

Colonel Rector and I chatted a bit before he left, and he asked where I hoped to be stationed on my return to the States. I hadn't given it much thought but mentioned that I'd like to do a lot of fighter flying and then fly another tour of combat. At that time we thought the war would go on for several more years. He asked if I had any college, and I told him that I had one year of engineering. He said that he had been testing fighters at Eglin Field, Florida, before he returned to China and that he thought I would make a good test pilot. He offered to write a letter of recommendation for me to the commander of the test group at Eglin, and I accepted gratefully.

Ed Rector became a good friend in later years, and he seldom misses an opportunity to tell this story whenever I'm about. He generally embellishes it by substituting a fox or raccoon tail for the hair ribbon, but is otherwise truthful. I don't know if our misadventure influenced his decision, but he never stationed a squadron at California.

There were four squadrons of CACW P-40s at Chihkiang, two in the alert shack next to ours at the south end of the runway and two at the north end. They took off in both directions to save taxiing, but we all landed to the north. We made it a point to be outside the alert shack whenever the P-40s on the north end took off toward us, after one Chinese pilot lost control on takeoff and skidded into the parking area behind the alert shacks, missing the corner of our building by a few feet. The pilot managed to stop without damage to the plane or anything else and, unperturbed, taxied onto our end of the runway, took off in the other direction, and caught up with the rest of the mission. About a week later another Chinese pilot had engine trouble on the takeoff roll, attempted to stop but couldn't, and ran off the end of the runway and over the clifflike slope at the end. When he hit the bottom, there was a terrific explosion and burst of flame. As we raced to the edge, I thought he had surely bought the farm, or in this case, the rice paddy. When we looked down, however, he was starting to climb the hill carrying his parachute, without a mark on him, as the P-40 blazed merrily away.

Late in December we escaped by a hair's breadth what could have been a disaster, again caused by an errant Chinese pilot taking off toward us. He lifted off a little farther down the runway than was normal, and as we watched him he reached down and, instead of pulling up the wheels, released the parafrags on his left wing. For a split second we were transfixed with horror, the same horror the Japanese we had parafragged must have felt. By great good fortune, the plane was quite low when the bombs released and the chutes didn't have time to open completely, so the bombs were not armed and didn't explode.

There was still a major problem: six of the world's touchiest bombs were lying on the runway. After losing Bellman, we weren't about to risk anyone else. We immediately evacuated the area and got the ordnance and armament officers together to work out a plan. A double wall of sandbags was placed around the bombs, with a small opening facing down the runway to the north. One of the ordnance officers fired a rifle at the bombs from more than a hundred yards away. The bombs exploded on the first shot without damaging anything but the sandbags. The ever-present Chinese repair crews came and filled in and leveled the crater in the runway, and it was once again open for business. To my knowledge no one ever asked the pilot what had caused him to drop the bombs; he would have lost several yards of face. We were lucky that about forty of our squadron didn't lose a lot more than face.

Doc Keefe in the meantime was doing his best to keep us all happy. He learned that tough, irascible Jesse Gray, who feared no one, was deathly afraid of hypodermic needles and would do almost anything to avoid taking a shot. Doc put up a notice saying that all pilots had to take shots for some disease he had made up and arranged that Jesse would be the third in line. Only the two pilots in front of Jesse were in on the plan. Each of them went into Doc's office separately and, once the door was closed, let out a terrifying scream and came out holding his arm and moaning. Jesse, with great reluctance and under pressure from those behind him, entered and shut the door. Doc was waiting with his hair askew, a wild look in his eyes, and a hypodermic needle that had been rejected for use on elephants because it was too big. As he advanced with needle poised, it was more than Jesse could face. Jesse burst out of the office and ran toward his hostel, with Doc chasing him brandishing the needle. Jesse barricaded himself in his room and refused to come out until Major Slocumb told him it was all a joke. To our surprise, Jesse's relief was so great that he didn't lose his temper but laughed along with the rest of us.

The Butcher decided it was time for some real entertainment, so he and I worked up a routine that became popular at all the squadron parties and other get-togethers. We performed on request and more often without request. He was the emcee, or more correctly the carnival barker, who introduced our act. He would shout, in his best carny fashion, "Ladies (wishful thinking) and gentlemen, let me present the singing, disabled war veterans, Lopez and Keefe, two legs between them! Yes, ladies and gentlemen, each of these heroes lost a leg in the great war, but did it deter them? No! Now hear them sing their great hit song, 'Samuel Hall,' two hundred years on the hit parade!"

We faced the assemblage with an arm around each other's shoulders, and holding our outside leg up behind us with our free hand, we hopped up and down in time to the song on our two legs between us. The song we sang a capella was an old English ballad with eight or ten verses, all in the same vein as the first and last, which went:

Oh, my name is Samuel Hall, Samuel Hall, Samuel Hall,
Oh, my name is Samuel Hall and I hates you one and all.
You're a bunch of bastards all, damn your eyes, damn your eyes.
Let this be my parting knell, parting knell, parting knell,
Let this be my parting knell, hopes to see you all in hell,
Hopes to hell you sizzles well, damn your eyes, damn your eyes.

My young wife was somewhat taken aback when, in 1949, at a 75th Squadron reunion in New York, Doc and I met in the lobby of the hotel and treated the startled guests and staff to our routine. If an agent had been present we might have made it to the big time, but Doc liked medicine and I liked flying better. Besides, we would always know that we had wowed them in Chihkiang.

17

A WARRIOR'S
MERCY

We do pray for mercy,
And that same prayer doth teach us all to render
The deeds of mercy.

Shakespeare, *The Merchant of Venice*

On January 19, 1945, I played a small part in a drama that was as tragic as anything William Shakespeare ever wrote. The scene was the airfield at Chihkiang; the time, midmorning; the weather, clear and perfect.

The 75th that morning was to escort, along with some CACW fighters, a squadron of 341st Bomb Group B-25s on a mission to bomb a Japanese airfield near Hankow. I briefed the pilots that they were to take off when we received a radio signal from the B-25s, which had taken off from their base far to the south, indicating that they were within fifteen minutes of Chihkiang. The radio room phoned our alert shack that the signal had been received, so I fired a green flare and our planes and the CACW, at the other end of the field, started their engines. Our twelve Mustangs took off first, followed by eight CACW P-40s that took off in the opposite direction. The fighters had joined formation and were circling for altitude when the flight of twelve B-25s appeared from the southwest. As they flew over the airfield, the fighters slid smoothly into position over them, and they slowly disappeared into the northeast.

Once they were safely on their way, I went into my office in the alert shack to work on the schedule for the next day. About thirty minutes later I heard a B-25 approach the field and begin circling. I didn't give it much thought, since both engines seemed to be running well. I assumed, correctly, that it had some minor problem and had decided to abort the mission and land at Chihkiang, rather than attempt the long flight back to its home base. I heard it throttle back to begin its landing approach from the far or north end of the runway.

I should mention again that the gravel runway at Chihkiang was about 3,200 feet long with a short dirt overrun at the north end. At the south end, however, the runway ended abruptly with a precipitous drop of about a hundred feet down to a mud flat that extended for several hundred yards to a river.

As I continued my work in our alert shack, on the south end of the field, I heard someone yell, "Hey, Lope, get out here. A B-25's going to crash!" I ran out quickly and saw the B-25, less than 1,000 feet from the south end of the runway, with its gear and flaps down, still trying to land. Its level attitude indicated that it still had plenty of speed to make a successful go-around, but the pilot forced it onto the runway less than 400 feet from the end. He still could have gone around, but he locked the main wheels with the emergency air brakes and skidded over the cliff at high speed. The locked main wheels caused the nose to pitch down violently as the nose wheel went over the ledge; the airplane disappeared from view and we heard a tremendous crash.

Four of us rushed to the edge and, looking down, saw that the B-25 had hit on its nose and right engine and had been brought to rest at almost the point of impact by the soft mud. The right wing had broken, the right engine had smashed into the radio compartment aft of the bomb bay, and smoke was pouring out of the right engine. We scrambled down the cliff as fast as we could and ran, in what felt like slow motion, through the gluelike mud to the plane. We could see movement through the waist windows. Two went to the waist window and two of us went to the nose. In the rear the radio operator had been crushed by the engine and was dead. The two other crewmen were walking around in the aft section in a state of shock, but with no apparent injuries. Fran Bailey, one of our four, found a landing strut from a previous P-40 crash and, working feverishly, managed to break the Plexiglas waist window and rescue the two crewmen. Fortunately, neither was badly injured.

Things were much worse up front. The Plexiglas nose, along with most of the windshield, had been completely ripped off, exposing the cockpit and the pilots, who were still strapped in their seats. The pilot, in the left seat, was semiconscious and was fumbling with his seat belt. The copilot was limp, covered with blood, and appeared to be dead. The flight engineer was lying face down between the seats with the lower part of his body covered in wreckage, but he was conscious and trying to extricate himself. The bombardier was trapped in the section behind the cockpit and was on his feet groping for a way out. Flames were now shooting out of the right engine nacelle, and fuel was beginning to pool on top of the mud. Knowing there was no fire-fighting equipment at Chihkiang except for a few small hand extinguishers, I hoped that someone would bring them before the fire got out of hand.

My companion and I freed the pilot and carried him a safe distance from the wreck, turning him over to some new arrivals on the scene. Hurrying back, we removed the copilot, who showed no signs of life, and carried him to the others, who now had a stretcher. As they started toward the cliff with him, we turned our attention to the flight engineer, whose situation was becoming more desperate as the flames increased.

We cleared away some of the wreckage in front of him, and then we each took one of his arms and tried to pull him free. He didn't budge an inch. We tried again and again but to no avail. Two more men came to help, but even with two tugging on each arm with all our strength, it was impossible to move him. Throughout this ordeal he remained calm, helped us as much as possible, and never indicated in any way that he was in pain or even worried about his predicament. He was incredibly brave.

Two fire extinguishers were brought up and discharged at the source of the fire, but the magnesium wheel had ignited and the fire continued unabated. Someone came up with a long wooden pole, and we inserted it under the wreckage that had the flight engineer pinned and tried to pry it up while others pulled on his arms. We were still unsuccessful, and as more pressure was exerted the pole snapped in half.

The fire was now burning furiously and the heat was becoming unbearable, so we switched our efforts to extricating the bombardier. About this time someone yelled that the bombs were still aboard, and many of the spectators wisely cleared the area. An ax had appeared, and we were taking turns trying to clear a passage big enough to drag the bombardier through. The heat was so intense that no one could work for more than thirty seconds at a time.

Suddenly there was a tremendous flash of flame as the gasoline on the ground ignited, and we all instinctively ran away from the crash. The bombardier said later that he had momentarily abandoned hope, thinking we had given up. We came back and frantically threw mud on the gasoline flames until we were able to get close enough to resume chopping. After what seemed like an eternity, we were able to make a hole large enough to drag him through. His arm was broken and he had numerous cuts and bruises and some burns from the hot metal, but he was able to walk away.

The flight surgeon, Dr. Keefe, had arrived, and by crouching behind blankets soaked in muddy water, we were able to get him close enough to the flight engineer to see if he could be freed by amputating a leg. That too was impossible, since he was trapped in the wreckage from the waist down.

By now the fire was completely out of control, and we were forced to back away. The ammunition began to explode and the machine guns to fire. We backed off still farther and were watching helplessly as the fire approached the trapped engineer, who never lost consciousness or, apparently, hope.

Colonel Dunning—commanding officer of the Fifth Fighter Group, CACW, and the ranking officer at Chihkiang—arrived on the scene from the headquarters building. He assessed the situation and asked if there was any way that we could save the engineer. We told him we had tried everything possible, but there was no hope now of saving him.

He walked up as close as possible to the raging fire, drew his .45 pistol, and carefully aimed it at the engineer. At that moment the engineer looked up at Colonel Dunning and said, "Don't shoot me, Colonel. I'm going to get out of here." Colonel Dunning holstered his gun, and the engineer, mustering all his strength, raised himself on his arms, as though doing a pushup, and looked down under his body to see what was holding him. While he looked down, Colonel Dunning drew his pistol, shot him in the top of the head, killing him instantly, and then hurled the gun into a nearby rice paddy.

Colonel Dunning told us to leave the area because the bombs could go off at any time. We all started walking slowly away, and that is all I remember from firsthand experience. I was told that I suddenly fell face down in the mud, unconscious, and when I came to a few minutes later, Maj. Glyn Ramsey of the CACW and another pilot were dragging me away. Although I was dazed, I was able to walk, and we went back up the hill together. In addition to some light burns on my face and hands, I had a large bruise and a burned-looking cut on the outer corner of my right eyebrow. Major Ramsey said that a machine gun had fired a round set off by the heat just as I fell, and I must have received a glancing blow from the slug.

I also learned that the pilot had returned because of an electrical problem and had landed so fast because he had a full load of bombs and almost a full load of fuel. He was accustomed to a much longer runway and hadn't realized how short ours was. Ironically, the copilot had instructed in B-25s for years and probably could have landed safely even under those conditions.

The next day we inspected the cooled wreckage and found that the engineer's legs had been trapped under the heavy armor plate, called the coffin, behind the pilot's seat and that the top turret had broken loose and was resting on the armor plate. It would have been impossible to free him without a powerful crane. Had it not been for Colonel Dunning's courageous act, the engineer would have burned to death slowly, from the feet up. The bombs were still aboard, but they had not been armed. They had broken loose and were partially buried in the mud, which must have kept them cool enough to avoid detonating.

I learned later that the copilot, whom we thought was dead when we carried him from the plane, was actually alive but had suffered a serious head injury. Dr. Keefe, who was an accomplished surgeon, was preparing to operate to relieve the pressure on his brain, but he died before the operation began.

Colonel Dunning never mentioned the incident, but it was obvious that he had been strongly affected by it. When he was ordered to Kunming to be court-martialed, every officer and man on the base volunteered to testify on his behalf. It was not necessary, as the court-martial was only a formality, as much to protect him from future prosecution as to adhere to military regulations.

Colonel Dunning was one of the finest men I have ever known—completely fearless, a brilliant pilot and tactician, and an inspiring leader. He went on to become a brigadier general and would undoubtedly have gone higher had he not died suddenly, in 1962, on the operating table from a reaction to an anesthetic. If there is a Valhalla, he is surely there, along with the flight engineer.

18

A DEVASTATING
LOSS

The war really wound down for me in the first few months of 1945. I began wending my way back to the west via Kunming, Karachi, Cairo, and Casablanca, and ended in Miami, where I had started my journey to the Far East nineteen months before. When I left the States the Italian government had just surrendered, but it took almost another year to drive the Germans out of Italy. Now Germany itself was on the verge of total defeat, and the United States in fierce fighting had retaken most of the territory captured by the Japanese early in the war.

Major Slocumb had pinned on my captain's bars on New Year's Day. Fourteenth Air Force policy required that an officer remain in China for at least two months after a promotion, so I stayed on as operations officer until late in February. The monsoon season was with us again, so there was not a whole lot of flying in January and February. The crew chiefs were able to spend all the time they needed to get our Mustangs in A-1 condition.

In early February we had a few snowstorms, which we all welcomed because China looked more like home when it was covered with snow. Some enterprising soul found two old P-40 nose cowlings, the part on which the eyes were painted, and pressed them into service as toboggans on a big hill behind our hostel, giving many of us the chance to act our age. They worked quite well, except that they were totally uncontrollable. At the end of the second day, when we had logged one broken ankle, one sprained ankle, one broken collarbone, and numerous other sprains and contusions, Slocumb reviewed the walking wounded and grounded all pilots from sledding. Being from Georgia, he didn't hold with them Yankee sports anyway.

Despite the bad weather the pilots on the schedule had to spend every day at the flight line, and I did also, since my office was in the alert shack and I usually stood alert as leader of the base defense flight. The low clouds, mist, and lack of flying didn't do much for our morale, but Doc Keefe was equal to the occasion. His ambulance was a primary means of transportation to and from the flight line, and on every trip he delivered a rapid-fire barker's spiel, describing the sights between the hostel and the flight line. We drove the same route every day, but he seldom repeated himself. One line I recall is "On our right we see the rolling hills and Slopi valleys of beautiful Chihkiang." "Slopi" is short for "Slopehead," the GI's epithet for the Chinese. I particularly enjoyed a line Doc used in one form or another as we approached the alert shack: "And now, ladies and gentlemen, we are approaching the lair of the famous man-eating 75th Fighter Squadron, every pilot in a separate cage. Please don't feed them. They only eat Japs."

Chunk Harrison, a regular passenger in the ambulance, would get nervous when Doc took his attention from his driving to point out scenes of interest. When Doc realized this, he introduced a new routine while we were on the curvy narrow road about halfway to the hostel. I always rode in the right seat of the ambulance because of my exalted position. Doc suddenly announced, "And now, ladies and gentlemen, for the first time anywhere, the famous trick driving team of Lopez and Keefe will attempt the dangerous feat of changing seats while driving." He stood up and started to shift over to my seat. I hadn't been briefed, but I slid under him and took the wheel. Chunk was horrified or terrified or both, and his reaction was so satisfying that we did it several times per trip, until Chunk abandoned the ambulance for a safer mode of transportation, Slocumb's jeep. Since the other passengers showed no fear, we abandoned the act. After I left, Chunk rode in the ambulance one day because it was the only transport available, and Doc unwisely tried his daredevil routine with another, less skilled, copilot. During the transfer they lost control, went off the road, and rolled the ambulance down the hill. By good fortune no one was injured, except for a bruise or two, and the ambulance suffered just a few dents. From then on Chunk would have crawled to the hostel rather than ride with Doc. He would, however, have been perfectly safe with him, since Doc was forced to drop the trick from his repertoire for lack of a dependable partner.

Slocumb was no slouch at providing thrills, either. One morning he made one of the hairiest takeoffs I've ever seen. We were short of drop tanks for the P-51s, which carried one under each wing on the bomb racks just outboard of the landing gear. Slocumb thought we might be able to fly with just one tank despite the asymmetric load, so he put his theory to the test. He had a tank installed on the left wing and filled it with fuel. To counteract the weight on the left side he planned to use full right aileron trim on takeoff, then gradually reduce the amount of trim as the speed increased. There was nothing wrong with the plan, but he inadvertently rolled in full left trim. On his takeoff run the right wheel came off the ground first, and as he left the ground he was in a steep left bank. He went roaring across, or actually through, the line of parked P-40s at the other end of the field as maintenance crews scrambled in all directions. Fortunately, his ability was equal to the task, and he was able to level out and climb away. After burning out some of the fuel, he landed, topped off the tank, and tried it again with the trim in the proper direction. This time the takeoff was completely normal, and he said it was not difficult to control. In the future the squadron often flew with just one tank.

One evening in late January or early February, four or five other pilots and I were in one of the hostel rooms—feasting on boned chicken and pineapple slices in lieu of the mess hall food—when suddenly someone walked into the dimly lit room. He was dressed all in black and appeared to be Chinese, except for his size. As he came into the light, we were happy to see that it was Jack Gadberry, one of the four pilots shot down over Hengyang on November 11. We had heard nothing of him since then and assumed that he had been killed or captured. Momentarily it was a bit embarrassing; we were just finishing off the last two cans of his private stock of food brought from India. His roommates had been eating it regularly for about a month, since we had given up hope of his returning. It was standard practice in the squadron to eat the food and divide up all but the most personal belongings of pilots who were dead or missing pilots that we had not been informed were safe. He was so glad to be back that the question of food never came up. The rest of the evening was spent listening to the harrowing tale of his bailout and escape.

He was extremely lucky to have escaped capture, and it is a credit to the Chinese and to Jack's fortitude that he was able to avoid capture. His Mustang was hit and on fire before he knew the enemy had attacked. He was forced to bail out directly over the airfield at Hengyang but by good fortune was carried about half a mile from the field by the wind before he landed. Some watchful Chinese peasants had seen him land, so they quickly led him a short distance to a farmyard, where they found an underground oven with a heavy metal lid in which to hide him. It barely accommodated him, even in a cramped fetal position, but he remained there for almost three days while the Japanese fruitlessly combed the area. Several times, as best he could tell from the sounds, Japanese on horseback and on foot were within a few feet of his hideout. They finally abandoned the search, and the Chinese were able to get him out at night and turn him over to the guerrillas, who led him out of Japanese territory by a long and tortuous route with many layovers. He had heard from the guerrillas that one of the pilots on his mission had gone down with the plane, but he did not know who it was. After the war we learned that Miller had been killed and Taylor had been taken prisoner.

Late in February, Slocumb told me to prepare to report to Luliang, where the administrative elements of the 75th were based, so that I could leave for home by the end of the month. Chief Sanford would be going home at the same time, as would Jesse Gray, who was already at Luliang. I was ready to go, since I could no longer fly combat and most of my closest friends had left.

The next night we had a big farewell party, with lots of drinking and singing. Our only other entertainment option in Chihkiang was singing and drinking. I pretended to take a few drinks to keep from having it poured down my throat, as had happened on several other festive occasions. GI lemonade powder and medicinal alcohol are hard to take under any circumstances, but it is especially rough when three people are sitting on you pouring it in your mouth. One of the pilots in some of the farewell oratory said, "Lope, when you leave, half our esprit de corps will be gone." I admit he had been drinking, but I appreciated it nonetheless. If true, the 75th would have been left with negative esprit, since more than half had left with Flash Segura.

The next morning Chief and I boarded a C-47, made our last farewells, and flew to Luliang, where we reported to Myron Levy, the adjutant. He said that our orders should be back from Fourteenth Air Force Headquarters in Kunming no later than the end of the month. Jesse had saved a bed for me in his tent, and he briefed me on the routine at Luliang. It was pretty dull. Except for the permanent administrative staffs of the forward-based squadrons, everyone was awaiting orders to leave China. He said that Earl Green was an assistant group operations officer and could help me get in some flying. There were a number of P-40s to be test hopped or ferried to nearby bases. Several pilots from other squadrons of the 23rd, whom I knew from training, were also there waiting for orders. Jesse and they said that the Luliang food was miserable, but there was a restaurant in Boomtown, a small cluster of buildings just off the base, that served good American-style Chinese food. The food was as good as they promised, so we ate there almost every night.

There were two fatal crashes in the short time I was at Luliang. In the first, an F-5, the photoreconnaissance version of the P-38, returning from a long mission, spun in on the final approach and the pilot was killed. I was up in a P-40 at the time and flew over the burning wreckage on landing. A few days later two P-51s from the 76th had buzzed the tents several times when the leader started a slow roll right on the deck with his wingman following. The leader let the nose drop, dished out of the bottom of the roll, and flew into the ground, followed by the wingman, who couldn't recover in time. The leader was the squadron commander, an experienced pilot who had flown to Luliang on squadron business, but the wingman was a new pilot. It was a tragic waste, two pilots dead and two airplanes destroyed to no purpose. It seems that regardless of age or rank, most fighter pilots are driven to demonstrate their courage and flying ability on all possible occasions.

Later that week, after eating at Boomtown and returning to the tents, Jesse and Danny Schiable, from the 76th, decided to take a jeep and go into Luliang to live it up a bit. They asked if I wanted to come along, but I decided to stay in the tent and finish a book I was reading, so they went on their way. Jesse hadn't returned when I finished reading about midnight, so I went to sleep. During the night I had a haunting dream that when I awoke in the morning and looked across the tent I saw Jesse laid out dead on a hospital or morgue table. When I actually awoke I looked across the tent and saw that Jesse's bed was empty and hadn't been slept in. I wasn't worried, since Jesse occasionally stayed in town. I dressed and strolled to the mess hall for breakfast. When I was about half finished, Earl Green walked in, spotted me, and asked if I had heard about Jesse.

I said, "No, what about Jesse?"

"He was killed last night in a jeep wreck on the way back from Luliang. It ran off the road into a rice paddy and turned over. Jesse was pinned under the steering wheel and drowned."

"What about Danny," I asked. "Wasn't he with Jesse?"

Earl replied, "Yes, but he was thrown clear. He was only banged up a bit and is in the hospital."

I was stunned by this shattering news. It seemed impossible that anyone as full of life and bursting with enthusiasm as Jesse could be dead. To lose such a close friend in a stinking rice paddy in a miserable little 40-horsepower jeep when he had been risking his life almost daily for the past several years in high-performance 1,500-horsepower aircraft was just heaping too much insult on injury. The enemy had fired thousands of rounds at him without effect, only to have him end this way. It was the lowest point of the war for me.

We had spent many hours in the last week talking about what we were going to do when we got home. Jesse came from a big family and from a very small town. He couldn't wait to see his parents and many siblings, and he couldn't wait to be idolized as the war hero of Stokes, North Carolina. He also planned to cut a wide swath through the female population. Now all his plans were shot to hell. It was some time before I could really accept his death. I kept expecting him to burst into the tent shouting, "By damn, Lope, I fooled you good this time."

We had been together from the first day we reported to Nashville and had planned to get together in the States and try to get into the same squadron if we went back into combat to invade Japan. I felt a small, nagging sense of guilt for a while because of my dream, as if it had somehow caused his death. It was completely irrational, but it took a while to shake the feeling. I wanted to get out of China as soon as I could. The war seemed to have gotten much worse since I stopped flying combat. First Bellman's tragic death, then the B-25 crash, and now Jesse. It seemed like friends were dying all around me.

In 1949 at Eglin Field I had a similar premonition in a dream. A young lieutenant had taken one of our squadron F-84s on a weekend cross-country flight. On Friday night I dreamed that his wife came up to me wearing a dress she had modeled in a fashion show the week before and said, "This dress is all I have left in the world." I didn't think anything about it until I learned the next morning that her husband had bailed out in a violent thunderstorm and been killed.

Earl and I went to see Danny Schiable in the hospital to see how he was and to learn the grim details. He was all right physically but terribly concerned that we understand that he had not abandoned Jesse. We assured him that we knew he had done everything possible. The jeep had sunk into the mud of the paddy, pinning Jesse beneath the wheel. Although Danny had tried desperately, he could neither pull Jesse out nor roll the jeep off him. The next afternoon we went to a simple memorial service for Jesse in Luliang, then Earl, Chief, and I flew to Kunming in P-40s to observe the burial in the same concrete vaults where Jesse and I had watched Ozzie's burial the past April.

February 28 had come and gone with no orders, so Chief and I were taking turns flying to Kunming to see if our orders were ready. Since Jesse's death I couldn't wait to leave. One day I borrowed a brand-new P-51D that had just arrived for the flight. It was a delight to fly in that bubble canopy. The visibility was remarkable, far better than anything I'd flown except the open cockpit PT-19 in primary. It also had six guns, mounted vertically so they would fire under high g loads. I would have liked to fly it in combat. The next day the Chief, not to be outdone, made the flight to Kunming in the D but forgot to lower the landing gear and bellied in that shiny new airplane. Chief thought it was funny, but he was the only one. By good luck our orders were ready, and he caught a ride in a C-47 back to Luliang with them. At last I had them in my hands.

The next day I packed and went up to Group to say good-bye to Earl and other friends. Earl said that he would have his orders in a few days and would join me at Landhi Field in Karachi, where I would be instructing before I left the theater for home. Just as I was leaving, the group operations officer casually said, "Lope, wait a minute. Have you been awarded any of your medals yet?" I said that I had seen the orders but not the medals, so he reached into his desk, got out a Distinguished Flying Cross and an Air Medal, and threw them to me in their boxes—a touching ceremony, one that I would long cherish. They were, after all, the first medals I had won since the Mary T. Browne Medal for the Best School Record from P.S. 114 in Brooklyn. The orders for the Silver Star and the Soldier's Medal had not yet been published. They were awarded to me a few months later in a formal ceremony at Eglin Field, Florida. Somehow, the offhand award of the medals in China epitomized the war in that theater.

Chief and I went to the flight line and caught a ride in a C-47 to Kunming, where we proceeded directly to the Air Transport Command dispatcher to show our orders for the trip to Karachi. We were hoping to leave that afternoon, but the dispatcher said returning air crew had the lowest priority over the Hump, and it could be a week or more before we could leave. What a way to treat hardened combat veterans. Somewhat daunted, we checked into the transient hostel for the night. Early the next morning we went to the China National Airline Company (CNAC) terminal, a Chinese government operation that used American pilots, many of them ex-AVG. A C-47 was being loaded, and we asked the pilot, a former AVG, if we could ride with him to India. He said, "Okay, hop in. We'll be leaving in about thirty minutes." Sure enough, in about thirty minutes we were airborne and on the way home. The Chinese copilot–radio operator spent his time after takeoff in the radio operator's seat, so I flew copilot for most of the trip. We didn't have to go much over 10,000 feet now that Myitkyina and its Japanese airfield in Burma had been captured and the southern route was safe. A few hours later we landed at the CNAC base at Dinjan in Assam. After thanking our benefactor profusely, we caught a ride in a weapons carrier to the ATC base at Chabua, where we learned that we could leave for Karachi by C-46 the next morning.

At the mess hall that evening we had a memorable meal of fried Spam with pineapple slices. For dessert we had ice cream, that American, cold, smooth, and creamy favorite, the first we'd tasted in about a year. It was even better than I remembered, if possible. My enjoyment of the meal was marred by the extremely insulting remarks Chief was making about the Air Transport Command pilots at the table as well as all other ATC pilots. I kept telling the Chief that they couldn't help being in the ATC, but he persisted. We got out unscathed, I'm sure, only because of Chief's six-foot frame of mean muscle, his mean mien, and his tied-down six-shooter.

The next morning we took off in a C-46 for Karachi, with a stop at Agra. I went up in the cockpit to talk to the crew and discovered that the pilot was a flying-school classmate of mine, although I had not known him there. He was extremely bitter that he had been commissioned for almost two years, had more than twice the flying time I had, yet was still a second lieutenant with no immediate prospects for promotion. He had not screwed up in any way, but he was in an organization that seemingly had no interest in its crews. I hope he was able to cash in on his experience after the war and become an airline pilot.

We landed at Karachi Air Base and boarded the truck for Landhi, where we would stay for a month or so, instructing newly arrived pilots destined for China. All new pilots in the theater passed through Landhi on the way to combat to be trained in combat tactics by pilots on their way home. The average stay both ways was about a month. When I was a student at Landhi, I thought it was a good way to impart combat experience to the new pilots. I now saw its value to the instructors, too. It was a good opportunity to transition from a combat squadron to duty in the United States.

We arrived at Landhi, checked in at headquarters, and were each assigned a private room in the barracks—a big private room. The room was identical to the one four of us had shared when we were trainees at Landhi in 1943. We cleaned up quickly and went to the mess hall, where we were welcomed by loud greetings from Moose Elker, Dick Jones, and a number of pilots I knew from other squadrons. We ate in the instructor-and-staff half of the mess hall, which was uncrowded and overmanned with waiters. Everything at Landhi was democratic, half for the students and half for the staff and instructors. The only problem for the students was that there were around eighty of them and only ten or twelve of us. They slept six to a room and were jammed into the same number of mess-hall tables that we used. We could get a jeep or weapons carrier every night to go into Karachi, while they were crowded into the back of GI six-by-six trucks. I recalled thinking it was a rotten deal when I was a student, but now, somehow, it didn't seem too bad. In fact, it was richly deserved.

Both Dick and Moose had their orders and would be leaving in a few days for the States. Moose said it was easy to get used to Landhi. He had reveled in the novelty of cake or ice cream every night, but he said, "After a week of it, I began bitching because we didn't have cake *and* ice cream." We spent most of that night in Dick's room discussing what had happened in and out of the squadron since Dick and Moose had left. They were shattered to hear of Jesse's death and of how he had died. It was even harder for them to accept than it had been for me, because I had been there. They had expected the two of us to arrive at Landhi together. Despite the initial shock, we all were soon laughing as we relived his many adventures and misadventures.

One of Jesse's stories that we all had enjoyed was about his father, who had worked as a crewman on a sailing ship when he was a young man. It seems his father's ship had been becalmed for several days, or as Jesse described it, he was caught in a no-winder. His father, not surprisingly, lost his temper and threw a $10 bill to the sea, shouting, "I'm going to buy me some wind." That night they were hit by a howling gale, and the ship nearly foundered. Jesse's father said that if he had known wind was that cheap, he would have thrown in only a dollar.

The nightly movies were much better than they had been in China, but I missed Andy Devine. I had begun to think that everyone talked that way. We even saw a few movies that I had read about in *Life* magazine only a few months earlier. *To Have and Have Not* was the first really good movie I'd seen in years.

Life at Landhi was easy to take, especially for the instructors. We worked only half-days, flying in the morning one day and the afternoon the next. The briefings for the students were long and detailed, and we led them in practice formation, dogfights, and ground attack missions. They were also introduced to shadow gunnery, firing at the shadow of another plane as it passed along the beach. For some reason, parafragging was not demonstrated in the United States, so we taught it at Landhi by dropping live bombs on a small rock island off the coast. I had my students circle above while I dropped my parafrags in the water, so they could appreciate the range and destructive power.

We flew P-40s and P-51As, the early Mustangs that were equipped with the Allison engine. I found an old friend I had never expected to see again on the flight line. It was the P-40K that I had ferried to Landhi from China almost exactly one year earlier. I flew it several times, and it handled well, seeming to appreciate an experienced, familiar hand on the stick. Some of the students who had trained on P-51s took a dim view of having to fly the old P-40s. They acted as though the P-40s were relics of World War I and never flew them enough to learn to love them as we did. They were not as fast as the newer fighters, but they were rugged, maneuverable, steady workhorses.

As combat veterans we were looked up to by the student pilots, just as we had looked up to the combat veterans who had shared their hard-won knowledge and experience with us. A major element of the fighter-pilot spirit is grudging respect for those who have cut the mustard in air combat, along with the feeling that you will do even better. In addition to the flight training, we spent a lot of time shooting the breeze with them at the flight line and in the mess hall.

Earl Green came in from China just in time for the farewell party for Dick Jones and Moose. I was glad to have such a good friend from the squadron to take their place. Chief, of course, was from the 75th too, but he and I had never been close, although we got along well.

On April 12, 1945, I slept late because I was flying in the afternoon. As I was walking to the mess hall, I noticed that the flag was at half-mast. I thought someone must have crashed that morning, so when I walked into the mess I sat down by Earl and asked who had augered in. "No one," he said. "President Roosevelt is dead." It was the end of an era. FDR had been president since I was nine years old and my commander in chief since I was eighteen. I could remember Hoover, chiefly from the 1932 election, but the words "President Roosevelt" were almost a tautology in the United States. I knew a little about the new president, Harry Truman, because of his work as a senator on the Truman Commission, but he, like most American vice presidents, was almost a nonentity. I had felt great pride in seeing President Roosevelt and flying in an airshow for him while I was a cadet. Although we all attended a memorial service at Landhi, it took some time to realize that someone else was president.

About a week later Joe Brown, Earl Green, and I were sent to the nearby Malir Field to instruct a group of U.S.-trained Chinese pilots, who were on their way to the CACW in China, in P-51As. Although they could speak and understand English after a fashion, it was difficult to communicate by radio because of their accents and, I suppose, our accents. Based on our observations of them in China, our main goal was to stay out of their way as much as possible. That precaution led to a strange accident.

Joe Brown was leading a flight of four Chinese on a minimum-altitude simulated attack across the adjoining desert. He had briefed them to stay several lengths behind him at all times. While flying only a few feet above the ground at about 250 mph, Joe looked back to make sure the Chinese weren't too close and flew into the ground. The Mustang skidded and ricocheted along the desert, shedding its propeller, wings, and most of the fuselage along the way. The remains of the fuselage slammed against a giant cactus, and the seat ripped out and slid to a stop with Joe still strapped in place. The Chinese were unable to get the tower to understand that Joe had crashed, and it was not until they had landed and calmed down that a search team went to look for him. From what the Chinese reported, we were sure he had been killed. I thought I'd lost another friend.

In the meantime, a group of Indians driving nearby had seen the crash and stopped to investigate. They found Joe, seemingly dead, covered with blood from a large scalp wound. They threw him into the back of their truck and headed for Karachi. Fortunately, an Indian was riding in the back of the truck with the "body," and after jolting along for a mile or two, Joe opened his eyes and began to stir. The Indian yelled to the driver, who turned into Karachi Air Base and delivered Joe to the military hospital. By some miracle Joe wasn't badly injured, except that his scalp had been ripped open.

Earl Green and I were able to see him the next day, and he was in his usual high spirits. He said that he had asked the surgeon to put a zipper in his scalp when he sewed it up so that he could pour his drinks directly into his brain and have them take effect faster. He was released from the hospital a few days later and left for the States almost immediately, sans zipper.

Strange things continued to happen. When we returned to Landhi we were told that it was to be closed and the Fighter Replacement Training Unit would move to Malir, a few miles away. We packed our belongings for what seemed like the thousandth time and sent them by truck to Malir while we flew the airplanes over. The night that we left Landhi, a C-46 caught fire in the air, crashed onto the ramp at Landhi, and exploded. All of our aircraft would have been destroyed.

The thought of going home loomed brighter every day, and after about a week at Malir, Chief and I got our orders for home. We checked in at ATC Operations at KAB and left that evening on a C-46 full of returning troops. The uncomfortable bucket seats seemed less uncomfortable as long as we were heading west. It landed for fuel at Abadan, Iran, which was ablaze with light from the oil refineries. Our next stop was at Cairo, and I saw the pyramids as we flew overhead. Fortunately, there was a one-day layover in Cairo, so Chief and I took a guided tour of the pyramids and the Sphinx. They were as impressive as I had thought they would be. How structures that massive could have been built 3,000 years ago without heavy machinery was beyond me then and still is.

The next day we flew to Casablanca, landing for fuel at Tripoli. We were on standby to leave for the States so were not able to visit the Casbah and Pepe LeMoko. There was an enormous backlog of troops from the CBI and the Mediterranean theaters waiting to return home, and we were told it could be as long as two weeks at the rate airlift was available. So near and yet so far. Two days later fortune smiled when an aircraft carrier docked and more than 2,000 of those ahead of us on the list were loaded onboard for the trip home. Chief and I were moved to the top and left the next day on a C-54. We landed at the Azores and, after a thirteen-hour flight into strong headwinds, at Bermuda before arriving at Miami on May 5, 1945, nineteen months after I had departed from that same airfield for my Asian adventure.

Even without the combat, it would have been quite a trip. I'd visited three continents and one subcontinent, crossed the Atlantic and the Equator twice, seen the Amazon River, the Nile, and the Yangtze. I'd flown across the Himalayas four times and seen the Sahara Desert, South China Sea, Red Sea, Arabian Sea, Bay of Bengal, Persian Gulf, Mediterranean, Gibraltar, Suez Canal, Hong Kong, Casablanca, Cairo, Calcutta, Taj Mahal, and the Great Pyramids and the Sphinx. About the only thing I'd missed was Kipling's great gray green greasy Limpopo River, all set about with fever trees.

Now after that great odyssey I was back in the best place of all, the United States. It is hard to describe the feeling of belonging that envelops a traveler returning after so long a time. Even though I was, in a sense, never out of the country while I was in an American military unit, it was a wonderful feeling to be in a clean country where everyone spoke my language and there were lots of American girls of about my age. It was especially rewarding to be wearing a uniform, wings, and ribbons at that time. It is hard to imagine, in the post-Vietnam years, the high regard in which servicemen were held. The whole country was behind the war effort; it knew what needed to be done and had the strength and courage to do it.

My orders called for me to report back to the Redistribution Center at Miami after a ten-day leave. I stayed on the airport and was able to get a seat on a National Airlines Lockheed Electra for Tampa that left almost immediately. After a short flight, my first on an airliner, we landed at Peter O. Knight Airport in Tampa, where I had learned to fly some three years earlier, although it seemed like an eternity.

I took a cab home and enjoyed seeing all the familiar landmarks on the way, but the house seemed smaller than I remembered. In the house, which was unlocked as always, I found a note telling me to call my mother at work as soon as I got in. She knew I was coming home but didn't know exactly when. In those days of gas rationing, she wouldn't have been able to pick me up at the airport anyway. She told me that my younger brother, Carl, had just completed the radar operator school at Boca Raton, Florida, and was now spending a few days on leave in New York, visiting my aunt and uncle. I decided to visit there right away so I could see Carl before he reported to his new duty station, the night fighter school at Fresno, California. At dinner I told my mother and brother Bruce as much as I could about my adventures in that short time. Afterward I went to MacDill Field and was able to catch a ride in a C-47 full of GIs on leave bound for Newark. We arrived after an all-night flight, and I took the subway to my late grandmother's house in Brooklyn where I had been born.

My aunt and uncle still lived in the house. We had always been close, since my brothers and I were the only children in the family and had lived around or with them until we moved to Florida in 1939. My uncle was unmarried, and my aunt's husband was commanding a Coast Guard ship in the Pacific. They both worked during the day, so Carl and I had a lot of time to catch up on things. In the afternoons he and I went to the officer's club in one of the New York hotels and picked up free tickets to Broadway plays. In the evening we met my uncle and aunt in Manhattan, ate, and then went to the theater. I'd never been to anything but a high-school play before, and these were much better. We saw Nancy Walker in *On the Town*, Beatrice Lillie in *The Seven Lively Arts*, and someone in *Up in Central Park*.

The second day that I was there, May 8, I visited my elementary school, P.S. 114, and it too seemed small. While I was chatting with some of my former teachers, the word came over the radio that the war in Europe had ended. All the students were called to the auditorium, and I had to mumble a few words, which were well received, since I was introduced as a real Flying Tiger. It was not lost on me that I was speaking from the same stage where I could have made the valedictory speech when I graduated, had it not been for terminal stage fright.

That afternoon Carl and I mingled with the crowds in Manhattan, who were celebrating the end of the war in Europe. They were somewhat subdued because the general belief was that the war against Japan would continue for several years. When my brother and I walked around in the city, people kept staring at us. We both looked young, and I looked especially young to be a beribboned captain. Once a pair of suspicious MPs even asked to see my identification card.

I spent a few days with my father in his Brooklyn apartment. I hadn't seen him since my graduation from flying school, and it was wonderful to see him again. I was pleased that he was no longer working as a welder in the miserable oil tanks and holds of ships. He still worked for Todd Shipyards, but his skill both as a welder and teacher had been recognized and he was now running the welding school. It was a much cleaner and safer environment. Since he was not so bone weary in the evening, he had taken up painting seriously. He was doing some fine work and had become a local celebrity in the shipyard. He had remarried and was happy, which of course made me happy.

One of my strongest memories of my elementary and high school years is of my father coming home worn out and chilled from welding all day in the tanks of oil tankers. Since my mother worked during the day and went to college at night, my father would cook our supper and often take us to a movie or some other entertainment despite his weariness. He was a wonderful man. He died in 1991 at the age of 93.

I left New York and returned to Tampa, again by military C-47. I enjoyed this flight more than the other because the crew let me fly for a while. My good friend Harold Williamson, of my Cub-flying days, had come home on leave from Italy, and we had a great time visiting our old flying instructors and dating some of the girls who had not yet married. After a week at home visiting with my family and friends in the neighborhood, I found that I could not wait to get back into the cockpit of a fighter. I felt more at home in a squadron environment than I did in a home environment.

I returned to Miami on schedule, where I received an intensive physical as well as a lengthy interview by a personnel officer on my combat and flying experience. I requested that I be assigned to Eglin Field in northwest Florida as a fighter test pilot. Colonel Rector had sent the promised letter of recommendation to the test group commander and had given me a copy, which I showed to the personnel officer. He was noncommittal but thought that my one year of engineering in college was a plus.

Except for the physical and the interview, the rest of my time was free. There were about five pilots from China there, and we spent the days on the beach and the evenings in the nightclubs. Finally, after a week of that, I saw on the bulletin board that my orders had been issued and could be picked up in the office. I zoomed there as fast as possible and found, to my delight, that I had indeed been assigned to the 611th Proof Test Group at Eglin and was to report there two days hence. I couldn't wait.

19

FIGHTER
PILOT'S HEAVEN

Eglin Field was paradise for a pilot, especially for a fighter pilot. I had the opportunity to fly all the first-line fighters in the Army Air Forces as well as some that were still experimental, some Navy fighters, and many bombers, transports, and trainers. It was also a primary center for weapons testing, so I could maintain and increase my proficiency in gunnery (both air to air and air to ground), bombing, and rocketry. At Wright Field, Ohio, airplanes were tested as airplanes. At Eglin they were tested as weapons.

In addition to the great flying, Eglin was located near one of the world's most beautiful beaches. A stretch of pure white sand runs along the Gulf of Mexico from Pensacola to Apalachicola. The Eglin Officer's Beach Club occupied a choice stretch of this beach about five miles east of the town of Fort Walton Beach. The beach, with its brilliant white sand and varying shades of blue and green water, was as lovely from the air as from the ground. I had ample opportunity to view it from the air, since most of our gunnery tests were run just off shore.

I reported to base headquarters on June 5 and was told to report to the 611th Proof Test Group. At Group I was told to report to the commanding officer of 611B, the Fighter Test Squadron, the next morning. Since it was just early afternoon, I went to the squadron right away and was taken in to report to the CO, Major Muldoon. He had a sardonic manner that he used to deflate hot young fighter pilots, although he himself was no more than twenty-five. He said,

"Not another damn P-40 pilot from China. Doesn't Rector ever quit?" In a demonstration of my brilliant repartee, I said nothing. "Well, I guess I'm stuck with you," he said. "Report to the operations officer, Major Schoenfeldt." I thought it was an unpromising beginning, but as I got to know him better I found him to be an excellent commander. He ran a taut squadron and demanded high performance from everyone, but he was always fair and had a fine sense of humor. He was also a world-class needler.

While I was talking to Major Schoenfeldt, someone said, "About time you were getting here, Lope." It was Dick Jones, who had reported to the squadron a week earlier. He said that Major Cruickshank, from the 74th Squadron in China, was also in Fighter Test. I began to understand Major Muldoon's remark. Schoeny told me to start reading the pilot's operating instructions on all the aircraft in the squadron, since I would have to pass a written test before I could fly any of them. Most of them were single-seat fighters, so no dual instruction was possible; the first flight had to be solo.

That night in the club Dick Jones introduced me to Maj. Barney Turner, one of the more experienced test pilots in the squadron. Besides being an outstanding pilot, he was one of the nicest people I've ever known. He went out of his way to help everyone. He said that there was an empty bed in his room that I could move into while his regular roommate was on temporary duty. By good fortune, his roommate's duty became permanent, and I roomed with Barney for several years. He, Dick Jones, and I became a well-known bachelor threesome and have remained good friends to this day.

The next day I told Schoeny that he had given me the pilot's operating instruction book to a Martin B-26 bomber by mistake.

"That's no mistake," he said. "We use a B-26 to tow targets, and everyone has to be checked out in it."

"I've never flown a bomber," I protested.

He replied, "Neither had any of the other pilots in the squadron before they got here."

A few days later, after I had drawn my flight gear, I saw my name on the operations blackboard. I was to fly copilot for Major Muldoon in the B-26 the next morning. I took and passed the written test that afternoon, and bright and early the next morning I attended the briefing and walked out to the B-26 with the CO. I climbed into the copilot's seat, and after strapping in, I said, "What do you want me to do?" "Nothing," he replied. That seemed easy enough, so I just kept my eyes on him to learn as much as I could.

We taxied out, checked the engines, lined up with the runway, and took off. It was much quieter and smoother than the B-25 I'd ridden in at Chihkiang, but I was a bit apprehensive because the B-26 had a bad reputation. I lived in Tampa when there was a B-26 group training at MacDill Field, and its slogan was "One a day in Tampa Bay," because of the many crashes. Actually, most of the problems had been solved by this time, and it was no longer considered a particularly dangerous airplane. We climbed up to the gunnery range and let out the target. Once we were flying on course, Major Muldoon said, "You've got it. Just hold this course." When we came to the end of the range, he took the controls, made the 180-degree turn, then let me fly it straight and level on the next run. Barney Turner was firing at our target from a P-38, testing a new gunsight, and he came up alongside and flew formation for a minute before going in to rearm. I had never been close to a P-38 in flight before. It was a magnificent sight, with its two counter-rotating propellers, twin booms and tails, and a pilot's nacelle in the middle. We used to kid P-38 pilots by saying that it was just two P-40s with a Link Trainer in between, but it was a fine airplane.

After almost three hours of that, we landed, and as we were walking in Major Muldoon said, "Well, Lopez, now you're checked out."

I asked, "What do you do if one of the engines quits?"

He said, "In this squadron engines don't quit," and he was right. We never had an engine failure while he was the CO.

It's strange, but pilots who were trained on single-engine aircraft are more worried about losing an engine in a twin-engine plane than they are in a single-engine. There are fewer options in a single-engine: a dead-stick landing, a belly landing, or a bailout. In a twin-engine the pilot often has to fly long distances on one engine, under the stress of higher power, and he has to make a proper approach the first time, because the plane usually can't go around for a second one. Until I had amassed a lot of twin-engine time, I always worried about losing an engine, but I never gave it a thought in a single-engine plane.

The next day I checked out in the P-63 Kingcobra and found it to be easy to handle and responsive. It was a delight to fly, but its limited range and ceiling were serious liabilities for combat flying. It flew almost exactly the same as the P-39 I'd flown once at Sarasota. Because the engine was behind the pilot, there was a long drive shaft under the seat. When the engine started it vibrated so much that the instrument panel was a blur and the liquid in the compass turned into a froth until the engine rpm increased.

To my amazement, the next day I found that I was to fly the B-26 with Dick Jones, who had never been in it, as copilot. We kidded that because we were both single-engine fighter pilots, we would each handle one of the engines. The flight engineer, a grizzled sergeant with hundreds of B-26 hours, kept an eagle eye on all these fighter pilots who were flying his airplane to make sure we did nothing too stupid. I shook him up a bit the first time I used the brakes, just after we started to taxi. I didn't know that they were power brakes, so I used a lot of toe pressure, as I did in fighters. The airplane came to a dead stop, but the sergeant didn't—until he hit the console and instrument panel. I apologized, but he said he should have been ready because almost all the fighter pilots did the same thing on their first flights.

The rest of the flight went well, with Dick and I sharing the flying, but I had a bit of a problem in the landing pattern. I put my base leg in so close to the runway that I couldn't turn tight enough to get lined up for landing. That is, I couldn't turn tight enough without making a vertical bank with the wheels and flaps down, and I didn't think that was done in bombers. On the next try, I made it, but I had to use such a steep bank that the flight engineer was sweating blood. The airplane felt all right though, and Dick, with confidence in my skill, wasn't bothered. The landing was fine, and now Dick was qualified as first pilot, too.

During the next ten days I was checked out in the P-47D, the P-38L, and the C-45 and was rechecked out in the P-51D. The Republic P-47 Thunderbolt was a powerful, 14,000-pound fighter powered by a 2,000-horsepower radial engine. With its eight guns and rugged construction, it was an excellent fighter bomber. Because of its large, oval fuselage, it was called the Jug. The Beechcraft C-45 was a twin-engine transport used, with modifications, as a bombardier and navigator trainer. I never liked flying it because the small control wheel and close-together rudder pedals made me feel as though I were flying a toy.

On June 21 I became a member of an elite group when I flew the first U.S. jet, the Bell P-59A Airacomet. The P-59 was powered with two small jet engines, based on the Whittle engine built by General Electric. Except that it was jet powered, the airplane had little to recommend it. It was not fast by jet standards and was a bit of a clunker to maneuver. It even looked like a clunker. It is a pilot's maxim that airplanes that look good, fly good, and vice-versa. Unlike many maxims, this one is true most of the time. The P-59 had little endurance, and the pilot's visibility was somewhat limited. Because of its lack of performance, it was used to train pilots to fly jets and never became operational. The P-80 was the first operational U.S. jet.

Despite its shortcomings, I was thrilled to check out in a jet. I climbed into the bathtublike cockpit, and Barney ran through the engine-starting procedures with me. The engines were unbelievably quiet at idle, except for a low whine, so I had to check the instruments to see that they were indeed running. The P-59 was sluggish on the ground, and it took a great deal of power to get it rolling. I taxied right into takeoff position, since engine runup and check are not required with jets. I opened both throttles to 100-percent rpm and then released the brakes, expecting a surge of acceleration. There was none; the airplane slowly gathered speed and, after an interminable roll, finally lifted off the runway. It was an eerie feeling. There was no apparent reason why the airplane was moving, with no engine roar and no propeller. It seemed as though I were in a glider with an invisible towplane and rope. Gen. Adolf Galland of the Luftwaffe described the feeling well after his first flight in the Messerschmitt 262, the first jet to be used in combat: "It felt like the angels were pushing." Since I could stay up for only forty minutes before running short of fuel, I climbed to about 20,000 feet and put it through what paces it had. It was stable and easy to fly but not very maneuverable. Its roll rate was quite low, which was not surprising because of its large wing area. When I went down to land I found that it decelerated slowly when throttled back, since it lacked the braking force of a propeller. It was a piece of cake to land, with its big wings and wide gear. I was proud to be a jet pilot but not impressed with jets, until I flew the P-80 early in 1946. The P-80's climbing speed was almost equal to the top speed of the P-40. Despite its performance, I had no idea of the tremendous impact that the jet engine would have on flying and on society.

In addition to the jets, we had at Eglin the first guided missile squadron in the country. The Germans had begun launching V-1 buzz bombs against England in 1944. The unpiloted, pulse jet-powered aircraft were crude but at least partially effective weapons. They caused fear in the tough British population because of their unpredictability; the people never knew when the engine would stop and it would dive into the ground.

Many V-1s were captured intact after D-Day and brought to the United States for testing. An almost identical model called the JB-2 was produced by the Ford Motor Company, and it and other more advanced models were undergoing tests at Eglin for possible use against the Japanese. They were launched almost daily from Santa

Rosa Island, a long strip of beach separating the Gulf from Choctawhatchee Bay. Booster rockets were used for launch, then jettisoned, and the buzz bomb continued straight south over the Gulf until the fuel ran out after 100 miles or so and it dived into the water.

Fighters were required to follow them until they crashed in order to shoot them down if the guidance system malfunctioned, as it often did, and the buzz bomb turned back toward land. Our squadron provided the fighter coverage with P-51s and P-63s, our fastest planes at low altitude. The bombs usually flew at about 1,000 feet. Following the bombs was a problem because of their high speed. We could not keep up with them in level flight for long, so we used two teams of two fighters each to follow them in shifts. The first two fighters circled at about 5,000 feet just north of the launch site until the countdown began. They then dived south toward the site at full throttle, timing it so as to be just behind and to the side of the buzz bomb as it was launched. The pilots climbed with the bomb and chased it until the momentum of the dive was lost and they fell too far behind.

The second team of fighters, which had been following along at about 10,000 feet, then dived into position behind the bomb and followed it until it dived into the sea. The first team followed at a distance too, since they could cut off the bomb and shoot it down if it headed for shore. Of course all the pilots hoped that the bomb they were following would malfunction so they could score an easy victory. The bombs were quite cooperative, and most of us were able to shoot down at least one. I was fortunate enough to get two while flying a P-51, and the next year I got two more while flying a P-80, which could easily outrun the bombs.

One thing I was apprehensive about was flying so far out over the Gulf at full power. The farther I got from shore the worse the engine sounded. As soon as the buzz bomb started its dive I turned north, throttled back, and started a slow climb. I could almost tell from the sound of the engine when the beach came into sight.

On one occasion in July one of the buzz bombs ran amok, pulled up suddenly to about 5,000 feet, almost stalled, then made a diving turn down to 500 feet and headed for the shore. The first two fighters couldn't keep up, and the high fighters had lost sight of it against the water until too late. They couldn't fire toward the land because of the possibility of killing someone. They chased it helplessly until it crashed in deserted country just after passing over the small town of De Funiak Springs, about forty miles northeast of the base. Everyone breathed a sigh of relief when the chase pilots reported it had crashed in a deserted area. Shortly afterward we received three separate reports of the crash through the state police, and two of the witnesses said they had seen the pilot bail out. So much for eyewitness reports.

The great flying continued unabated. I was logging more than fifty hours a month and had checked out in several more planes, including the P-47N, a long-range version of the Thunderbolt designed for the Pacific. Barney had recently flown one on a simulated combat mission of more than twelve and a half hours. I also flew the Northrop P-61B Black Widow, the P-51H, and the Grumman F7F Tigercat, a twin-engine Navy fighter that the AAF was testing. I was test officer on the F7F and found it to be a rugged, fast, heavily armed fighter but deficient in high-altitude performance. The Black Widow was the first airplane designed as a night fighter. All previous night fighters had been designed for another purpose, then modified for the night fighter mission. It was a large, twin-engine plane armed with four 20-millimeter cannon and four .50-caliber machine guns. The three-man crew included a pilot, radar operator, and gunner. It came out late in the war but saw combat in most theaters.

The Gulf Coast area has buildups of cumulus clouds almost every afternoon, and they gave me some of the most beautiful and pleasurable flying I've ever experienced. Often in the late afternoon, Barney, Dick, and I would take off in three fighters (sometimes all the same type, usually some mixture of P-51, P-38, P-63, and P-47) and rat race through the cloud valleys and over the cloud mountains. We would zoom up one side of a steep cloud, then roll over the top and dive down the other side, do a roll or two through the valley, and then zoom up over the next mountain. There was no conscious thought of flying behind the leader; we just followed him, and the airplane was a part of the pilot. The beauty of the clouds and the sun was surpassed only by the shadows of the airplanes on the clouds surrounded by a rainbow halo. If I had to do only one thing for the rest of my life, I think that would be it. It was what heaven should be like for fighter pilots.

On August 6 we learned that the first atomic bomb had been dropped on Hiroshima. Not having seen the films of the mushroom cloud, we couldn't imagine a weapon that destructive. The power of the bomb was just a number to us. On August 9, the second bomb was dropped on Nagasaki, and we began to think that the war might actually end this year without the need for an invasion of Japan. The papers and the radio said that negotiations for surrender were under way, but we didn't know if more bombs would be required. We were not privy to the fact that no more atomic bombs were available.

On August 15, we were attending a 611th Group party at the beach club when the word came over the radio that Japan had surrendered. The war was over. It had touched almost every part of the world and had lasted almost six years, two years longer than World War I. Untold millions had been killed or maimed, and for the first time a large proportion of them had been civilians. We hoped that the end of this global carnage would also be the end of major wars. So far it has been, but there has been instead a continuous procession of smaller wars that often have the world teetering on the edge of another major and perhaps final war.

EPILOGUE

In addition to my combat experience, much of what I have done since the end of the war has helped to prepare me for my present position as deputy director of the Smithsonian's National Air and Space Museum.

I completed the Air Force Test Pilot School and spent almost six years testing fighters. After a tour in the Pentagon, I earned a bachelor's degree in aeronautical engineering at the Air Force Institute of Technology and a master's in aeronautics from the California Institute of Technology. The next five years I spent teaching aeronautics at the U.S. Air Force Academy. I retired from the Air Force in 1964 and worked as an engineer on the Apollo and Skylab space programs. In 1972 I took over the Aeronautics Department at the Air and Space Museum and became deputy director in 1983.

My personal life has been equally satisfying. I married a lovely southern blonde, a course that I recommend highly, and we have two children and a wonderful granddaughter.

Despite the dire predictions of the cadets in 1942, I have never been sorreee.

APPENDIX A
Unit Citation for 23rd Fighter Group

Headquarters Fourteenth Air Force
APO 287, c/o Postmaster
New York City, New York

27 August 1945

GENERAL ORDERS)
Number 118)

1. *UNIT CITATION*: Under the provisions of War Department Circular No. 333, dated 22 December 1943, the following named unit is cited for outstanding performance of duty in action against the enemy:

23RD FIGHTER GROUP

The Japanese were sending 70,000 crack troops down the Siang River Valley in Hunan Province, China, aiming at the capture of Hengyang, vital communications center and mid-way point in the Japanese strategy to drive an inland corridor across China. A major defense stand by ill-equipped Chinese ground forces was planned at Hengshan, 25 miles north of Hengyang, to attempt to stop the drive. Between 17 June 1944 and 25 June 1944 the 23RD FIGHTER GROUP threw its total effort into battle. On all but three days during this period the weather was adverse to aerial operations, with an overcast arched over the river valley and resting on the mountains that lined both sides of the valley. Demonstrating extraordinary heroism, the pilots flew nearly half of their missions during this period through this "tunnel" created low above the valley. The valley floor was studded with machine guns, anti-aircraft guns and thousands of rifles in the hands of the troops, forcing the pilots to fly through deadly curtains of machine gun and small arms fire. Despite the extreme hazards, the Group's pilots flew 538 sorties, strafing and bombing the enemy spearhead forces. They killed 1,640 troops and destroyed approximately 780 cavalry and pack horses. Striking at the supply lines immediately behind the front, they destroyed 377 small boats and damaged 372 more; sank fifteen large river vessels 100-or-more feet in length and damaged eight. They destroyed 91 motor trucks and damaged 50. They also sank three and damaged two heavily armed gunboats that the Japanese had rushed into the area to protect their water supply lines. In addition, they wrought extensive damage among supplies and equipment in the 100 or more compound storage centers they destroyed and damaged. In four encounters with enemy aircraft, the Group's pilots shot down seven enemy planes, probably destroyed seven more and damaged eight, losing none of their own aircraft. This lone, gallant stand by the 23RD FIGHTER GROUP against 70,000 enemy troops, despite adverse weather and even after the Allied ground defense stand at Hengshan failed to develop, is expressive of the extraordinary heroism, gallantry, determination and esprit de corps in keeping with the highest traditions of the American military service.

BY COMMAND OF MAJOR GENERAL STONE:

Clayton B. Clauson
Colonel, G.S.C.
Chief of Staff

OFFICIAL:
/s/ Henry A. Beasley
/t/ HENRY A. BEASLEY
Lt Col., A.C.D.
Adjutant General
TRUE COPY

APPENDIX B
In Memory of Jesse Gray

Following the publication of the first edition of this book by Bantam in 1986, I tried without success for several years to locate Jesse Gray's family in North Carolina. Finally, in 1988, a good friend of mine, John A. Watkins of Kill Devil Hills, North Carolina, located one of Jesse's sisters in Williamston, North Carolina. Through her I found that Jesse had five surviving siblings, three sisters and two brothers. I sent them each a copy of the book, and we arranged to meet in Washington on October 29. They were wonderful people, just what I expected of Jesse's family. Although we all knew him as Jesse, the family called him Jake. The following is an excerpt from a poem written by his sister Lucille Uzzell, of Charlotte, North Carolina, to commemorate that meeting:

A VERY SPECIAL DAY

We had descended upon Washington to meet Don Lopez and his wife,
He would share his knowledge of Jesse's army life.
Jesse, our brother, was a casualty of World War Two,
Don and Jesse were members of the same fighting crew.
Don is Deputy Director of the National Air and Space Museum,
It is housed in the Smithsonian Institution where we met him.
We were delighted that Don was accompanied by Glyn, his wife,
Together they told us the story of Jesse's army life.

From enlistment, through training, war and how he died,
He loved life so much, yet longevity he was denied.
Don showed us slides and explained each of them,
He showed us a great video made from original film.
We discussed *Into the Teeth of the Tiger*, Don's memories in his book,
He gave us all a copy so we could get another look—
At how they participated as pilots in a war that wasn't a game,
And how their squadron's outstanding fighting reached a level of fame.
Their off-duty time seemed to be centered around sports,
They played softball, volley ball and on all kinds of courts.
It was in 1945 when we had reason to weep,
That's when Jesse was drowned in a rice paddy beneath a jeep.
To have weathered 100 dangerous missions without getting a scratch,
It's ironic that he would die in a Chinese rice patch.
Some good comes from the bad is how the story goes,
It's better late than never that the good is disclosed.
We possibly would have met the Lopezes if Jake were still alive,
But chances are of this meeting we would have been deprived.
Don suffered, I'm sure, when Jake's life came to an end,
It's a traumatic experience when one loses a friend.
Out of a family of ten children, Jake was the first of five to die,
So helpless—no body to deal with—thank Goodness we could cry.

> Thoughts by Lucille Uzzell
> Washington, D.C.
> October 29, 1988

INDEX